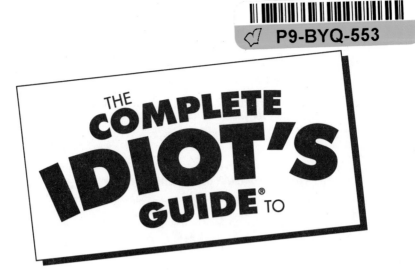

THE COMPLETE IDIOT'S GUIDE® TO

Horses

by Sarah Montague and PJ Dempsey

ALPHA

A member of Penguin Group (USA) Inc.

For mum, who kept my horse dream alive, and Michael,
who made my horse life a reality.
I love you both,
Phyllisjo

Copyright © 2003 by Sarah Montague and Phyllisjo Dempsey

International Standard Book Number: 0-02-864460-3
Library of Congress Catalog Card Number: 2002116797

05   04   8   7   6   5   4   3

Interpretation of the printing code: The rightmost number of the first series of numbers is the year of the book's printing; the rightmost number of the second series of numbers is the number of the book's printing. For example, a printing code of 03-1 shows that the first printing occurred in 2003.

Printed in the United States of America

Note: This publication contains the opinions and ideas of its authors. It is intended to provide helpful and informative material on the subject matter covered. It is sold with the understanding that the authors and publisher are not engaged in rendering professional services in the book. If the reader requires personal assistance or advice, a competent professional should be consulted.

The authors and publisher specifically disclaim any responsibility for any liability, loss, or risk, personal or otherwise, which is incurred as a consequence, directly or indirectly, of the use and application of any of the contents of this book.

Publisher: *Marie Butler-Knight*
Product Manager: *Phil Kitchel*
Managing Editor: *Jennifer Chisholm*
Senior Acquisitions Editor: *Mike Sanders*
Development Editor: *Michael Thomas*
Copy Editor: *Jeff Rose*
Illustrator: *Chris Eliopoulos*
Cover/Book Designer: *Trina Wurst*
Indexer: *Heather McNeil*
Layout/Proofreading: *Angela Calvert, John Etchison*

Contents at a Glance

Contents

Foreword

Horses are a dream. Quite literally, as when they visit you in sleep, a vision in the dim distance of flashing manes against the pasture fence. And metaphorically, when they represent the only kind of future you can or want to imagine, a future where you and a horse are bound together completely. It is a powerful dream. Sometimes the power is yours; suddenly you are five feet taller and a thousand pounds stronger and faster than you were. Sometimes the power is his, as in that one swift moment when you are reminded of an irrevocable fact of nature, with luck not too painfully. But both make up the totality of one of the loveliest unions in the universe.

How odd, then, that *books* should be such an important part of this (indeed) earthy relationship. Yet they are. The complete library of volumes written on every aspect of horses is one of our oldest and biggest. And if you are interested in horses, not a single one is too arcane.

When I was a horse-crazy child, before I had ever learned to post properly (and I own several books that definitely inform me I still do not know how to post properly), I was consulting the likes of one of America's greatest riders, William Steinkraus, in the pages of his 1961 classic, *Riding and Jumping*. It was so easy to fancy that it was only a matter of time before I would be putting the contents of the chapter on "Advanced Schooling over Fences" to work for me and my bold and honest mount. That such a mount never quite materialized—not to mention any opportunity to show my perfect balance on approach to a fence—did nothing to diminish the pleasures of being lost in such a dream. I studied Sam Savitt's elegant drawings illustrating "Correct position at the gallop" in Gordon Wright's 1966 *Learning to Ride, Hunt, and Show*, a book I received for my eleventh birthday, and I could feel that thrilling contact with a sensitive mount as the great churning of hooves beneath me made the most seductive music I would ever hear.

That treatise began by repeating the truism that "no one can learn to ride by reading a book." Inarguable; yet so is the fact that the desire to ride may first be ignited by reading. In books, we encounter the deeds of individuals who make us long to know for ourselves a Misty or a Stormy, a red pony or a Top Kick, a Man o' War or a Seabiscuit, a Smoky or Black or Little Vic. You think you are touching horses through the words on a page. And then you touch a real horse and realize you did nothing of the sort, for here is a different horse, unlike any other, and this moment has not yet been written.

You will, as it were, take up your own pen to author the horse story of your dreams. It will join that great library that becomes any true horse-lover's treasure. It contains things you need and want to know. And you start by turning the page.

Melissa Holbrook Pierson
author of *Dark Horses and Black Beauties*

Introduction

First off, we know you're not an idiot. But you probably are a busy professional, or student, or active retiree, or parent. You know how to learn things, you've been doing it all your life; and yet it's difficult to know where to begin sometimes, especially when the subject—horses—takes you into a completely different world.

Horses aren't just animals, but our companions in work, pleasure, and sport, with a history as complicated as our own. We've tried to treat this subject thoroughly and entertainingly, beginning at the beginning:

🐎 Where did horses come from?

🐎 How have we worked with them throughout history?

🐎 What are the breeds and what do they do?

Today, more is known about horses than ever before, and we want to share this knowledge with you:

🐎 How do horses think, move, and react?

🐎 What should we feed them?

🐎 How do we care for them?

🐎 What about common ailments, behavior problems, gender issues?

We assume you're reading this book because you're contemplating lessons, or even horse ownership, so here are some other things you're probably thinking about:

🐎 What types of riding are there?

🐎 How do I learn?

🐎 What kind of horse should I buy? Where do I find him?

🐎 How much is all this going to cost?

These are many of the same questions we had when we started out, buying our own horses and competing with them, and we've learned a lot in writing this book. We've tried to cover, not only the basics for those of you who are just starting out, but some of the more complex information, and a wealth of detail about different breeds and disciplines. Since the "horse world" is really many worlds, we think there'll be something for everyone to discover. Most of all, we hope it will help to make you a horseman, sharing a special bond with this fascinating creature.

What's in This Book

Think of this book as a ride, with different roads to follow, different hills to climb. The journey's end is up to you, and so is the route. We've divided it into five "trails," and depending on where you are in your riding life, you may want to amble through some and gallop by others.

Part 1, "The Horse Through the Ages," takes you through the ancient history of horses, their place in our developing civilizations, the horse breeds in all their colorful variety, and the place of the horse today.

Part 2, "Body, Mind, and Soul," teaches you all about the horse, inside and out. How they're built, how they move, what to feed them, how to care for them, and, most important, how they think and feel. Knowing this will help you make the most of your riding.

Part 3, "Preparing to Ride the Beast: Grooming and Saddling," focuses on you—how to handle a horse safely, groom him, saddle and bridle him, and prepare for your ride, including what you'll want to wear for security and comfort.

Part 4, "School Days: Learning to Ride or Drive," takes you through the various horse sports, and will help you to choose a school and instructor who will help you to pursue the discipline of your choice. We also tell you about programs for children and those with special needs.

Part 5, "Horse Heaven," takes you step by step through the process of becoming a horse owner, from where to keep him to how to find and judge prospects to how to deal with dealers and come away with the right horse at the right price. We'll also discuss a special member of the eqine population—the senior horse.

And there's more ...

We know this book is only the beginning of your journey with horses, so we've provided information about where you might want to look next—organizations, books, catalogues, and websites. We're also sure that you'll come to feel as strongly as we do that *every* horse deserves a decent life and a loving home, and we've listed some worthy organizations that are trying to make that possible.

Extras

Throughout the book you'll find a variety of sidebars. Some of them highlight important points in the text, and others contain new information we thought fun and useful.

Horse Sense
Tried and true techniques for making your horse life happier, healthier, safer, better!

Horse Whispers
Sometimes others said it better. Our favorite horse quotes from teachers, riders, poets, and others are sprinkled throughout the text.

Horse Lore
Equine history, heroes, legends, and fascinating facts.

From the Horse's Mouth
Deciphering the terminology and lingo you'll encounter in the horse world. What those special terms mean, and where they came from.

Whoa!

Falls we don't want you to take, literally or otherwise. Here we'll point out important safety tips, and warn you about common mistakes and pitfalls.

Horse Friends (Acknowledgments)

Quite specific thanks are due to the cadre of professionals who helped us get to this book—our agent who made it possible, Sheree Bykofsky and her associates Janet Rosen and Megan Buckly, Mike Sanders of Alpha Books for taking a chance on us, Michael Thomas, our editor, for catching everything we threw. And special thanks to Sally Eckhoff—we are indebted to your heroic, articulate contribution to the text.

We are personally grateful to Maria DiBello, Karen Donley, Jeff Kleinman, Bob Langrish and his staff, Suzy Lucine, Dusty Perrin, and Lori Steffensen, for responding so quickly to requests for vivid, memorable, horse-worthy pictures and to the owners and riders who have graciously permitted us to reproduce them. To friends old and new who graciously took time out of their busy lives to share photos and stories of their lovely equine friends, Fred Boberg, Susan Lee Cohen, Judith McCarthy and her family at Waterford Farm, and Bryna Watson. To Leah Patton of The American Donkey and Mule Society and Karen Winston of Solar Wind Miniature Horses, who shared their knowledge and entrusted their photographs to total strangers who asked for help over the Internet. Thanks also to Sandra Hilderbrand of the Gilcrease Museum, and Adam and Emily Gershberg for providing pictures for the book.

Blacksmith Hilary Cloos kindly shared the tricks of her trade, and Linda Robinson has brought a lifetime of breeding, training, riding, showing, and judging horses to her careful reading of our manuscript.

Sarah feels she walked in a lot of big hoofprints to get here, and thanks the generation of thoughtful horse people who proceeded her, as well as her articulate, demanding instructors—Jane Armour,

Adam Gershberg, Eric Horgan, Margaret Hutchison, Helen Isherwood, and Susan Reichelt. Most of all, of course, she thanks her horses Winchester and Jonathan Swift for summing up in two bodies what it has taken 325 pages to try to say.

Topping PJ's list are Lois Butz and Linda Robinson of Lo-Lin Arabians. I can never repay the education you have given me and the patience you have afforded me over the years. My loyal instructor, Gayle Zanders, who has made it possible for me to never leave the show ring without a ribbon (OK, except for once), and her husband, and my farrier, Dave Zanders. The gang at Chestnuthill Arabians, Joe Alberti Jr., Joe Alberti Sr., Rob Janecki, Gregg Briner, and Jody and Jamie Gray of Sultana Stables (who sold me my wonderful horse) for their moral and technical support at shows and at home. My fellow horse buddies, Elizabeth Zayatz, Donna Gantz-Kanton, Cate Collyer, Geri Petty, Lynn and Dan Oswald, JoAnn and Gabby Russo, who make this sport fun.

I am also grateful to George deKay, who graciously allowed me to take time off the job so this book could be completed on time. Thanks, too, to my family, Stan, Tom, Deb, Jeannine, Stan, Ken, Erin, Brett, Alex, Uncle Syl, Michael, Kathy, Tony, Christina, JoAnn, Bob, Lee, Courtney, Scott, Betty Jane, Donna, and Betty and Jim Hall whose phone calls and emails of encouragement were greatly appreciated. And, to LH Endless Luv, my spotted friend and fairy-tale horse come to life.

Special Thanks to the Technical Reviewer

The Complete Idiot's Guide to Horses was reviewed by an expert who double-checked the accuracy of what you'll learn here, to help us ensure that this book gives you everything you need to know about the world of horses. Special thanks are extended to Linda Robinson.

Claiming that the love and dedication to horses is a disease and/or addiction, Linda Robinson has spent a lifetime learning, loving, and living with horses. Now co-owner of Lo-Lin Arabians in Stroudsburg, Pennsylvania, she has owned, shown, bred, and judged Arabian horses since her teens. Horses she has exhibited include a

Canadian Reserve National Champion Country English Pleasure Horse, regional champions in hunter pleasure, halter (conformation), and Western pleasure. She has been a breeding manager at two large breeding farms, a judge in all-breed and Arabian horse shows, a horse show manager, and a member of several equine associations for many years. When not acting in an official capacity, she has raised and trained many of her own horses to go on to such other activities as competitive trail champions, hunter/jumpers, dressage horses, and, most important, best friends. Linda and co-owner Lois Butz have been active consultants to the equine world in several states.

Trademarks

All terms mentioned in this book that are known to be or are suspected of being trademarks or service marks have been appropriately capitalized. Alpha Books and Penguin Group (USA) Inc. cannot attest to the accuracy of this information. Use of a term in this book should not be regarded as affecting the validity of any trademark or service mark.

Disclaimer

This book represents the views of the authors on the subject. It is not, however, meant to replace the services of competent professionals in either the areas of riding instruction or horse care and management. There are physical risks involved in riding and working with horses, and it is assumed that readers will proceed with caution and after receiving proper guidance and training.

Part  The Horse Through the Ages

Horses have been part of our lives for 60 million years. They've led us into battle, pulled our carts (and barges, and trains!), tilled our land, and helped us to see the world. In Part 1, we'll show you a little bit of *their* world, both ancient and modern.

As cultures developed and climates changed, breeding became specialized, and today there are well over 100 breeds of horses, each with a unique history and special attributes—strength, endurance, dazzling gaits—not to mention every color and pattern from gold to polka dot! We'll introduce you to some of the most influential, the most popular, and the cutest!

Descalo, Arabian Stallion (owned by Dan and Lynn Oswald, Reeders, Pennsylvania).

(© Jerry Sparagowski)

From Prey and Pack to Park and Puissance

In This Chapter

- The prehistoric horse
- Horse meets man—food or beast of burden?
- Early attempts at riding
- From war horse to work horse to race horse to companion

We know you're eager to meet your first real horses, but it's worth spending a little time getting to know their ancestors—and yours. Next to dog and man, the relationship between horse and man is among the oldest, though not always the coziest, in nature. Once we got over the idea that they were simply food, we began our first tentative attempts at domestication. And the rest is the history you will find in this chapter.

Back to the Drawing Board

The magnificently muscled, fleet, and proud animal we know as the horse began, some 60 million years ago, with the *timorous hyracotherium* or *Eohippus* (meaning "Dawn Horse"). This small (approximately 12 inches high) four-toed ancestor more closely resembled a cross between a deer and a lapdog than what we think of as "horse."

As the genus Equus evolved, it went though several incarnations on its way to the model we know today. Fundamentally these changes allowed for its transformation from a creature of camouflage and concealment to one of detection and flight, the same instincts that dominate the nervous forebrain of today's horses.

The final "test model" for today's horse, Pliohippus, evolved 12 to 6 million years ago, and appears to have reached its final form on the North American continent—Americans were go-getters even then! Pliohippus was taller than his predecessors: The lapdog was now a small pony (48 inches), and a longer head and greater depth of shoulder hinted at the horse to come.

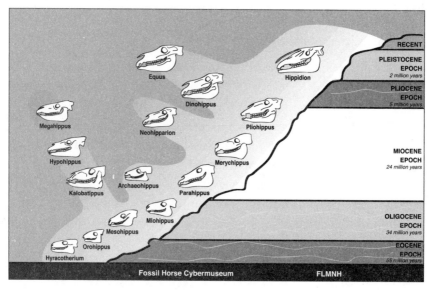

Horse genus names and migratory chart.
(Reproduced with permission, Florida Museum of Natural History)

The Model T

It took some five million years for *equus caballus*—the official scientific name for "horse"—to develop from Pliohippus, and this busy grandfather species was also the beginning of zebras, asses, and half-asses.

Equus caballus, your basic model T horse, migrated from North America to Asia, Europe, South America, Africa, undergoing subtle alterations as it adapted to different climates and terrain. The isthmus connecting North America to Asia and Europe disappeared at the end of the Ice Age (9000 B.C.E.), isolating the continent. As land masses settled, and the earth's various zones began to develop distinct characteristics, so did the rapidly spreading strains of Equus.

Horse Whispers

Our History was written on his back.

—C. J. Bucher

In the Beginning ...

This dissemination and migration, most experts agree, resulted in three distinct types of early horse from which most of today's breed types derive: the Forest Horse, the Tarpan, and the Asian Wild Horse (more commonly known as the *Przewalski's Horse* after the Russian explorer who discovered it in 1879), which, amazingly, is still with us today.

From the Horse's Mouth

The **Przewalski Horse** (Asian Wild Horse) is native to Mongolia and the Central Asian Steppes, in which regions it is also known as *Taki, Tag,* or *Kertag*. With their massive, blunt heads, chunky bodies, and pot bellies, they uncannily resemble prehistoric Pliohippus, giving us an astonishing window into the past. And there, apparently, they prefer to stay—they have never been successfully tamed!

To simplify a very complex set of relationships, the Forest Horse, which had thick legs, a burly body, and a shaggy, gnomelike coat, is probably the ancestor of today's draft breeds (see Chapter 4), while the lighter horse breeds descended from the lithe Tarpan and the chunky Asian Wild Horse, respectively.

Flight to Farm

Eventually (around 4000 B.C.E.) tribesmen in Eurasia began to domesticate them, breeding them, like cattle today, for meat and the milk of the mares. At around the same time, some bright lad probably saw the potential for horses as pack animals, as these early hunter/gatherers began alternating agricultural settlements with nomadic migrations.

From the Horse's Mouth

We don't mean to be rude, but **half-ass** is the colloquial translation for an Onager, or Hemionid—a subspecies of Equus sharing both horse and ass characteristics. The Onager preceded the horse proper as both a draft animal and a mount—the Mesopotamians (around 2000 B.C.E.) controlled it using a nose ring.

Drive Time

The wheels were turning, all kinds of wheels, and the period from 3000 to 2000 B.C.E. saw the creation of a variety of vehicles—plows, sledges, war wagons, and chariots—with early experiments in yoking and driving involving oxen, asses, and onagers (wild *half-asses*) according to archaeological evidence from the Near East. But as swift, horses were imported from the north (the steppes of Southern Asia), these became the draft animal of choice.

Living in Tents

Early civilizations were a restless and contentious lot, and much interaction with horses was in support of fighting and moving on. No one really knows who first said, "Hey, why don't we get on them?" but the earliest known evidence of mounted riders comes from the Ukrainian Steppes—horse teeth with possible bit wear. These unlettered nomadic tribes left only these scant physical traces—it is in the historical records of the "civilized" Near East that we get our first glimpse of an equestrian culture in the making.

In the meantime, the horse was experiencing a second migration, this time not as primate prey paralleling the slow ascent of man, but as increasingly indispensable pack animals—and eventually, as mounts. Herds spread from the high Steppes of Central Asia, into Europe, the Caucasus region of Russia, and then into two of the lands we most associate with equestrian glamour, Arabia and China.

If the early riders were casual opportunists, or, as some evidence suggests, lowly messengers, the demands of war, which regrettably, seems to go hand in hand with civilization, soon saw the establishment of the first cavalry ranks, and with them, the first codification of horsemanship in the form of training regimes. Several empires contributed to this growing culture, using horses both as mounts and to pull chariots, which allowed for swift, effective invasions. Among these were the early Egyptians, the Kassites and Elamites, who conquered Persia, and the Hittites.

Horse Whispers
A good rider has a thinking mind, fine emotions and a sensitive hand.
—Tu Yu, 72 B.C.E.

The Complete Idiot's Guide, circa 1345 B.C.E.

The first horse-training regime was created by Kikkuli, the horse-master to the Hittite King Suppililiuma, an ambitious monarch set on conquering the rival Mitannians. Kikkuli's seven-month program, which survives in the form of clay tablets known as "The Kikkuli Text," outlines a training program that would be the envy of any competitive professional today. It includes instructions on developing strength and fitness using progressive workouts at the trot,

canter, and gallop (first using chariots before the horses were mounted), swimming, warm-ups and cool-downs, and stable management including diet of mixed grains (oats and barley) hay, and legumes (leafy grasses) very similar to today's recommended staples.

Kikkuli's know-how died with him, but similar equestrian forces were being built up all over the East, giving rise to the first selective breeding programs, which were practiced by the Babylonians, Egyptians, and Assyrians. These early experiments may have reached their apex in the Nisean horse, an ancestor of the modern Arab that enabled the rapid—and sustained—spread of the Persian Empire from the sixth to the third century B.C.E. In addition to their use in war, the horse was becoming a symbol of wealth and status, used by the aristocracy for hunting, racing, and polo. They were also a valuable commodity, demanded in tribute by the Persian king from the various tribes and provinces that made up the empire.

Horse Lore

The Parthians, famous for shooting their arrows over the backs of their horses, gave us the term "Parthian shot"—the zinger that is loosed just when you think someone is retreating.

The Empires Strike Back

The Persian Empire was succeeded by the Greek Empire. Classical Greece produced the greatest equestrian partnership in history, that of Alexander the Great and his horse Bucephalus, and the first completely preserved riding manual, *The Art of Horsemanship*, by the Greek cavalry commander and diplomat Xenophon (430–356 B.C.E.). In addition, they developed an impressive cavalry to help speed their conquest of the Persians, and established chariot racing as a national sport.

Horses were already part of the lore and literature of warring civilizations, with the epic poet Homer recounting the conquest of Troy (with the help, of course, of the hollow wooden "Trojan horse" from which the concealed Greek soldiers emerged at night to sack the city), the breathtaking chariot races in honor of the warrior Patroclos, and many scenes of horses in battle.

When in Rome ...

Despite Hollywood's love of a good chariot race, the ancient Romans were not the natural horse people the Persians were, and tended to hire mercenaries to support their cavalry. However, they are credited with establishing breeding practices that resulted in many of Europe's eventual foundation breeds, and management of an Empire, with its sheer scope, brought horses into general practical use as pack animals, mounts for couriers, and the power behind (or in front of) wagons and mail coaches.

As Rome slowly developed the might and sophistication of its cavalry, it became the key to many of its conquests, including that of Britain in 54 B.C.E., but eventually (451 C.E.), in a pattern common in military history, the Empire fell to Attila the Hun, whose fleet forces had benefited from the riding traditions of the Near East, the nomads, and the Chinese Empire they had spent years bedeviling.

The Year of the Horse

China's first great contribution to equestrian culture was related to driving, rather than riding: the breast-strap based harness that allows free air passage for driving horses. They also invented the single horse vehicle. And those Currier & Ives prints of horses driving through picturesque landscapes one behind the other owe their existence to ancient China, which began this practice to free up their roads. But, as with the Roman empire, the perpetual gadfly of marauding nomads eventually drove one emperor (Wu Ti, 141–87 B.C.E.) to inaugurate an aggressive program to increase the supply of quality horses, and to use them to create an effective light cavalry, in one instance sending an army more than 3,000 miles to obtain precisely that many horses for breeding from Ferghana (now Turkestan).

Horse Lore _____

The deep golden color of the Tang Dynasty glazed horses is not just an artist's rendering—these favored horses of Emperor Wu Ti were really the Golden Horses of Samarkand, also known as the Heavenly or Celestial Horses and, more creepily, as the "blood-sweating" horses because of a microorganism that actually caused them to sweat blood in warm weather.

This program of improvement naturally focused the culture's ingenuity on the craft of riding. By the early fifth century C.E., the stirrup was invented to increase the range an army was able to travel and to aid in stabilizing the rider for more effective use of his weapon. Soon, however, the use of the stirrup spread to Northern China and Asia, aiding the swift and destructive force of the nomadic archers making up the ranks of the Goths and Huns who brought down Rome.

(Horse) Culture Clash

Next to Greece and Rome, the most pervasive and influential of all dynastic movements was the spread of Islam in the seventh and eighth centuries, and Islamic conquests in the East and North Africa insured the spread of Arab bloodlines—mixed with indigenous stock—that would influence the shape of generations of horses to come. Mohammed enlisted the horse in his holy war—"Who feeds the horse for the triumph of religion makes a magnificent loan to God," he wrote, and the conflict between Islam and Christianity can also be seen as a clash between the swift Arabs and the European heavy horses favored by the crusaders.

The Light Horses of the Dark Ages

While the early part of the Middle Ages is often depicted as an intellectual black hole, rife with plague and superstition, it was a turning point in the history of the horse in Europe, as it was adapted to an increasing number of uses from jousting to plowing. But if heavy horses were the SUVs of the equine world, palfreys and coursers were the compacts and sports cars, respectively, and all of these contributed to an increasingly diverse horse population, as did the selective breeding encouraged by growing estates and social stability.

Horses in High School

The Renaissance, with its resurgence in intellectual life and the rediscovery of classical traditions, brought about the creation of a "classical riding" tradition known as *haute ecole*. The first important riding academy in Europe was opened in Naples in 1532 by Federico Grisone, whose manual *The Rules of Horsemanship* created an ideal in which a supple and obedient horse could be taken through a range of gymnastic exercises demonstrating collection, extension, and obedience, like ballet for horses.

A number of famous riding masters elaborated on this tradition, including Antoine de Pluvinel (1555–1620), Louis XIII's riding master; William Cavendish, the Duke of Newcastle (1592–1676), riding instructor to Charles II; and François Robinchon de la Guérinière (1688–1751), equerry (riding master) to Louis XIV, whose *Ecole de Cavalerie* (*School of Horsemanship*), published in 1733, became the basic manual for the most famous classical riding academy in the world, the Spanish Riding School in Vienna.

Real Men Do Ride Horses

As you can probably guess from the grand associations of the classical riding masters, the art of horsemanship was still very much the province of nobility and the upper classes—not just because they were responsible for the defense of their realms, but because riding became one of the attributes of a gentleman. In addition to academic riding, in the areas of sport, pleasure, and travel the horse became part of the evolving ritual of genteel society.

I'll Race You

Because humans have been competitive since we first stood upright, it probably wasn't long after the domestication of the horse and the first tentative attempts to tame him that someone suggested finding out who could go faster. Races, both mounted and driving, still take place in many areas of the world. "The sport of kings" refers specifically to the flat racing industry that was begun by James the First at Newmarket and impelled the establishment of the Thoroughbred in the early eighteenth century (see also Chapter 3), which vastly influenced the development of other breeds and disciplines. In addition to flat racing, steeplechasing, and harness racing grew out of the field hunting and driving traditions, respectively.

Horse Lore

Horse racing was America's favorite pastime until the mid-nineteenth century. It was so common that many towns today still have a "Race Street."

The Carriage Trade

For decades after the dissolution of the Roman Empire, which had built a sophisticated network of well-maintained roadways, the five o'clock commute was a nightmare of rutted roads pulled by rudimentary wagons. But gradually transport began to improve, as trade routes opened up, and the wheel and the horse were slowly brought together more efficiently.

As usual, some progress was from the top down. While the peasants were still bumping along in their primitive carts (when they weren't walking), Anne of Bohemia, bride of Richard II, introduced the sophisticated Hungarian *kosci* (from which we get the word *coach*) to England in 1351, and this influenced the design of lighter, more flexible vehicles. By the mid-eighteenth century, in England and Europe carriages and coaches were the dominant mode of transport for both goods and people. Well-to-do families traveled in private coaches to their homes in the country, fashionable young men raced phaetons in the park, and genteel young ladies visited each other for lunch while waiting for the advances of the fashionable young men. But democracy was creeping in, courtesy of the post office. The mail coaches that supplanted single riders could also take a limited number of passengers, and this proved such a successful sideline that commercial firms began to run passenger coaches by the early nineteenth century.

Working Like a Horse

The horse was the key link between the past and the Industrial Revolution, which, with its surge of early technology and industry, signaled the start of the modern era. Horses were used in the building of railroads both in Europe and the United States, and even pulled the trains and streetcars in some areas. In others, especially in rural England, docile "boaters" pulled passenger barges along the canals (freight barges traveling the Erie canal, opened in 1825, helped expand the American West), "pit ponies" and mules worked the coal mines, and horses were the literal "horsepower" behind many machines. In the increasingly crowded cities, horses delivered goods and private passengers in the earliest form of the ubiquitous taxi, pulled trams and buses, galloped to fires, and paced solemnly to funerals.

Horse Lore

The first humane societies were begun during the Industrial Revolution. Even back then, people tried to protect working horses and circus animals from being mistreated.

Similar advances in the agricultural sciences—improved plows and harvesters, crop rotation systems, the increased demand for food—gave the horse a leading role on farms, finally supplanting the ox. The heavy warhorses of the medieval era were the basis for the gentle draft horse giants that made up teams of anywhere from two

to thirty-six horses. Horses were made obsolete in their turn by tractors and other motorized equipment (although they are still used on small farms, especially in Europe).

American Beauties: Horses on This Continent

When the last Ice Age had finished redesigning the face of the earth, the land bridge that had once linked Asia and the Americas (through present-day Alaska) disappeared, leaving behind prehistoric horses that did not survive the change.

Eight thousand years later (in 1519), the Spanish conquistador Hernan Cortés landed in Mexico with the 16 horses that would re-establish the species on the American continent, famously proclaiming that "Next to God, we owe our victory to our horses." The natives he encountered perceived his mounted troops as terrifying armored man-beasts, and their dread contributed to their submission. Three hundred years later, Native Americans were among the most skillful and sensitive riders on the continent, mounted on the descendants of Cortés's 11 stallions and 5 mares.

Horse-Drawn Country

Horses contributed to every facet of the burgeoning new continent. In the East, patterning itself after its European models, horses were bred for racing and use under saddle, with the first race course being inaugurated by New York's English governor in 1668, and stud farms were firmly established, first in Rhode Island, and later Virginia, by the mid-eighteenth century. In the West, the Spanish settlers helped to establish the first American cattle ranches, and with them the start of the great American tradition of the cowboy.

"Camptown Racetrack Five Miles Long ..."

Until the mid-nineteenth century, horse racing was the leading sport in America. Quarter Horse racing was in evidence a century earlier, flat racing gained its premier event in 1875 with the running of the first Kentucky Derby, and the smooth-gaited trotting horse, one of the earliest to be developed on the American continent, was adapted for harness racing, producing famous sires like Dan Patch and Hambletonian. In a more sporting preamble to the Civil War, the North and South used to compete in a series of races called the Intersectional Match—with the fastest from each region going up against each other.

George Catlin, Catching the Wild Horse, *oil, #0126.2174.*
(From the collection of Gilcrease Museum, Tulsa)

Horse Power, U.S. Style

Here, too, horses were the muscle of the Industrial Revolution and the boom in agriculture, dragging logs, trains, barges, and ploughs. The first draft stock (for establishing American draft horse breeds) was imported in 1839, and an aggressive breeding program began after the Civil War. And here, too, the post office was a prime architect of the new horse culture, establishing the famous Pony Express in 1860, to carry letters the 1,966 miles between Missouri and

California. The Pony Express rider faced unfriendly terrain and frequently unfriendly Indians. The Pony Express lasted only two years, and was succeeded by Wells Fargo, trains, and the telegraph.

Trains, Planes, and Automobiles

By the late-nineteenth century, the U.S. horse population numbered in the millions, but this same century gave birth to myriad inventions that would slowly replace the horse in many aspects of industry and society—the car, tractor, and telephone. In one area, however, both here and overseas, the horse remained the stalwart companion to man: war.

Charge!

Famous—and infamous—cavalry battles included the Battle of Waterloo, the Charge of the Light Brigade, and Custer's Last Stand at Little Bighorn River. Less celebrated are the many battles of World War I, in which more than six million horses were deployed and at least half of them died from diseases, exhaustion, mismanagement, and sheer firepower. Horses are still used today in desert conflicts where machinery remains impractical.

Sad as it is to think of the loss of so many innocent equine lives, the cavalry tradition was the foundation of many modern equestrian disciplines. Already the centerpiece of such equestrian sports as racing and hunting, between and after the two world wars horses partnered with a cadre of professional and amateur riders competing in a wide range of equestrian sports. The National Horse Show (held at Madison Square Garden until 2002) was first held in 1883. In 1912, 2,500 years after those first furious chariot races of ancient Greece, equine events—including dressage, three-day eventing, and jumping—returned to the Olympics.

Horse Lore

Comanche, a tough brown gelding, was the only U.S. Army survivor of Custer's Last Stand. He was pierced with seven arrows and lay on the battlefield for two days, his dead owner still clutching the reins. (Warriors, fearing bad medicine, could not take a horse so closely tied to its owner.) In his 125 years on display at the Natural History Museum, the University of Kansas at Lawrence, Comanche has also survived other calamities. One was a kidnapping attempt by students and the other was a near "drowning" when a plugged drain on the floor above him flowed water onto his exhibit.

Ranches and Rituals

Riding had another face in America. On the Plains and all over the Southwest, two parallel equestrian traditions had grown up around the culture established by the original Spanish settlers. Native Americans had begun to establish their own herds from horses acquired from white settlers through trade, theft, or capture, developing fleet and intuitive riding skills to accommodate the buffalo hunting and migration patterns that dominated their lives. The same Spanish conquerors began the cowboy tradition using enslaved Mexican Indians—their rancheros were the blueprint for the American beef industry that gave rise to a whole cowboy culture of rugged independence, rough living, and lonely vigils over vast herds of cattle. The first rodeos grew out of competitions between cowboys, and eventually grew into a vast professional circuit.

The other areas in which the horse continued to maintain a presence was in law enforcement (mounted police), popular entertainment (including circuses and the movies), and ceremonial contexts such as parades and displays at shows and fairs—often of the vanished world of which they themselves were the most potent symbol. Indeed, as the horse slowly ceased, throughout the early part of the twentieth century, to be the practical mainstay of life in town and country, he became something more precious—a companion.

The Least You Need to Know

- Eohippus, the Dawn Horse, appeared on the earth 60 million years ago.

- The horse was domesticated circa 3000 B.C.E., and became indispensable in war, agricultural, and industry.

- The Greek general Xenophon (430–335 B.C.E.) is considered the father of classical equitation.

- War helped to develop the breeds we know today as the swift Eastern horses were bred with the heavier European stock.

- The Spanish conquistadors reintroduced horses—and brought the tradition of cattle ranching—to the Americas.

- As society became more industrialized, horses were used increasingly for sport, entertainment, and recreation.

Chapter

Don't Fence Me in: Today's Horse

In This Chapter

- The horse census
- The evolution of the horse from industrial machine to pet
- How horses earn their keep today
- Horses on call: helping people with physical disabilities and emotional problems

Horses don't have to fill out those irritating forms the government sends once a decade to find out who and where we all are, but rest assured that in the United States, Big Brother, in the form of the Department of Agriculture, has his eye on the stable (at least on the farm), and other industry and breed organizations have also made it their business to keep head counts. So we pretty much know how many horses there are and to some extent how they're being used.

Early Twentieth Century

From 1900 to 1910, the U.S. horse population grew 70 percent (outpacing people!), peaking at 24 million (and 4.5 million mules) by the start of World War I. Even with the loss of more than a million horses to the war effort, the Census of Agriculture recorded 21.5 million horses at work on farms in 1918. At the same time, horses were growing as the accessory of choice for the newly affluent American moguls and their socially conscious and ambitious wives, encouraging both foreign imports of fashionable breeds and domestic programs.

But while horses were holding their own on farms and down the avenues of the country's growing cities, Henry Ford had other ideas. Launching an aggressive campaign for tractors, as well as the ubiquitous Model T, he persuaded millions of farmers to trade in their hay-burning matched pairs for gasoline-guzzling tractors. By 1929, draft horses were disappearing at the rate of 500,000 a year, and by 1954, for the first time, tractors outnumbered horses on farms. Changes in military practice had already caused the U.S. Army to disband its cavalry in 1948.

Horse Lore

In 1954, it finally happened—farmers owned more tractors than horses. But today history is repeating itself as the working horse again returns to the farm.

Horses survived the transition from pre- to post-industrial society, and post–World War II affluence fueled a generation of eager consumers of gas-guzzling cars, labor-saving devices, and more important, pleasure in all forms.

Breed registrations and participation in horse shows climbed steadily from the 1950s to the 1980s, when economic downturns and changes in tax laws (not to mention the high cost of gasoline for hauling horse trailers around to shows) flattened the curve. According to the last comprehensive survey done by the American Horse Council (in 1996), there are approximately 6.9 million horses in the United States. And some individual *registries* have shown modest increases, though the latest figures (from 2001) show a drop in seven of the ten largest, with fewer new horse purchases as well. Some of these were in surprising areas—there is a growing movement championing the return of draft horses, spearheaded by the very farmers who were eager to reject them in the 1920s!

From the Horse's Mouth

A **registry** is usually kept by a breed organization to keep track of the birth and parentage of each purebred horse or recognized crossbreed.

The Many Roles of the Modern Horse

Despite the decline in horses on farms and in the military after the advent of industrialism, there are many horses in the United States still working for their supper, and the industry contributes $112.1 billion to the economy according to the AHC.

Giddy Up

Every year thousands of eager children—and adults in touch with their inner child—make the pilgrimage to riding camps and dude ranches around the country to try their hand at riding. For many, this is a first-time experience, and legions of patient horses and ponies are pressed into service to see that the experience is a pleasant one.

The Surrey with the License Plate on the Back

Although the Golden Age of carriage driving is long gone, and today's romantic heroine is more likely to hail a taxi than a *hack*, a modest carriage trade still exists in many big cities, suburbs, and small towns. There are firms that specialize in carriage hire for weddings and other festive occasions (just check the Yellow Pages). In

From the Horse's Mouth

A light horse used for riding is called a **hack**, but so is a carriage for hire. Trail and pleasure riding is referred to as hacking.

rural areas and resorts, horses can still be hired to pull sleighs and wagons for hay rides, and other special occasions.

Horses on Parade

Organizations as unalike as the Royal Canadian Mounted Police and the Anheuser-Busch company use horses for a variety of ceremonial occasions such as parades, fairs, and horse shows. The Mounties have their own breeding program for horses used in their famous musical ride, an intricate drill they have performed since 1887. Like many of today's sport horses, the RCMP horses are now a combination of thoroughbred and draft horse bloodlines, and must be black.

Anheuser-Busch owns the largest herd of Clydesdales in the world. This magnificent horse has been its most recognizable corporate symbol since 1933.

Other show-stopping favorites on the parade route include the showy Palominos with their golden coats and flaxen manes and the flashy pintos with their attention-getting spots.

There's a Horse Lover Born Every Minute

The American circus tradition has been in place since the mid-nineteenth century. In the "old days," big operators like Barnum and Bailey and Ringling Brothers (before they merged) used as many as 750 horses to pull the brightly painted wagons that acted as advance advertising for the shows, as well as in the many equestrian acts that have charmed and dazzled spectators for more than 150 years. Elegant gray Percherons and the white Liberty horses (the ones with the plumes on their heads), who dance by themselves, were favored mounts, but all kinds of horses have appeared in circuses over the years, because agility and intelligence count for more than looks.

In 1858, Black Eagle, billed as "The Horse of Beauty" by Howes and Cushing circus, toured the United States and England demonstrating the waltz and polka and walking on his hind legs. In recent years, the French New Age Circus extravaganzas Theatre Zingaro and Cheval are dazzling audiences in Europe and America with mystic tales "told" by a company of trained riders and horses—their acts, which include horses sitting and galloping on command, as well as intricate horse/human gymnastics, are often old circus tricks wearing chic new clothes.

Ready for My Close-Up

Horses have been involved in "popular" entertainment since chariot racing, but in nineteenth-century America, no theme captured the public's imagination like the American West. Buffalo Bill's Wild West was the traveling show that set the standard. It not only made Buffalo Bill Hickok, Annie Oakley, and Sitting Bull into the first entertainment superstars, it created a true niche for the performing horse that survives into the twenty-first century. As with people, film and television employs both "star" and "stunt" horses, who are handled by special trainers. It is these horse actors that inspire the dreams of kids. And the horses don't even have to be real—the Mustang Stallion, Spirit, hero of the DreamWorks film, is an animation!

Riding the Range

No matter how technically advanced the world becomes, cattle move the same way they did 2,000 years ago, and horses remain the most practical way to round them up, check on them, and get them moving in the direction they are supposed to go. Although the Quarter Horse is still the range ride of choice, there are cow ponies of mixed stock descended from wild Mustangs, Appaloosas, and other Western breeds. Arabians, too, have shown that they have an innate *cow sense* with their ability to herd and cut cows.

Like the cowboys who ride them, cow ponies need to be hardy, willing, able to think on their feet, and dependable, but with an independent streak. With its even temperament and willingness to work, the cow pony made an enormous contribution to the taming of the West. Today, the modern cow pony is just as essential to the ranch business as its ancestors. This intelligent, docile, and patient creature also works hard helping legions of tenderfoot dude-ranchers in their quest for a genuine Western experience.

Back to the Land

Henry Ford didn't manage to replace every working horse. On small farms, areas where land is steep or threatened by erosion, in national parks and logging communities, horses are still performing their old tasks of hauling and plowing. The most recent Census of Agriculture figures (for 1997) placed 2,427,277 horses on farms. In addition to their actual work, many of these horses also go on to other lives, while at home they compete in driving and logging competitions, showing off their skills to an appreciative audience of people for whom a lively look backward beats pay per view any day.

Go Ahead, Make My Hay

Many state and regional law enforcement agencies still have mounted police forces, for crowd control as well as ceremonial appearances. Police horses are often donated after completing other careers, and need to be as unflappable as their riders, who attend special classes to learn to work with them. The horses, too, receive special training to be taught, among other things, the intricacies of herding people.

They're Off!

Three hundred thirty-four years after the British governor of New York opened the country's first race course, the single largest employment of professional horses in the country is in the flat and harness racing industries. There are 69,500 racetracks (according to the American Horse Council) involving 725,000 horses. As the working life of a racehorse is short and swift, many of these fine animals go on to other careers as competitive show horses.

Passing the Buck

The first official rodeo (the unofficial ones were what bored cowboys did on their days off) was held in Prescott, Arizona, on (surprise) July 4, 1886, and it proved to be one of the most successful creations of American culture. Today, there are more than 800 formal rodeos in the United States that employ many valuable horses from bucking broncos (the Frankies and Johnnies of the riding world, encouraged to do their worst—bucking, kicking, fishtailing) to the highly trained and talented horses in events like team penning, cutting, roping, steer wrestling, reining, and barrel racing.

Pay *Attention*, Class

Anyone who rides owes their riding skills and sometimes both their best and worst memories of riding to school horses. These wise and patient schoolmasters come in all shapes, sizes, colors, ages, and breeds. Because no one breeds something called "the school horse" (although maybe they should), these four-legged instructors are usually retirees, or giveaways, or horses who didn't quite work out in other fields, or dealers' specials of the day. There is no exact count of riding schools, but of the estimated 2,970,000 horses classified as "recreational" a considerable percentage are available to teach you that there is no difference between "Stop" and "Go" and "Right" and "Left" unless you know how to ask.

But Will You Respect Me in the Morning?

In the horse world, a one-night stand is commonplace and does not reflect badly on your reputation—in fact, it's the norm. Since the earliest empires, horses have been bred for specific looks, specific

colors, specific jobs, and specific sports, and never more so than today. New and more aggressively competitive disciplines, as well as a renewed interest in traditional breeds, have inspired many breeding programs.

Number of Horses and Industry Participants by Activity

Activity	Number of Horses	Number of Participants
Racing	725,000	941,400
Showing	1,974,000	3,607,900
Recreation	2,970,000	4,346,100
Other	1,262,000	1,607,900
Total	6,931,000	7,062,500

Source: *The Economic Impact of the Horse Industry in the United States, the American Horse Council (1996).*

Our "Other" Best Friend

Think there's no political correctness in the animal kingdom? Think again. We used to call them "pets," but now our domestic animal population is increasingly referred to as "companion animals." This term used to refer largely to cats and dogs, and has spawned a number of organizations and research into the human/animal bond. However, it is now often applied to horses as well, although legally horses are still classified as livestock by the federal government.

What's the difference? The language says it all. Livestock is something you count, not something you cuddle, something you work, not something you work with. Since the 1950s, as mass affluence and mass transit allowed the middle class access to material pleasures (such as horses) that were once exclusively the province of the very rich, the number of recreational riders in this country has increased considerably. Some surveys have estimated that there are as many as 20 million people for whom riding is a good time, rather than a livelihood. And for them, a horse is a friend, a partner, a lifetime commitment (it's that marriage thing again). Even professional competitive riders view their bonds with their mounts as a tremendously important part of their success.

This changed view of the horse has spawned an entire industry, changed the way horses are trained and riding is taught and practiced, and inspired everything from books to massage therapy (as we'll see in the pages to come).

Though dogs have earned the title "man's best friend," horses, too, are naturally programmed to be companions. Their herd instincts revolve around the notion of close contact and bonds with other horses at the same social level (horse society is very stratified). These bonds are easily, if not always clearly, reestablished with humans.

For this blanket designation there are no real formal categories except those defined by the riding styles and disciplines we'll be discussing later on. The horse as companion is a partner on the trail, in the hunt field, in the show ring, and in the barn late at night. An estimated 2,600,000 people own horses—or, because companionship is a two-way street, are owned by one.

Horse Doctors

Although it's not totally borne out in research, having a bond with an animal reduces stress, and the risk for stress-related disorders such as heart attacks and high blood pressure. While hard data is sketchy, there is enough anecdotal information, and, let's face it, generations of gut instinct, to have spawned an entire therapeutic movement based on the horse.

The therapeutic riding movement got its start after a polio sufferer, Liz Hartwell, won a silver medal for dressage in the 1952 Olympic Games. This inspiring triumph prompted a Norwegian therapist, Mrs. Boothker, to start the first riding program for children with disabilities. The establishment of other therapeutic centers in the

United States and Europe soon followed; the North American Riding for the Handicapped Association was founded in 1969.

Therapeutic riding encompasses a number of different disciplines and therapies that assist in the improvement of muscle tone, balance, posture, coordination, motor development, and most important, self-esteem.

Hippotherapy

In classic hippotherapy, the movement of the horse's hips and pelvis is used to help the impaired rider gain musculoskeletal and motor response to the horse's action. In recent years, *hippotherapy* has come to be utilized to complement a wide range of therapies addressed at improving not only motor responses, but psychological, cognitive, social, and behavioral functions. And because of the complex wiring of the human body and mind, even speech patterns can be affected, so that sufferers who are disassociated from the everyday world can, in ways that are affecting and empowering, both speak and listen to horses.

By comparing MRI Scans, Dr. Daniel Bluestone, a former Pediatric Neurologist at UC San Francisco, found that the repetitive movement of riding prompts physical changes in the brain. Like other types of pet therapy, the emotional bond that is formed with the horse cannot be downplayed, either. We know that hippotherapy helps lengthen attention spans and sharpen memory and concentration. And as a bonus, it's fun.

> **From the Horse's Mouth**
>
> Why "hippo"therapy, you ask? It was the Greeks, as early as 460 B.C.E., who recognized the therapeutic value of the horse, and the Greek word for horse is *hippos*.

Developmental Riding Therapy

Therapeutic riding teaches actual riding skills to people with disabilities in general. This more diverse group might be taught, in the course of therapy, how to handle a horse, basic riding skills, and such disciplines as vaulting (basically, gymnastics on horseback), and dressage (see Chapter 16).

Because of the challenge facing disabled riders and the need for increased safety precautions, the varying forms of hippotherapy often involve teams. These might include a physical therapist, a riding instructor, and side walkers.

Horse Lore _____

It seems that the rhythmic, repetitive, but variable pace of the horse is attuned to our own movements, specifically the movement of the pelvis. For riders with physical disabilities, trying to maintain their balance on a moving horse tones, strengthens, and stretches the same muscles they would use if they were able to walk on their own. No machine can duplicate this movement or provide better results.

Riding in the 'Hood

Equine Facilitated Psychotherapy (with a licensed/credentialed mental health professional) and Equine Experiential Learning both work in the same way as forms of horse therapy used to combat depression, low self-esteem, learning disabilities, ADD, anxiety, substance abuse, eating disorders, memory impairment, autism, Tourette's syndrome, schizophrenia, and post-traumatic stress disorder. Not totally centered on riding, the goal here is to help individuals explore their feelings and behaviors while being responsible for the care and well-being of a horse. This type of therapy uses interaction needed to brush, walk, communicate with, and discipline a horse to promote psychosocial healing and growth.

These programs are now in place in inner cities, prisons, and mental health institutions and have helped troubled individuals improve their self-esteem and self-awareness, develop trust, become more aware of their own body, learn problem-solving and goal-setting,

and experience positive sensory stimulation. Some of these programs also help rehabilitate and restore trust in rescued horses, and, in an inspired mix of two kinds of "endangered species," some programs use the endangered wild Mustang as the basis of their efforts. The results are amazing and benefits help both the person and the horse. For some in the program, it is the first time they have ever successfully related to another living being. How's that for companionship?

The Least You Need to Know

- Although overall numbers declined after World War I, horses were vital to work and the economy until the 1930s.

- Post–World War II affluence produced a new, more demographically various generation of recreational riders, with established horse shows increasing to more than 14,000.

- Of the country's estimated 6.9 million horses, nearly 5 million are involved in recreational riding and showing, but more than 1 million still do other sorts of work, including farming, harness work, law enforcement, and therapy work.

- The most significant change in the twentieth century with regard to horses was the transformation of the horse from worker to companion.

All Sizes, Shapes, and Colors: Horse Breeds

In This Chapter

- The difference between hot, cold, and warmblooded horses
- How each horse breed came about
- The physical and temperamental attributes of each breed
- Learn what each breed does best

If the early history of the horse seems crowded with breeds, it is nothing compared to the teeming landscape today. While any two horses can produce a horse, and there are certainly a fair number of horses out there whose father is the boy next store, dedicated breeding programs have been driven by the racing industry and the exponential growth of leisure riding after World War II.

These combined pressures have dictated which breeds have made the top 10 list. You'll want to become familiar with them, but it's worth looking as well at some of the up and comers, who may well change the face of riding in the future.

In this chapter, we'll give you a pocket-size portrait of each breed, so that Thoroughbred will come to mean more than off-track betting, Lusitano won't sound like a foreign resort, or Mini a small car model.

How Many Are There?

They're all winners, but the American Horse Council, which tracks breed registries, has identified the country's leading breeds (figures are for registrations for the year 2000 and do not reflect total populations).

The Ten Most Popular Horse Breeds

Quarter Horse

Paint

Thoroughbred

Tennessee Walker

Standardbred

Appaloosa

Arabian

Anglo and Half-Arabian

Morgans

Saddlebred

Source: Equus Magazine, *Trend issue, November 2002*

Horse Whispers

What is a horse, but God's subtle way of proving the attainability of perfection.

—Anonymous

Climate Control

Horses don't come with thermostats, but in the horse world people are apt to refer to them as "hot," "cold," or "warmblood" horses, terms that have come to have recognizable historical and culture meanings. Here's a brief overview:

- **Hotbloods** refer to the ancient Arabian and Barb horses from the East that were the foundation for the modern Thoroughbred, which is also considered a hotblood.

- **Coldbloods** refers to the heavy European draft horses, to which light horses were often bred.

- **Warmbloods,** as you might have guessed, are what happens when you mix hot- and coldblood lines, but the term has come to be used principally in connection with horse breeds perfected in Germany, England, the United States, the Netherlands, and Scandinavia.

As with all impressionist terms, some anecdotal meaning has also attached to these names. Hotbloods are small-boned, streamlined, and swift, and considered bold; coldbloods are big, heavy-boned, and powerful, and thought of as stolid; warmbloods—the light breeds— are bred for a specific purpose such as racing, eventing, jumping, and pleasure, and are both steady and responsive. It doesn't really make much sense until you get to know one. So let's do that.

A Horse of a Different Color

Horses come in so many fabulous and fascinating shades that it ought to be possible to order them with swatches, like wallpaper. In Chapter 5, we'll discuss the various coats in more detail, but two types of color/breed classification are actually among the country's leading registries.

Seeing Spots: Pinto and Paint

Spots on horses, as on other animals, were probably originally a form of camouflage, but these eye-catching patterns have always been thought of as special. The cave painters of 20000 B.C.E. recorded them long before the horse was domesticated, and in both the former Soviet Union and Egypt, Pintos were revered in antiquity.

Where they come from: The first two Pintos to set foot in the New World were brought to Mexico from Spain in 1519 by Hernan Cortés, and helped establish today's Pintos, Paints, and Appaloosas.

Pintos, along with Palominos and Buckskins, belong to a classification of horse known as "color breeds." What this means is that no matter what the breed, if it has spots, it can be registered as a Pinto. The Paint horse, on the other hand, is considered a breed even though its coat colors and patterns are the same as Pintos.

 Horse Sense

The difference between these two types of spotted horses depends only on bloodlines and has nothing to do with color or coat pattern. In order for a spotted horse to be registered as a Paint, it must be of documented and registered Paint, Quarter Horse, or Thoroughbred breeding. This means that a Paint may also be a registered Pinto but a Pinto cannot always be a registered Paint. Got it?

What they look like: Pintos and Paints look like casualties from a good paintball game. Like snowflakes, no two coat patterns are exactly alike, not even on Pintos related to one another. The two common types of Pinto markings are Tobiano (*tow-bee-ah-no*) and Overo (*oh-vair-oh*). The Tobiano is the most common. The easiest way to tell them apart is to think of Tobianos as dark horses with white spots and Overos as white horses with dark spots. Tobianos always have dark-colored heads and dark eyes, and Overos have mostly white heads and may even have blue eyes. There are even gray-and-white Pintos (although these horses, like solid grays, turn all white as they age) and Palomino Pintos. The terms *piebald* and *skewbald* simply mean black and white and brown and white, respectively.

 From the Horse's Mouth

Conformation means basically the structural relation of the parts to the whole, and how that whole compares to the standard for its breed.

Other than that, their *conformation* varies depending on the contributing breed. Because their derivation was more often from the Western areas of the country, many are cow pony and Quarter Horse types, but some may more closely resemble the Thoroughbred.

What they're like: Because Pintos come in every breed, size, and shape there is no one type of personality that describes them. The personality of any spotted horse, Pinto or Paint, will depend on its breeding, be it horse, pony, mini, or longear.

What they do: Pintos are classified into four types:

- **Hunter-type** are those of Thoroughbred breeding. Ponies will resemble the Connemara (see "The Celtic Pony: The Connemara" in Chapter 4).

- **Saddle-type** have Saddlebred, Tennessee Walker, Hackney, or other gaited-horse breeding. Their conformation and action are true to those breeds. Ponies are of an English type, displaying the animation, action, and carriage of these breeds and the style of the modern Shetland and Hackney ponies.

- **Pleasure-type** are those of Arabian or Morgan breeding. Ponies have the conformation of Arabians, Morgans, or Welsh ponies.

- **Stock-type** are the typically Western horses of Quarter Horse breeding and conformation.

How many? The American Paint Horse Association, founded in 1962, has issued pedigree certificates for more than 660,000 horses. The Pinto Horse Association of America maintains a registry of more than 109,000 horses, ponies, and minis.

Horse Lore

Overo Pintos and Paints that have white heads and have color only on their ears, or on and/or around the ears, are called Medicine Hats, because it looks like they are wearing hats. Some tribes of Native Americans thought horses with this type of marking would bring them good luck.

The Yellow Horse: Buckskin

Nonhorse people think this is a fashion statement, but Buckskin is the term for yellowish or tan bays with black manes and tails.

Where they come from: Although technically a color breed, the Buckskin horses native to the western United States can trace their ancestry back through the Mustang to the Spanish Barb, brought to this country by the Moors who came to the New World to escape King Charlemagne, who gave them two choices if they remained in their homeland: convert to Christianity or be killed. Eventually, their whereabouts were located, and in the fifteenth century, Queen Isabella dispatched soldiers to kill them. Their horses were claimed by colonists and Native Americans or escaped into the wild. Other Buckskins who were brought to the United States later were descendants of the Norwegian Dun or Tarpan horses.

What they look like: The look of each Buckskin depends upon his breeding. They are all, however, within a color range called "yellow," which ranges from a very light cremello/perlino through shades of yellow to a chestnut/sorrel. Some Buckskins have black points (mane, tail, legs, and ear frames), dorsal stripes, or other *primitive marks*, and others do not.

From the Horse's Mouth

Primitive marks include a stripe down the back (called a dorsal stripe), a stripe over the withers, and stripes over the knees and hocks. Dorsal stripes can be black, brown, red, or gold, and can occur on any color coat. Horses with a dorsal stripe are said to be linebacks. These primitive markings can occur in any combination on any horse color.

What they're like: Because Buckskins may be of any breed, their personality, talent, and size depends on their specific breed type.

What they do: Again, though more concentrated in the Western states, Buckskins are as versatile as their respective breed types, and can be found both in the pleasure ring and on the hunter course.

How many? There are approximately 30,000 registered Buckskins, including such variations as the zebra dun and the blue-slate colored grullo (*grew-yo*).

The Golden Horse: The Palomino

When we think of a Palomino, the first horse that comes to mind is Roy Rogers's horse, Trigger, who is credited with popularizing this breed in modern times. But Trigger was only one striking example of this exquisite shade. Golden horses, thought to have links to the sun, have been revered by ancient tribes and ridden by Greek gods, prized through the ages by royalty, and featured in many historical paintings.

Where they come from: Palomino is a genetic phenomenon rather than a breed, and today is most often found in American breeds like the Quarter Horse.

What they look like: The Palomino (which may come from the Spanish *palomilla*, a cream-colored horse with a white tail) is technically a yellow dun, but the breed registry prefers this horse to be dealt with as a separate color breed, requiring a flaxen (light-colored) mane and tail. All Palominos are some shade of gold (technically yellow) and Smutty Palominos (a mixture of yellow and black hair) may be as dark as chestnut. (If there were red hairs in the coat, the color would be considered chestnut.) It is also common for the coat to be dappled. Skin color is dark (except on the face or legs where white hair is present), but occasionally there is a Palomino with pink skin. The eyes are usually dark, accentuating the dramatic color.

What they're like: Like the other color breeds, the personality and type of each Palomino depends upon its breeding—acceptable crosses (for the Palomino breeding register) are with Quarter Horses, Arabians, American Saddlebreds, or Thoroughbreds, but a horse of any breed between 14.0 to 17.0 *hands* can be registered as a Palomino, and types vary accordingly.

What they do: Palominos are divided into three types that are defined in the same way as Pintos: Saddle-type, Pleasure-type, and Stock-type (see "What they do" in the Pinto section).

How many? According to the Palomino Horse Breeders of America, there are 76,820.

Spot on: Appaloosa

One of the most distinctive horse breeds in the world, the Appaloosa may trace back, through its various ancestors, to the famous prehistoric cave paintings at Lascaux, France.

Where they come from: Although all American breeds owe a debt to Hernan Cortés and his small band of horses, the link with the Appaloosa is especially clear. Early descendants of herds established by Cortés and other conquistadors were "liberated" by the Plains Indians, and these came to form the foundation stock for the Nez Perce Indians in Washington State and Idaho. The name "Appaloosa" is a corruption of the name of a local river (and related tribe), the Palouse. By the early nineteenth century, the Nez Perce horses, products of rigorous selective breeding, were well known, but were almost rendered extinct during successive battles over land with the government. Happily, enough survived to form the basis of a revival spearheaded by the Appaloosa Horse Club, founded in 1938.

From the Horse's Mouth

The name Appaloosa comes from the Palouse River in the Northwest, were the Palouse and Nez Perce Indians who established the breed held their lands. Settlers referred to them as "Palouse horses" or "a Palousey" or "Appaloosey," which was officially shortened to "Appaloosa" by the breed's horse club.

What they look like: Would you believe spotted? Actually, there are six different recognized patterns and eight variations, leaving the Appy, as they're called by fans, as dazzling as any spring fashion line-up. In terms of conformation, they reflect the dual standards of the Nez Perce: decorative and practical. They have compact bodies, strong legs, and especially strong hooves, with stylish black-and-white vertical stripes. Necks are relatively straight, but well muscled, and the ears prick forward appealingly, as if they are still looking out over the Plains from which they once came. Their wispy manes and tails were supposed to keep them from getting tangled in brush. Height: 14.2 to 16 hands. Color: The patterning combines with every coat color, though Appaloosas must display mottling of the skin around the muzzle and genitalia and prominent white sclera surrounding their eyes.

Horse Lore

During the Nez Perce War of 1877, Appaloosas were instrumental in helping Chief Joseph and his tribe hold off the cavalry, traveling more than 1,300 miles. The hardy horses that survived the tribe's final losing battle are the forerunners of today's Appys.

The Appaloosa has six coat patterns:

- **Spotted blanket.** A "blanket" of spots over loin and hindquarters, with dark head, neck, and back.

- **White blanket.** A solid white blanket over loin and hindquarters, with dark head, neck, and back.

- **Marble (varnish roan).** A pattern of white hairs either concentrated into a blanket pattern or distributed all over the horse.

- **Snowflake.** A pattern of white spots on a dark coat that changes with age and may not appear until after maturity. Generally, they continue to increase in number—although this can stabilize at some point—but they may even disappear altogether over time.

- **Leopard.** What it sounds like: dark spots all over a white background.

- **Solid.** A solid-colored Appaloosa has no spots, but must exhibit mottled skin in addition to other recognizable characteristics of the breed (striped hooves, etc.).

What they're like: Hardy, willing, and versatile.

What they do: Appys are the sixth most popular breed in the country, and have been used in almost every discipline. Given their Northwestern heritage, they are naturally prominent in stock and trail riding, but are solid, dependable jumpers, good in pleasure classes, and have added a decorative pizzazz to the dressage ring. They also race short distances, like Quarter Horses.

How many? According to current registry figures, 630,000.

The Desert Horse: The Arabian

The origin of the Arabian is one of history's mysteries, but we do have records going back 3,500 years documenting this ancient breed, the oldest of all purebreds and considered the foundation of all breeds. First and foremost the Arabian was bred to be a warhorse and it was the mares that were chosen for their stamina and bravery.

The beginning of the Arabian breed is told in the story of Al Khamsa (The Five Mares). The story goes that the Prophet Mohammed wanted to test the obedience of his mares. He chose 100 of his finest and kept them confined without water for a couple of days and then released them near a stream. As they raced toward the water, Mohammed blew the call to battle on the bugle. Five mares spun around and galloped to their master. It was these five who

Mohammed chose to mother the breed. This tale illustrates the strong bond Arabians have with man. The tribesmen of Arabia, called the Bedouins, were the first and most famous Arabian breeders. They valued this beautiful animal above all other possessions because it was crucial to their survival in the harsh, lonely desert. Man and horse lived as friend, even sharing the same tent. This interaction with people over the centuries has given the Arabian an innate ability to bond with humans.

The Arabian is considered to be the most intelligent breed of horse. The bulge between its eyes (called the *jibbah*) is thought to allow for a larger brain.

During the Crusades of the Middle Ages, the heavily armored Christian knights mounted on their Draft-type horses were no match for the Muslims on swift, brave Arab mares. When the knights returned home in defeat, they brought word of these amazing little horses and the part they played in winning battles. It wasn't long before Arabians were brought to Europe and England and crossed with the native horses to produce the breeds we know today.

What they look like: An Arabian is refined and beautiful in appearance, with a dished face, large, dark, expressive eyes, arched neck, large nostrils, high tail carriage, short back (allowing them to carry great weight for their size), and hooves of steel. Height: 14.2 to 15.2 hands. Color: gray, bay, chestnut, and black.

What they're like: The Arabian is an intelligent horse with a good memory and an eagerness to learn (and it learns quickly). Here is a horse that bonds as easily to people as it does to other horses. Talk to any Arab owner and you'll hear stories about how these horses seem to possess the ability to read minds. They are also very curious. If there is a horse in the barn who can figure out how to open his stall door, it will be the Arab. What's more, being the social creature he is, he'll proceed to open the stall doors of all of his buddies! Arabians are wrongly thought to be difficult horses; the problem usually stems from an owner who is not as smart as this horse.

What they do: Arabians are a long-lived and versatile breed (considered in their prime at 20!). You'll see them in all types of English and Western activities, including reining, pleasure, and harness classes, and increasingly in hunt and dressage as well. But, not surprisingly in this ancient desert breed, what they really excel at is endurance riding. The American Endurance Ride Conference (the official governing body in North America) estimates that more than 70 percent of their members ride Arabian horses.

Horse Lore

George Washington rode an Arabian in the Revolutionary War, but didn't show any interest in breeding them. It was an entirely different story with President Ulysses S. Grant, who was presented with two Arabian stallions, Leopard and Linden Tree, by a Turkish sultan in 1873. Leopard sired the first American-bred Arabian foal in 1890.

How many? The Arabian registries are among the largest in the United States. The International Arabian Horse Association, founded in 1950, has registered 392,000 Arabians, 313,500 Half-Arabians, and 9,100 Anglo Arabians registered in North America, while the Arabian Horse Registry of America lists 578,488 registrations.

The Peacock: The National Show Horse

The National Show Horse is a relatively new breed (its registry officially began in 1982) and refers to a combination of the Arabian and American Saddlebred. Known as "the peacock of the show ring," the National Show Horse is thought to combine the beauty and stamina of the Arabian with the Saddlebred's extremely long neck, high-stepping acting and charisma. To qualify for registration, foals must have at least 25 percent Arabian blood. (See Arabian and Saddlebred sections.) There are currently 14,975 registered.

The Little Engine That Could: The Morgan

The first documented American breed, the Morgan's origins seem to be a quintessentially American story of pluck, luck, and hard work.

Where they come from: All Morgans descend from a single stallion, probably the most famous (outside some of the great Thoroughbred legends) in American equine history. Originally called Figure, this diminutive (14 hands) dark bay colt was born, probably in 1789, in Massachusetts. Experts can't agree on exactly what mix of horse he was—possibly some combination of Thoroughbred, Arab, or Welsh cob. He was eventually sold to the impoverished sometime music master who would give him—and the breed—his name: Justin Morgan. It wasn't long before he was demonstrating incredible strength and versatility as a plough horse, harness horse, racer, and, as his reputation grew, a sire, standing for a number of different owners after Justin Morgan's death. Three of his sons, Sherman, Bullrush, and Woodbury, carried on the line.

What they look like: Whatever Justin Morgan's breeding was, the result was the dainty and curvaceous powerhouse we know today. Morgans still run small, though selective breeding has produced a somewhat larger animal, but all are short-backed and have distinctive curved necks, round bodies, and wide but delicate faces. Two types of Morgans are now bred: Park, with higher leg action like that of the Saddlebreds to which Morgans contributed; and Pleasure, a calmer, smoother ride. Height: 14.1 to 15.2 hands. Color: bay, black, or chestnut.

What they're like: Just what you'd expect from New England— hardy, willing, affectionate, but unfussy.

What they do: Everything. At one time the chosen mount of the army, Morgans are shown in almost every type of show class there is, both riding and driving, including English and Western pleasure (see Chapter 16), hunter, jumper, dressage, reining, and cutting.

They were the first breed to represent the country in a World Pairs Driving competition.

How many? Approximately 90,000, according to the American Morgan Horse Association.

Faster Than a Speeding Bullet: The Quarter Horse

In a tribute to the form that makes reining and rodeo so spectacular to watch, Quarter Horses, which got their name from the quarter-mile races they were originally bred to run, are said to be able to run, "turn on a dime, and toss you back nine cents change."

Where they come from: Here, actually. The Quarter Horse is the oldest officially established American breed, and despite all those cowboys we picture aboard, its origins were in seventeenth-century Virginia. At the time, local horses were descended from various combinations of English pony stock and Spanish horses with Arab influence brought over by the conquistadors. Not everyone agrees about who married or influenced whom, but some combination of this sort was eventually bred to the influx of English Thoroughbreds and began to generate a line of horses that were distinguished by their muscular compact bodies and powerful thrust at the start of a race. To suit the action to the horse, and to save land for farming, English settlers began establishing quarter-mile races, giving this fledgling breed its name.

The Thoroughbred stallion Janus, imported from England by Virginia planter Mordecai Booth, was responsible for much of the Quarter Horse line, passing along his strong bones and large, powerful hindquarters. Another influential sire was Sir Archy, but the breed actually has 11 foundation families, with the sort of down-home names—The Shiloh, Old Billy, Steel Dust, and in the twentieth century, Joe Bailey and Peter McCue—that reflected the next stage of the Quarter Horse's career.

With flat racing increasingly established in the southern and eastern states, Quarter Horse racing fell out of favor, and the dominance of the breed moved, like much of the country itself, westward, where its speed and agility were much appreciated on cattle ranches.

What they look like: Quarter Horses are the Carl Lewises of the horse world, with a little Arnold Schwarzenegger thrown in—powerfully built sprinters with a chunky, compact pumping-iron look, large hindquarters for that explosive spring, and strong, short legs. Another distinguishing characteristic is the flexion through the tapering hock joints (like a sort of backward knee) in the hind legs—this gives them the ability to flex deeply, a skill in demand in reining and cattle roping. Squarish heads on shorter, muscular necks contribute to the can-do look. Height: 14.3 to 16 hands. Color: all solid colors.

What they're like: Like cowboy, like horse. A calm, reliable sort with occasional streaks of stubbornness. Comfortable alone, and good in crowds.

What they do: Considered the ideal trail horse, the growth of rodeo and the Western horse show circuit has given them more performance-oriented roles as pleasure, reining, roping, and barrel-racing horses, as well as being used as eventers. In recent years, Quarter Horse racing has regained its popularity, with purses that give Thoroughbred flat racing a literal run for its money. And in the ongoing horse recipe hunt, if Thoroughbreds are cream, Quarter Horses are flour, adding bulk to various crossbreeds.

Horse Lore

The Hobby, first mentioned in a reference in 1375, is the oldest recorded ancestor of the Quarter Horse. Many Hobby horses were imported to the United States in the seventeenth and eighteenth centuries. Hobby was a general term used to describe any small farm or cart horse and is probably responsible for the naming of the favorite child's toy—you guessed it—the hobby horse!

How many? A lot. There are more than 4,574,000 registered Quarter Horses, making this the world's most popular breed. The Quarter Horse is the largest breed registry in the United States, with no close second.

Every Gait but Neutral: The Saddlebred

The American Saddlebred has the in-your-face animation of a high fashion model, but enthusiasts say it's an all-around pleasure horse. Both facets of its character come from its early history.

Where they come from: Like the Standardbred, the Saddlebred is a cocktail of early pacing horses (the Canadian and Narragansett, Thoroughbred, and Morgan), but the same ingredients produced quite a different result. The Saddlebred, known as both "the American Horse" and "the Kentucky Saddler" was bred by Southern plantation owners to be both practical and elegant—able to spend a long day in the fields and still drive you to church in your Sunday best. So successful were their efforts that the first documented mention of the breed is in a letter from an American diplomat stationed in Paris, trying to obtain one as a gift for Marie Antoinette (let them eat hay).

Its pacer ancestry has given the Saddlebred its most striking characteristic: its showy gaits with elevated knee action. As recreational and exhibition riding succeeded day-to-day work, the horse was bred to show these to advantage. In addition to the three "natural" gaits, some of the horses are taught two additional four-beat gaits, the *stepping pace* (slow gait) and the *rack*, producing a three-gaited and five-gaited variety. Around these have grown an extensive show culture of pleasure riding and driving, and an immediately identifiable look.

From the Horse's Mouth

The **rack** is one of two four-beat gaits—the other is called the **stepping pace** (slow gait)—that are taught to the naturally high-stepping Saddlebreds. In each, the legs are brought up level or above level with the barrel, almost as if the horse were a marionette, and the rack is as furiously quick as a piston engine.

What they look like: If they were starlets, Saddlebreds might almost be termed voluptuous. They have long, sweeping backs and high, rounded necks and haunches, with delicate heads and small, curved ears. The head is set naturally high on the neck, as if already anticipating those show ring antics, and they have exceptionally long pasterns (the ankle bit of the horse), which helps those lightning-bolt strides to seem actually comfortable. The trademark high "action" of the legs and knees is usually implicit from birth, though training brings it out. Height: 15.2 to 16.2 hands. Color: Any, although chestnuts and bays are most common, with spotted versions becoming popular in recent years.

What they're like: As they churn through their paces in the show ring, they appear flashy and high-strung, but fans claim they have a kinder, gentler side, as is evidenced by their many other uses.

What they do: Saddlebreds are shown both under saddle and in harness in gaited classes, but, like their Kentucky forebears, they are versatile, and are also used in dressage, jumping, and Western pleasure classes, and without all their makeup on, make comfortable trail riding partners.

How many? There are 246,600 registered American Saddlebreds.

Pacemaker: The Standardbred

The term Standardbred, first used in 1879, comes from the "standard" speed required for a horse to be accepted to the breed registry. Originally 3:00, it was later reduced to 2:30 for trotters and 2:25 for pacers. Of course, today's surging racers easily surpass these.

Where they come from: If you think multicultural is a trendy term invented to describe contemporary society, meet the Standardbred, the world's leading harness-racing horse. On the father's side, all

Horse Sense

Most horses trot (the intermediate gait after the walk and before the canter) using diagonal pairs of legs; but pacers, which make up the majority of Standardbreds in harness racing today, move using lateral pairs of legs.

Standardbreds trace back to a Thoroughbred aptly named Messenger, but the female line includes Morgans, two defunct breeds—the Clays and the Narragansett Pacer, which were popular in the American colonies—and Spanish Jennets brought by the conquistadors. This was one of several "ambling" breeds, with rideable shuffling gaits, and these lines helped to create one of the most distinctive variations in the breed—some horses pace rather than trot.

Standardbreds have two racing gaits: trotting, where the legs move diagonally, as with most horses, and the unique "pace," where they move laterally.

Messenger was imported to the United States in 1788; 60 years later his ill-tempered grandson Abdullah sired the most important horse in Standardbred history, Hambletonian. His dam (mother to you) traced back to the smooth-gaited Norfork Trotters, and this combination of pace and speed gave the young horse impressive times on training tracks, although he never raced formally. In one of the horse world's many rags-to-riches stories, Hambletonian had been purchased from his original breeder, Jonas Seely, by a farm hand, William Rysdyk, for $125. In retrospect, this seems as neat a deal as the celebrated purchase of Manhattan Island: By the end of his life, the horse had earned more than $200,000 at stud, and sired 1,335 foals—the Casanova of horses.

Hambletonian sired a dynasty, and also gave his name to the premiere event in harness racing, second only to flat racing in popularity. Though trotting fools, Standardbreds have also been used for crossbreeding.

What they look like: The most distinctive thing about the breed is the extremely strong legs able to withstand the strain of pulling in harness. Like a good sports car, Standardbreds are built long and low, with a lean, straight physique that is less voluptuous than a Thoroughbred, and a croup (or rump) that is usually higher than the shoulder, giving the horse its driving power. Standardbreds look long all over, in fact, as if they were ironed Thoroughbreds. Height: 14 to 16 hands. Color: Usually bay, but other solid colors are possible.

What they do: Well, duh. The majority of Standardbreds are still used for harness racing, but they make tractable saddlehorses and have been used in such disciplines as trail riding and dressage successfully, in addition to providing the basis for a variety of crossbreeds, such as the National Show Horse, which is at least 25 percent Arabian and American Saddlebred.

How many? Figures vary. The United States Trotting Association estimates the current population at between 90,000 and 100,000, but *Western Horseman*, in a recent issue on top breeds, came up with a figure of 500,000 from multiple sources. These horses go into the general population after their racing careers end and are harder to track.

Easy Rider: Tennessee Walking Horse

The fourth leading horse in the country, Walkers still retain the stylish looks and easy strides for which they were originally bred.

The Tennessee Walking Horse has three gaits: the flat-foot walk, running walk, and canter. The first is a distinct, even four-beat gait with long strides. The second is basically a speeded-up version of the first, but, because the front foot strikes the ground just before the diagonal hind foot, gives the rider the sensation of gliding—a horse

can travel up to 10 to 15 miles an hour at this gait over short distances. A Walker's canter has a distinctive rocking motion, and is sometimes called a "rocking horse" canter. At the walk, the head bobs rhythmically in time to the movement, and in arrested motion it looks as if the animal is trying to shake your hand!

Where they come from: Early plantation owners in Tennessee and surrounding areas were looking for a good riding horse that could carry them through a long day on the plantation, where hours in the saddle could make the usual up-and-down thrust of a horse's trot uncomfortable. Like the first Saddlebred breeders, they looked to the universal donor of gaited horses, the extinct Narragansett Pacer, and combined these bloodlines with Thoroughbred, Morgan, Saddlebred, and Standardbred. The Stardardbred Black Allan, born in 1886, is considered the breed's foundation sire. He was bred as a trotter, but seemed only capable of a strange skimming gait that became the hallmark of the breed.

What they look like: Someone you'd want to take a good long walk with. A deep body tops sturdy, rather than elegant, legs, and it carries its neck much lower than its flashy cousin the Saddlebred. Horse people sometimes seem stuck with nineteenth-century snobberies, and the Walker's head has been referred to as "plain"; but sensible, like a good pair of shoes, is the better interpretation. And speaking of shoes, Walkers, like Saddlebreds, usually have pads and rounded toes for the show ring, to help sustain and highlight the walk, though these are not used for pleasure horses. Height: 14.2 to 17.0 hands. Color: If you ask anybody to picture a classic Walker, they will probably have in mind a tangerine-y chestnut with a dark or blonde mane, but actually black is by far the most popular color, and they also come in other solids, including gray.

What they're like: Walkers are famous for their exceptionally gentle dispositions, perfect for children and nervous new riders. Like a good soft-shoe man, they seem to be able to create their stylish gait without sacrificing a calmness of motion and disposition.

What they do: Even without plantation rows to delicately maneuver through, Walkers are still as smooth a ride as you can get. The breed association modestly declares them "World's Greatest Show, Trail, and Pleasure Horse," and they are shown in both English and Western tack in trail and pleasure classes. It is a measure of the breed's popularity that the annual show held in Shelbyville, Tennessee, is referred to as the "Tennessee Walking Horse National Celebration," and attracts a record number of entries.

How many? There are 410,000 registered Tennessee Walking Horses.

Kissin' Cousins: Missouri Fox Trotter

"It only happens when I'm dancing with you." Not quite as popular as the Walker, this Ozark-bred gaited horse, crafted by nineteenth-century Western pioneers, has some Walker in its pedigree, as well as Saddlebred, Thoroughbred, and Arabian. First bred to navigate rough roads, it is now distinguished by its natural dancing gait. It walks with its front legs and trots behind, making it perhaps the last of the true "amblers," and one of the smoothest rides around. It is used in a variety of trail and Western pleasure contexts, and is happiest when doing something with the family. Height: 14.0 to 16.0 hands. Color: All colors, although chestnut and black are common.

How many? There are 69,000 registered Missouri Fox Trotters.

Class Act: Thoroughbred

All horses are equal, but some are more equal than others, and the flowing lines, bold temperaments, and colorful history of the Thoroughbred may make it the quintessence of "horse."

Where they come from: The name says it all: a horse that is a triumph of selective breeding. Royal patronage of racing by Charles II (1660–1685) and later Queen Anne (1702–1714) led to the quest for improved racing stock, and following a fashion that had gotten its first push during the Crusades, English breeders began crossing their local

mares, many derived from draft stock, with "hot" horses from the East. This eventually produced a range of horses, not yet specifically designated as an official breed, known as "running horses," and these horses were in turn bred to the three official "foundation" sires from which all registered Thoroughbreds must show descent. (With us so far?)

These are as well known in horse lore as any Biblical patriarch, and with family trees almost as big (if not as troublesome). The earliest (1690) was the Byerley Turk, a war horse who later stood at stud in County Durham. The Darley Arabian was purchased (by Mr. Darley) from Sheik Mirza II in 1704 (the Sheik, perhaps realizing his mistake, later tried to welsh on the deal). The third sire was the Godolphin Arabian, owned by Lord Godolphin. From these horses derived the first real "Thoroughbreds" who are the actual start of the various stallions from whose bloodlines most Thoroughbreds descend: Herod, Eclipse, and Matchem.

> **Horse Lore**
>
> "Eclipse First, the Rest Nowhere" was the catchphrase coined to celebrate the Thoroughbred's most influential stallion, Eclipse. Foaled in 1764, this unbeaten racehorse sired 335 winners, and 90 percent of all thoroughbreds trace back to him.

After 1770, the Thoroughbred was considered sufficiently established in England for breeders to dispense with the services of Arabian stallions.

In America, racing and stud farms were well established by the eighteenth century, especially in Virginia, and the breeding industry really expanded after the Revolutionary War. The studs first relied on imported stallions such as Bulle Rock (the first Thoroughbred in America) and Diomed (winner of the first English Derby), who sired the first great homegrown stallion, Sir Archy, whose career as a father lasted 23 years.

What they look like: Thoroughbreds are both elegant and tough, with strong, well-muscled (when fit) backs and loins; long, powerful legs with large flat joints (like good machinery, this makes the interplay of sinews over bones smoother); well-laid, back-sloping shoulders, and fine heads well set on sloping necks. In motion, this produces a powerful sweeping action. The various breed lines have produced a range of signature "looks"—some Thoroughbreds have large, noble heads, others more delicate and tapered ones, hinting at their Arab ancestry. They are also thin-skinned, in both senses of the word, which usually produces lustrous coats. Height: 14.3 to 17.2 hands. Color: any solid color.

What they're like: Large hearts and a great deal of nervous intelligence. Adept at learning, but in need of reassurance about the world around them, and you.

What they do: Run, of course. Early races were up to 12 miles, and these horses still offer virtually unbeatable combinations of speed and stamina. In addition to use on the racetrack, their power and grace has earned them a place in competitive disciplines such as hunter/jumper, three-day eventing, and dressage (see also Chapter 16). And the successful outcome of inspired cross-breeding, they are being used in their turn to create a new generation of sporting horses through their union with a wide variety of breeds—like adding a little cream to a recipe to enhance its richness and elegance.

How many? There are 1,593,000 registered Thoroughbreds.

The Exotics

In a country as large as this one, many of the world's breeds are represented in some form, but a few are beginning to gain ground as popular favorites to judge by publicity and their registry numbers.

Peruvian Paso

Known as the "Peruvian Stepping Horse," this breed has a high head and downward-sloping back, and exhibits naturally the same type of eccentric lateral pace as the Missouri Fox Trotter. Of mixed Arab,

Barb, and Andalusian blood, this rugged trail horse is now used for pleasure and parades. Height: 14.2 to 15.2 hands. Color: Mostly solid colors and gray, but occasionally roan and Palomino.

Paso Fino

The cameo version of the Paso, bred in Puerto Rico, although it may have originated with horses brought to the Dominican Republic by Christopher Columbus. It has a unique four-beat gait, a broad head and alert expression, and is very popular as a trail, driving, and pleasure horse, where their glamorous long manes and tails make an impressive show. Height: 14.0 to 15.0 hands. Color: Most colors.

How many? There are 35,540 registered Paso Finos.

Andalusian/Lusitano

These romantic-looking Iberian breeds (the Andalusian hails from Southern Spain, the Lusitano from Portugal, but they now share the same registry) trace back to the early Barbs of North Africa, and eons before that to the horses of the prehistoric cave paintings. They have short, study legs that contribute to the agility needed for bullfighting, one of their primary jobs. But their strikingly beautiful heads, with wide-apart eyes, their rounded contours, and their big movements have made them a favorite with photographers and artists, and they have an increasing presence in high school dressage competitions and, of course, ceremonial occasions. They are well mannered and intelligent, probably setting a good example for the many celebrities who own them. Height: 15.1 to 16.0 hands. Colors: mostly solid colors, especially gray, and occasionally roan.

How many? There are 5,600 registered, and all purebreds trace back to the stud books of Spain and/or Portugal.

The Least You Need to Know

- Quarter Horses are the most popular breed in the United States.

- Horses come in a great array of colors, but some patterns, like Pinto, Paint, and Palomino, have their own registries, and Paint is considered a breed as well as a coloration.

- The American gaited horses, Saddlebreds, Tennessee Walkers, and Missouri Fox Trotters, share common ancestors.

- The Morgan was the first documented American breed.

Chapter 4

Big, Small, and in Between

In This Chapter

- The major and most influential breeds of draft horses
- Miniature horses
- Common pony breeds
- Warmbloods and sport horses
- Asses and mules

From horses who weigh more than a ton to those small enough to be walked like dogs, from the ponies who start many people on their riding careers to today's equine athletes—this chapter provides a look at some of the most interesting specimens at the extremes of the equine world. We'll also look at donkeys and mules, some form of which accompanied the earliest horses across the frozen tundras and preceded them as pack and harness animals.

Draft
17-21

Horse
14.3-18.0

Pony
10-14.2

Miniature
34"-38"

All shapes and sizes: The Mini could fit inside the Shire.

Gentle Giants

No one quite knows what qualified as the first draft horse, but the heavy-boned breeds that evolved from the European Forest Horses took different forms depending on the culture and the way history shaped its needs and breeding programs. Even today, almost every nation that works with and supports a horse population has one or more draft breeds.

Land Mass: The Shire

The largest breed of draft horse, this one-ton wonder originated in the Middle Ages from a now extinct breed called Old English Black, or Great Horse, mixed with a lighter German draft breed called the Friesian (see the later section). The early version, like the early knight he carried, was much smaller than today's massive version, which did not really come into being until the sixteenth century. Even then it was a work in progress, and the Shire's foundation sire, the Packington Blind Horse, didn't begin his career until the middle of the eighteenth century.

From the Horse's Mouth _____

Draft beer and draft horses both have big heads, but also share a common ancestry: brewery wagons. "Draft" is the term for any horse who draws a heavy vehicle, but has come to be applied generally to the massive breeds, with their huge hooves and long silky hair, known as "feathers," on their lower legs, who generally shouldered these burdens.

By the nineteenth century, the breed was renowned for its equitable temper and amazing pulling ability, still to be seen at exhibitions and parades today. It is also used as a cross to produce today's sport horses. Distinctive feature: Roman nose. Height: 16.0 to 18.0 hands. Color: black, bay, brown, and gray.

"This Clyde's for You ...": The Clydesdale

A late-comer in the draft stakes, the Clydesdale began its formal life in the eighteenth century as the result of the simultaneous aggressive breeding programs of the Duke of Hamilton and John Paterson of Lochlyoch, working with Flemish horses that they had imported. This interbreeding resulted in a coincidence of the two lines in a horse with the industrial-sounding name of Glancer 335, the breed's foundation sire. He was followed by Clyde, who gave his name to this now world-famous breed, whose straight knees, feathery legs, and large animated heads have endeared it to, among others, generations of Budweiser drinkers. And this is no accident, as Clydesdale breeders were enthusiastic marketers abroad. Distinctive feature: White blaze or stripe on face and stockings on legs. Height: 16.3 to 18.0 hands. Color: bay.

Horse Sense _____

Clydesdale judges often look first at the horses' feet, which are meant to be very wide and flat, with well-developed frogs (the springy underside of the hoof) to withstand concussion on city streets (sort of like being born with tennis shoes on).

Belgian by Any Other Name: Brabant

Ironically, the Belgian Draft Horse barely exists in Belgium anymore, but deserves mention here both because of its historical influence and because it is now much more popular here than in its home country. An old breed (Julius Caesar mentioned a version of it in his war memoirs), it has influenced many other breeds. Of the three main lines that established the breed in the nineteenth century, one stallion was fittingly called Orange I, because the coppery chestnut coat of the Belgian is one of its most notable features, along with a classically arched neck. Noted for their strong legs, they are still used for farming. Distinctive trait: dimpled hindquarters and (frequently) sunny chestnut coats. Height: 15.3 to 17.0 hands. Color: Most are chestnut or sorrel with flaxen manes and tails.

From the Horse's Mouth

What's in a name? This breed is known today as the Belgian Heavy Draft but is more popularly referred to as the **Brabant**, from the region in Belgium most responsible for it. One of the oldest draft breeds, it has also been referred to as the Flanders Horse, and may trace its ancestry directly back to one of the four primitive "foundation" horses, *Equus sylvaticus* (Forest Horse).

Arabian Knights: The Percheron

The most elegant and possibly the most popular of the draft breeds, the Percheron (from the Le Perche region of Normandy) still shows

Horse Lore

Percherons are the holders of two equine records: the unofficial world pulling record (3,410 pounds) and the world's biggest horse, Dr. Le Gear (21 hands).

hints of the Arab blood that helped shape it at the time of the early wars against the Moors in 732 and later in the Crusades. It has a strikingly arched neck and refined features, with a free walk that has made it popular in circuses and as a cross with other breeds to produce sport and stock horses. Distinctive feature: Elegance in a big package. Height: 16.2 to 19.0 hands. Color: gray or black, frequently dappled, with blue-tinted hooves.

"The Best Things Come in ...": Miniature Horses

"If I wanted a dog, I'd be reading a different book," you're thinking. But don't ever let a mini enthusiast hear you say so. This fast-growing breed, in a time-, space-, and money-conscious age, is meant to encapsulate the best traits of the horse in a small package—34 to 38 inches, depending on which registry you consult. And Minis are not all that recent a phenomenon. Established in the nineteenth century, they came from a variety of bloodlines including an Argentinean version called the Falabella, pit ponies from the mines, and, most influentially, the Shetland Pony.

These days Minis can look like little Arabians or little Quarter Horses, but the important thing is that they look and act like little horses. And you can do as much with them as you can with their full-size cousins, as long as you don't mind being on the sidelines. Minis drive, jump, show in harness, are fun to dress up, and are naturals for children, seniors, and as therapy horses. So come on, what were you going to do with your backyard, anyway? Distinctive feature: That they be of horse-type conformation and not that of a pony. Height: 34 inches (to qualify for the American Miniature Horse Association) to 38 inches (for the American Miniature Horse Registry). Minis are measured from the last hair at the base of the mane to the ground. Color: all colors.

Horse Lore

Minis, like the pit ponies from which they are partly descended, were sometimes used in coal mines, and even today a fit Mini can pull a 200-pound man in a cart.

(© Karen Winston)

Persia has one eye on the camera and the other on Mr. Snowman's carrot nose (which became lunch the minute this photo was snapped). Persia is a 17-year-old, 32¹/₂ inch, silver-dappled mare, and the mother of Savannah, pictured in the color insert. Owned by Solar Wind Miniature Horses, Perkasie, Pennsylvania.

Little Devils: Ponies

Nature seemed to think there was good reason to keep some things small. Among the first equine types to emerge from the final prehistoric stages were two *pony* types, distinguished, like today's models, by being hardy and waterproof. From these tough diminutive beginnings emerged some of the many pony breeds, which became the focus of selective breeding in the nineteenth century. In case you missed them when you were 12, following are some popular favorites. For many, a pony was both a dream come true and a small hell—they are determined, mischievous, willful, and fast—but can be the best teachers any child could have.

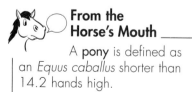

From the Horse's Mouth

A **pony** is defined as an *Equus caballus* shorter than 14.2 hands high.

Everybody's Favorite: The Shetland

There are two types of Shetland Ponies: British and American. Even though the American Shetland is a descendant of the British pony, it is a very different animal.

Where they come from: The British Shetland Pony is thought to have been with us since the Bronze age. It evolved on the Shetland Islands, about 100 miles off the northern coast of Scotland, where it remained as a pint-size draft animal until brought to the mainland in the nineteenth century.

What they look like: A little like a Vietnamese pot-bellied pig. The Shetland is the smallest of the British breeds and stands only 40 inches at the withers, with a low sloping back and prodigious amounts of hair compared to body mass. Height: 10 hands. Color: mostly black but also brown, chestnut, gray, and pinto.

What they're like: This is a tough little pony who evolved on a cold island with limited food in supply. It is versatile and adaptable.

What they do: Over the years it was used as a pack and harness animal, as a children's pony, as an attraction in public parks, and as a lawn ornament on some of the great estates. It was the Shetland who was pressed into service in 1847 as a pit pony in the coal mines.

As a popular child's pony, this breed has taught many children to ride and given them their fondest (or worst) memories of the experience. There's no doubt that the Shetland is smarter than the majority of children it hauls around.

How many? Shetlands have been exported all over the world, in particular the United States, Canada, and Europe. All have large populations and operate their own studbooks. The breed is also the basis for the miniature horse.

The New Breed: The American Shetland

You know us—build a better mousetrap. The American Shetland was created by selecting the more refined types of Island Shetlands and crossing them with Hackney ponies. The offspring were then crossed with Arabians and small Thoroughbreds. The result was a Shetland much flashier in appearance than its stocky British cousin and one that bears no resemblance to the original Island pony.

Where they come from: Within about 50 years of the arrival of the first 75 Shetland Ponies in America in 1885, two separate breeds emerged: The Pony of the Americas (see the following section) and the American Shetland, which has had its own breed club since 1888.

What they look like: The American Shetland is a Hackney type with a high stepping action, more of an elegant little cart or show pony than its roly-poly counterpart. Height: 11.2 hands. Color: all colors and pinto patterns.

What they're like: With the influx of Hackney, Arab, and Thoroughbred blood it took to transform the original Shetlands, a somewhat more animated animal resulted—in mind, as well as in body; more like a little horse.

What they do: The American Shetland is extremely versatile. It is shown in harness, drawing two- and four-wheeled buggies and also races in lightweight sulkies. It is also ridden in either English or Western tack and a hunter type jumps small fences. There is also a show pony who competes with weighted shoes and set-up tails, in a style similar to that of the gaited horses such as the American Saddlebred—a look that would astonish its hard-working, plain-shod British cousin.

How many? It's the country's most popular pony, with more than 50,000 registered.

The Colorful Pony: Pony of the Americas

Growing in popularity, these made-in-America ponies are valued for their stylish looks and versatility.

Where they come from: The second descendant of that first batch of imported British Shetlands, the Pony of the Americas was the result of a one-man crusade. Leslie Boomhower of Mason City, Iowa, set out to produce an attractive child's riding pony that could be used in every activity whether ridden in English or Western tack. The breed's foundation stallion, Black Hand, was foaled in 1954, sired by a Shetland stallion out of an Appaloosa mare. Subsequent offspring were crossed with Arabians and Quarter Horses.

What they look like: Well, genetics isn't always straightforward, but the POA breed standard is just what you'd expect from its past: a pony who looks like a miniature Quarter Horse–Arabian cross with some Appaloosa features and markings, and physical characteristics. Their pert faces extend out of strikingly curved necks. Height: 11.2 to 13.2 hands. Color: polka dots. (See the Appaloosa section in Chapter 3 for color description.)

What they do: Live up to their founder's expectations—a good all-around pony, with smooth gaits and a pleasing personality; they don't care what the tack looks like as long as there's a child aboard.

How many? Registrations are now more than 45,000.

The Celtic Pony: The Connemara

If the Shetland grew in isolation, Ireland's only native pony, the Connemara, named for its region, thrived on invasion and interference. They originally resembled Shetlands, but in the sixteenth and seventeenth centuries there was an infusion of Spanish Jennet blood and then that of the Barb in the nineteenth century, producing leaner, more refined types with that hallmark ambling gait that was the Jennet's gift to all its descendants.

Popularity took its toll, however: By the end of the nineteenth century, the quality of the Connemara had deteriorated along with the standard of living of the farming communities in which it lived. This may be one of the few breeds actually saved by a government inquiry, which began in 1887, and determined on a controlled breeding

program to bring the Connemara back to its former self and forward into the future.

What they look like: The reinvented, reinvigorated pony combines Hackney and Thoroughbred blood among other influences such as Arab, Welsh Pony, and Irish Draught. The result is a handsome animal with a deep shoulder and phenomenal toughness and jumping ability, and an elegant free stride. Height: 13.0 hands to small horse size. Color: Many solid colors, including traditional dun, and some roan, but most often thought of as gray or gray roan, probably a romantic association with its stormy coastline and most famous foundation sire, Cannon Ball.

Horse Lore _____

Among the "new" Connemara's foundation sires, the gray stallion Cannon Ball easily has the most colorful history. He worked in harness throughout his life, still managed to win a local race 16 years in a row, and the story goes that he regularly trotted home from market while his owner, Harry O'Toole, slept off his liquid supper in the bottom of the cart. Cannon Ball's death was marked with a traditional Irish Wake.

What they do: With typical Irish flair, the Connemara takes naturally to performance, and is seen frequently in children's hunter and jumper classes. Crosses with Thoroughbreds and Arabians have produced strong event horses as well, hardy and full of heart, with a kind temperament, and strong enough to carry adults as well as children. They also make stylish harness horses.

How many? There are 5,000 registered with the American Connemara Pony Society, but this is also a popular import.

The Beauty: The Welsh Pony of Cob Type

The Welsh Pony lived in the hills of Wales long before the Romans got there. Like other ponies of the region, he subsisted on meager amounts of food, but continued to thrive and evolved into the sturdy, intelligent pony we have today. The Welsh even managed to survive the edict of King Henry VII that all horses smaller than 15 hands be destroyed.

Through the years the Welsh Pony has served many masters: He pulled chariots, worked in coal mines, delivered mail, and was even a ranch horse.

What they look like: The Welsh has been called the most beautiful of the native British ponies, and owes some of its fairytale looks to Arabian, Thoroughbred, and Hackney influence, although the Welsh cob tradition has given it a hardy constitution. The ideal type has large dark eyes, a delicate head, small ears, short back, high-set tail, strong hindquarters, and slender, elegant legs. Height: Because of their size and talents, the registry divides these animals into four sections: Section A (also known as the Welsh Mountain Pony): 12.0 to 12.2 hands; Section B: not to exceed 14.2 hands with no lower height limit; Section C (also known as the Welsh Pony of Cob Type): may not exceed 13.2 hands; Section D (the Welsh Cob): 13.2 hands with no upper height limit. All colors are acceptable, except for pinto markings.

(© Lori Steffensen; rider: Christie Schnurr)

A Welsh pony doing what ponies do best—teach children.

What they're like: The Welsh Pony has a friendly personality, is intelligent, alert, and usually has an even temper. This is a pony that can be trusted. He responds well to good treatment and shows respect for the person (old or young) that shows respect for him. The Welsh is an ideal mount for a growing child, but it also has the spirit and endurance to challenge an adult.

What they do: One of the most versatile of all breeds, the Welsh is perfect for all types of riding and driving, for both children and adults.

How many? The Welsh Pony & Cob Society reports that more than 34,000 have been registered and that all of these animals are descended from animals registered with the Society in England.

The Storybook Pony: Chincoteague

Legend has it that in the seventeenth century, Barb horses swam to safety after the Spanish vessel in which they were being transported from Africa to Peru capsized off the coast of Virginia. Other sources, skeptical of the convenient romance of the shipwreck, think it is more likely that the ponies descended from stock abandoned by colonists. Either way, there was definitely some early Spanish influence.

The first ponies, breeding on one of two then-connected islands (Chincoteague is Native American for "beautiful land across the waters"; the other island is Assateague), survived on meager rations of coarse beach grasses, weeds (even poison ivy!), and twigs, and drank salt water. One of the few genuinely feral herds, by the time they were discovered in the 1920s they suffered badly from defects caused by inbreeding.

Arranged Marriages

Today the herd (actually there are two herds, one on Assateague Island and one on Chincoteague) is managed, and Pintos, Arabians, and Welsh ponies have been introduced over the years to broaden the gene pool and improve the stock.

In July of every year, the Chincoteague Volunteer Fire Department, in a tradition begun in 1924, herds the ponies off Assateague Island at slack tide and they swim to Chincoteague Island where the foals and yearlings are auctioned off. In 2001, one pony went for more than $10,000!

Horse Lore

Marguerite Henry, through her book *Misty of Chincoteague*, published in 1947, is credited with giving this real-life pony, and its island home, the popularity they have enjoyed in recent years (there was a also a film version of the book in 1961). Every year dozens of horse lovers journey to Chincoteague and neighboring Assateague to participate in the annual pony penning she made famous. The Chincoteague is America's only indigenous pony, and perhaps in honor of this, the original Misty, a Pinto, and two of her descendants had a shoulder marking that looked like a map of the United States.

What they look like: Chincoteagues are likely to display a range of types reflecting the donor breeds that have made an impact over the years, including Arabians, Welsh, Shetlands, Pintos, and Mustangs, but generally they have large, expressive heads (perfect for making up a story about!) on short, round bodies with low hindquarters. The years of existing on food with very little nutritional value has made these ponies into very easy keepers, and it is said that the Chincoteague can get fat off a cement slab. Height: 12.2 to 14 hands. Color: primarily Palomino and bay Pintos, with some solid black and a Mustang-y sorrel.

What they're like: Like any feral population, they have an independent streak, but are increasingly gaining a reputation for being clever and trainable.

What they do: Leaving behind their island paradise for the rigors of civilization, Chincoteagues, some now bred on the mainland, are increasingly used in English and Western Pleasure classes, under harness, in dressage, and even as hunters. Misty would be astonished!

How many? There are approximately 180 privately owned Chincoteague ponies in the United States and Canada. (The registry was founded in the 1980s by Gale Park Frederick.) But the number may grow as today's Chincoteagues extend their own legend and mainland breeders increase the available numbers.

SUVs: Warmbloods and "Sport Horses"

It's possible to carry the car/horse analogy too far, but today's warmblood really is bred to be the equine equivalent of the sports utility vehicle—large, dependable, with four-wheel drive and off-road capability. But if the advertising jargon is new, the model is not. Warmbloods (you remember: they're the combination of hot, i.e., Thoroughbred/Arab, and cold, i.e., draft, horses) have been around in Europe since the eleventh century, and for much the same reason: a need for a solid all-purpose horse. Of course, the purposes were different, and the earlier warmbloods were often a combination riding, driving, cavalry, and sometimes even farm horse, while today's version is used for dressage, jumping, and three-day eventing. (See Chapter 16 for detailed descriptions of these disciplines.)

From the Horse's Mouth

Sometimes used interchangeably with "warmblood," **sport horse** is a term often used more casually than accurately to describe horses of some draft/warmblood/thoroughbred derivation being bred or shown specifically as sports performance horses. The Irish Sporthorse is a specific type—Irish Thoroughbred and Irish Draught—but you will now read of Arab or Appaloosa sport horses, for example, and many dealers suddenly seem to be offering this type of animal.

Warmbloods are more than a simple mix of draft horse and Thoroughbred. In the countries where they originated—Germany, Denmark, Sweden, the Netherlands, France, Belgium—rigorous selective breeding programs combining a number of different strains, including those of other warmbloods, resulted in a range of versatile horses. In general, however, especially as the market has grown in the United States, there is a significant dose of Thoroughbred.

Warmbloods first attracted the attention of twentieth-century competitive riders because of their strong performance in the dressage ring—they are naturally big, graceful movers. As interbreeding has added more Thoroughbred to many of the breeds and lines, they became increasingly in demand as jumpers—combining the responsiveness and agility of the Thoroughbred with sturdiness of bone and a calmer temperament, though they can be stubborn and have been described as having a strong survival instinct, making them less generous than their hot-headed colleagues.

Brave Little Belgians

Definitely the youngsters in the warmblood tradition, these (relatively) small horses were fashioned in the 1950s in response to a need for a lighter, more performance-oriented horse than the traditional heavy farm horse. Contributing breeds include the Holsteiner, Anglo-Arabs, Dutch Warmbloods, and Thoroughbreds, making the shapely Belgian a competitive answer to international challenges. An increasing presence on the jumping and dressage teams, more than 4,500 are foaled each year. Distinctive features: elegant head and legs. Height: 16.2 to 16.3 hands. Color: any solid shade.

Universal Donor: The Friesian

Among the earliest of established breeds—they are mentioned as brave and competent, but ugly! by the Roman historian Tacitus (55–120 C.E.)—Friesians, considered a light draft horse, have contributed to many other breeds and are enjoying a surge of popularity as dressage and driving horses, and for cross-breeding. Bred in the Netherlands, they almost became extinct in 1913, but fuel shortages in World War II made Dutch farmers see the value of horse power

over—well—horsepower. Distinctive features: High head carriage on muscular necks, animated trots, exceptionally long, thick manes and tails, and prominently feathered feet. Height: 15 to 16 hands. Color: like the original Model T, any color so long as it's black. There are only 3,400 registered in North America.

"H" Is for Hanover: Hanoverian

The Hanoverian is one of several breeds that got its start by royal decree. George I of England was also the Elector of Hanover, and he decided to combine the best of his two worlds by cross-breeding native horses with imported English Thoroughbreds. His son George II founded the stud at Celle that formally established the breeding program, based on 14 Holsteiner sires; from the eighteenth century onward, detailed pedigree records have been kept on every horse bred at Celle. The type of horse produced varied with the need of the times, and early Hanoverians, needed for both plough and parade, were heavier and less graceful. Today, with even more Thoroughbred blood in their veins, they are both strong and elegant, with down-sloping hindquarters that help give power to their jumps. The Hanoverian is a horse for serious riding. He is a world-class athlete, with 13 medals won in the 1992 Olympics. Height: 15.3 to 17.2 hands. Color: all solid colors. There are 6,000 are registered with the American Hanoverian Society.

Horse Lore

Hanoverians, one of the best-known of the warmblood breeds, is not only a brand name, but actually branded. Genuine Hanoverians have a brand on their lower hip, an impressionistic "H" topped by two horse heads that was inspired by designs on breeding farms in Saxony.

That Certain *je ne sais quoi:* Selle Français

Literally "saddle horse," this especially versatile warmblood, begun in Normandy in the nineteenth century with mares descended from the great Norman war horses, is the usual combination of Thoroughbred plus, but in this case the plus includes more Arabian and trotter blood, giving the competition version of the horse (they are also bred for racing and general trail riding) particular scope as jumpers. This combination of elegance and spring is making them popular as event horses also. In some circles the Selle Français is considered the world's greatest show jumper. This is a talented and courageous horse, which means that he needs an equally courageous and expert rider to show off his talents. Height: 15.3 to 17.0 hands. Color: Chestnut and bay are the most common (would Saint-Laurent approve?). There are only 150 of these magnificent horses registered in the United States.

Swedish Modern: The Swedish Warmblood

We're joking. Actually, the Swedish Warmblood traces right back to native ponies of the Bronze Age, though the Royal Stud that guaranteed the refinement and continuation of the breed wasn't founded until the seventeenth century, as soon as Sweden gained its independence from Denmark. Like several other warmblood breeds, these include some Friesian blood, and like their equine neighbors they were bred for both the cavalry and the farm. By the nineteenth century the breeding programs had diverged, and the riding version of the breed, infused by more Thoroughbred, Hanoverian, and Trakehner lines, was set to make twentieth-century history as the first horse to win a medal in the modern Olympics in 1912. This helped set the breed on its path as modern performance horse, which in recent years has become more athletic. Their rhythmical gaits and strong personalities have helped continue their winning streak. Height: 16 to 17 hands. Color: all solid colors.

Add Water and Mix: Trakehner

Another warmblood that can trace its ancestry clearly back to ancient pony breeds, the Trakehner hails from an area that used to be Prussia, and was originally the product of breeding by no less than the Order of Teutonic Knights in the thirteenth century. This program received the royal stamp of approval in 1732 when

Friedrich Wilhelm I founded the Trakehnan Stud. The indigenous Schweiken pony was successively, and successfully, crossed with various combinations of Thoroughbred and Arabian, fed off famously nutritious marshlands, and grew into an elegant coaching and riding horse that in turn contributed to other warmblood breeds. Prized in the dressage ring, the Trakehner stallion Abdyullah, whose name hints at those long-ago Arabians in his bloodlines, is an Olympic silver medalist in show jumping. The Trakehner is the prettiest and most versatile of all the warmbloods. Height: 16 to 17 hands. Color: mostly bay, chestnut, black, or brown; some gray.

There's More ...

These are but a few of the distinguished warmbloods who seem as set on making their mark on the future as they have on the past. Other breeds include the Oldenberg (a real rescue, this German coaching horse was almost extinct until revived recently as a sport horse breed), the Dutch Warmblood, the Westphalian, and the Cleveland Bay.

"A Mule Is an Animal ...": Donkeys, Asses, and Mules

Bing Crosby gave the mule a bad name in *Going My Way*, though mules may have helped by their famous disinclination to go anyone's way. Nevertheless, donkeys and asses (they are the same thing) have been around as long as horses, and mules as long as early civilizations, where they were often prized above horses.

The original donkey is part of the family *Equus*, originating in the Old World and migrating to North Africa. Ancient Egyptians and Mesopotamians were using asses around 4000 to 3000 B.C.E., and early Israelite kings rode mules, which were considered more dignified than horses.

Boy Meets Horse, and Vice Versa

Mules are the result of what must have been among the earliest breeding experiments, though the experimenting may have been on their part as much as ours. A mule, strictly speaking, is a cross between a male donkey and a female horse, while a hinny (yes, a hinny) is a cross between a male horse and a donkey mare. The latter is much rarer and less physically hardy than the mule, so many people have not heard of the hinny, and wouldn't know the difference if they saw one.

Mules and donkeys have been used throughout history as pack and plough animals in both war and peace, but have a sizeable following in many countries as friends of the equine family. Today they are still used in agriculture, but also for trail rides, especially in hot and rugged climates, in parades, as part of regional displays and celebrations at agricultural fairs, and as tourist attractions.

What they look like: *Donkeys:* Though there are various types, including miniatures, the basic configuration includes a straight back, round tummy, tapered face with a masklike white around the eye, big ears, and, oh yes, that bray. Almost all also have a hair growth pattern running from head to tail and across the withers known as "the cross."

Mules: Because mules can be bred from any horse or pony breed, looks vary, but the basic look is bigger bodied than a donkey, with more shoulder, and large head with a Roman nose, topped by large ears, and a generally kindly expression. The most familiar cross, the "Missouri" mule, is a donkey crossed with a Belgian draft mare, making the mule offspring all chestnut in color.

What they're like: Patient and brave. The famous stubbornness of mules is thought to be a strong instinct for self-preservation.

What they do: Everything we've every asked of them. Grand Canyon tours are done with all mules. Mules and donkeys generally have working lives of more than 25 years.

(© Leah Patton)

Wjf Jubilation T (Curly), a mule out of a quarter pony mare, owned by Leah Patton, Mesquite, Texas.

(© Leah Patton)

Historique de Wsf (Thor), a half-bred Poitou Donkey gelding. This rare breed from France was almost wiped out in the 1970s. Owned by Leah Patton, Mesquite, Texas.

From the Horse's Mouth _____

Watch your language. Ass, as in *Equus asinus* (from the Latin words for horse and animal), is the correct term for this species. Donkey may have come from a reference to the coat—which is a cross between dun and gray—and the suffix "kin" meaning small, and did not appear in general usage until the eighteenth century when saying "ass" was likely to get you misunderstood in polite society. While burro often sounds like the cuddly form of donkey, it is correctly used to describe feral donkeys in the Southwest. In all versions, "jack" is the male, "jennet" the female.

The Least You Need to Know

- The heavy horses known as "draft" were once common laborers, but are now contributing to the breeding of sport horses.

- Miniature horses are just that—not ponies, but horse talent and temperament in a small package.

- From the sturdy Shetland to the elegant Welsh, a pony is the best riding teacher a child could have.

- Warmbloods, the horse world's SUVs, are the result of crossing draft breeds with Thoroughbred/Arabian types.

- Donkeys have been around as long as horses, and both donkeys and mules have been our patient, hardworking companions for centuries.

Part

Body, Mind, and Soul

Horses were once worshipped as gods—and no wonder. All that beauty and power had to have some supernatural origin, right? Unfortunately, it's taken us a long time to learn how to really appreciate and care for these complex animals. We'll share the results of years of research and observation about nutrition and health—what to feed horses and how to care for them so that they'll keep going strong.

That healthy body should be wrapped around a sound mind, so we'll also talk about horse behavior. Are mares really moody? What happens when training goes against instinct? How does the way horses act together effect the way they act with us? Can they "talk" to us, and can we understand when they do? We hope this part will help you form a strong bond with the horse in your life—one in which you are both master and friend.

Mtn. Laurel Maximillian, Morgan Stallion (trained by Luman Wadmans).

(© Suzy Lucine)

Body Beautiful, Body Equine

In This Chapter

- The physical makeup of the horse
- Horses come equipped with four-speed manual transmissions
- Choose your model, color, and amount of chrome
- The unique workings of equine vision and hearing
- How long do they live?

The sports fitness craze has taught us that "know thyself" includes knowing how the body works. "Know thy horse" requires the same approach. The more you understand about how horses are built and how they see, hear, move, and eat, the better a rider, and the more intelligent and sympathetic an owner you are likely to be.

Because the layman's horse and the veterinarian's horse differ, a range of terms has grown up around the domesticated horse that are the ones you'll hear about, and read, most often. At first, they'll make you feel like a landlubber in a sea of nautical terms (the gaskin? What's that about?), but you'll soon be murmuring knowledgeably about fetlocks and croups with the best of them.

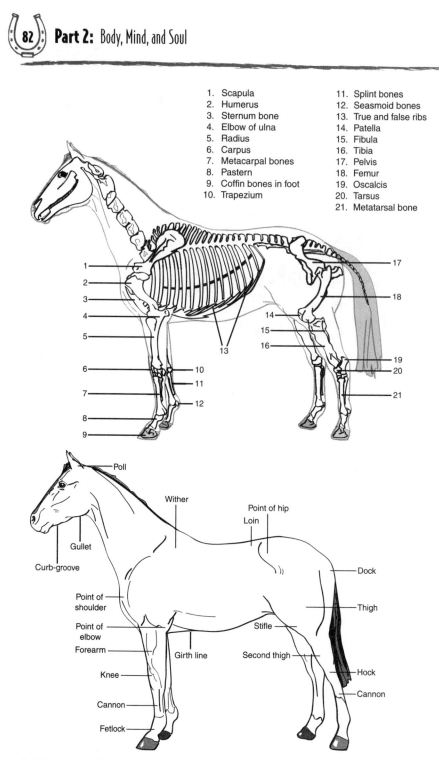

1. Scapula
2. Humerus
3. Sternum bone
4. Elbow of ulna
5. Radius
6. Carpus
7. Metacarpal bones
8. Pastern
9. Coffin bones in foot
10. Trapezium
11. Splint bones
12. Seasmoid bones
13. True and false ribs
14. Patella
15. Fibula
16. Tibia
17. Pelvis
18. Femur
19. Oscalcis
20. Tarsus
21. Metatarsal bone

Poll
Wither
Point of hip
Loin
Gullet
Curb-groove
Dock
Point of shoulder
Thigh
Point of elbow
Stifle
Forearm
Girth line
Second thigh
Knee
Hock
Cannon
Cannon
Fetlock

Inside and out: the parts of the horse.

Body Language

While different breeds have the varying characteristics of the horse in different proportions, the basic animal is long-bodied, with a neck about a third the length of the back and croup (the top of the rump), a deep rib cage, and deeply muscled haunches in relation to other parts of the body. The proportion and relationship of these parts is what determines the soundness and capability of the animal—in other words, its future. And the overall look will be affected by its type and breeding—in other words, its genetic past.

Rules of Hoof

We talk about someone having "a good figure," which in these post-feminist times means more than 36-24-36. In horses, we hear about "conformation," which means basically the relation of the parts to the whole, and how that whole compares to the standard for its breed. Beauty is still in the eye of the beholder, but it does help to know how to sharpen that eye.

Heads Up

The head should be in proportion to the body and have an even, strong jaw without noticeable overbite. The actual shape depends on the breed—drafts and warmbloods horses often have "Roman" or dramatically convex noses. In an old-fashioned prejudice every bit as unreasonable as afflicts human society, these are sometimes considered a sign of "commonness," but many a fine hunter has had a nose that would do Jimmy Durante proud, so go figure. More important is that there be sufficient distance between the eyes and large nostrils—the better for breathing, my dear.

A horse's wide-apart eyes increase his peripheral vision; his alert ears, which flick back and forth in response to his environment, help keep him alert to friend, foe, and especially, you. The broad nostrils draw in air—whether as a draft or racing animal, the horse is the last word in anaerobic fitness.

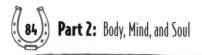

Neck and Neck

Round, well muscled, but not too muscled. A shapely neck contributes to not only an aesthetically pleasing horse, but a balanced one. (Balance is as big in the horse world as in the gymnast's.) There is actually an ideal ratio for the neck, though it's doubtful that any but the most rigorous buyers and breeders actually confirm it; most horse professionals, like most good cooks, begin to trust their "feel." In an ideal world, however, the neck should be one and a half times the length from the top of the horse's head behind the ears (known as the "poll") to the lower lip.

Full Frontal: Chest and Shoulders (Forequarters)

Another magic measurement: the length from the point of the shoulder, which is toward the front of the chest, to the anterior (sometimes called false) ribs should be about twice the distance from the rear of the withers to the croup. Do people go around measuring this? Probably not, but a horseman's eye automatically seeks relationships of this kind.

You won't have much trouble spotting a narrow, compressed chest, but what you're looking for is one "well sprung" (an old-fashioned term meaning the rib cage is roomy and generous) but a good shoulder is a little harder to see. It should be sloping—not too straight, because this usually means a shorter, choppier motion. This area includes the withers, which you'll get to know well. The withers are the ridge between the shoulder blades; from the outside it is the bony bit behind which the saddle rests. Too little, and the saddle slides off; too much, and it gets rubbed by all but tailor-made tack.

The Seat of Power: The Back

This is the region that varies most from breed to breed, so what is most important is that it be proportionate to the rest of the animal. Some horses, like Saddlebreds, are naturally long-backed, while Quarter Horses, and most ponies tend to be short-backed. Long backs are elegant, but sometimes weak; short ones, like straight shoulders, don't give the easiest ride.

In all cases, the back should be reasonably well muscled (when horses lose condition, this is often where you can spot it first. Strength is important—this is, after all, the area that carries the rider, and because it links all the other parts together it is sensitive to numerous outside influences, from an ill-fitting saddle to a worn-down shoe. Two common flaws are inversions of one another: sway back (an exaggerated dip) and roach back, like an angry cat.

V8 Engine: Hindquarters

This is where the power in horsepower comes from, and you usually want to look for good muscle and definition, especially in the thighs. In many breeds this section is also a little higher than the withers, but actual size depends on the type of horse and the type of work it has been doing. Because horses aren't drawn to the robotic pleasure of pumping iron, they are rarely muscle-bound; but an excessively heavy rump, aside from indicating that the horse is probably unfit, sometimes tops a horse whose legs bow out and has a shortened stride.

You will hear more from us, and any of your riding teachers, about how the horse should and does push from behind—the engine is in the rear. And, in fact, the best place to judge the rear is from the rear, where you are looking for a gradual swell of muscle.

Leg Room

And what, precisely, is he driving? Straight, strong legs both front and hind are as much of a guarantee of soundness as you are going to get. And again, what you see from the outside can signal a lot about what is going on on the inside. Much of the strain of carrying around this vast animal (as well as us) is taken by the round joint above the hoof, known as the fetlock joint, and how well it does this is where biomechanics comes in: This joint is connected to the hoof by what you might perceive as an ankle, but is actually called a pastern, and its

angle should be about 45 degrees in slope from the joint. Otherwise, movement is literally bone-jarring, and the animal will pay for it in later life.

> **Whoa!**
>
> A horse's (not inconsiderable) weight goes down the leg into the pedal bone, which is suspended inside the hoof. If the walls of the hoof are not at the correct angles, or are uneven, the horse is at risk, not only for lameness, but a variety of related problems with alignment. The front feet should be at an angle of about 45 to 50 degrees from the ground; the rear 50 to 55. The front hooves should also be round in front, the rear more elongated, and each pair should be the same size.

The two halves of the leg, above and below the knee, should be relatively equal; the knee should be flat in front and flexible, the lower leg should be shapely and blemish-free, and the whole should taper down to a strong, symmetrical hoof. In the rear, the folding joint that corresponds to the knee is called the hock, and these should be large and flexible, as they take much of the strain of pushing off, reining, and jumping, for example.

These Hooves Are Made for Walking

The horse world is full of salty old sayings, but there isn't a truer one than "no foot, no horse." Although good shoeing (see Chapters 6 and 7) and proper care can help maintain a horse's feet, nothing can really repair faulty conformation or old injuries.

The really tricky thing is that so much of what is crucial in a hoof is happening on the inside. The hoof, you'll remember, was one of the last things to change the family Eohippus into modern Equus, and it is a miracle of adjustable complexity. The outer covering is hard horn, surrounding sensitive fleshy tissue called "laminae." This in turn surrounds the major bone in the foot, the pedal bone, which, as the name implies, is a flexible bone designed to absorb stress. The underside of the hoof has a fleshy, cleft ridge called the "frog" (goodness knows why), which acts as a shock absorber and helps stimulate circulation, while the sole should be relatively flat and clean.

Because the feet get so much pounding, the right shape is even more crucial for them than for us, and if horses got drafted, a 4-F classification would mean the perpetual threat of stress and lameness. Uneven feet make for an uneven walk, which causes stress all over the body. Beware, too, of tight, pinched heels (just like us, it looks as if their shoes don't fit properly); this means the frog can't hit the ground properly, and there is likely to be too little blood flowing to the foot. And a very flat foot will bruise easily.

Walking the Walk: Gaits

When man stood upright, everything began to go wrong, which is why we are a generation of slumpers with lower back pain and hip replacements. But the horse evolved more efficiently, and has four useful, and when he is sound, graceful, natural gaits:

- **The walk.** A four-beat gait in which each foot is picked up independently of the others in the following sequence: off hind, off fore, near hind, near fore. The horse walks at approximately four miles an hour.

- **The trot/jog.** A two-beat gait in which the horse moves alternate pairs of legs: near hind and off fore; off hind and near fore. (Pacers move these legs laterally, rather than diagonally.) Horses trot at approximately six miles an hour.

- **The canter/lope.** A three-beat gait with a rocking motion, in the following sequence: left hind, left fore and right hind simultaneously, right fore. (This is for a "left lead" canter;

From the Horse's Mouth

In Western riding, the trot is called a jog, and the canter is called a lope. And in addition to these basic gaits, as we've mentioned, gaited horses have additional paces such as the running walk, slow gait, fox-trot, or rack, depending on the breed.

for a "right lead" canter the sequence would be reversed.) Horses canter at 8 to 10 miles an hour.

The gallop. An extended version of the canter, though at very high speeds it becomes a four-beat movement with a dramatic moment of suspension when all four legs are off the ground. Speed varies depending on horse and circumstances: 25 miles per hour is average for a sprinter, but the average horse having a brief tear is probably going more like 10 to 15.

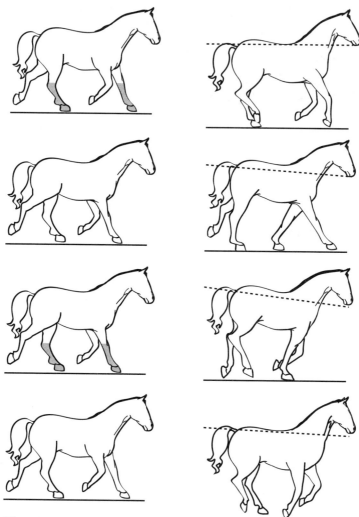

The gaits.

Skin Deep

A horse's skin is so sensitive he can feel a fly landing anywhere on his body, which is why the experience of riding in high summer sometimes is a little too much like a visit to Disney World, with your irritable mount torqueing like a roller coaster. As with people, the inner and outer layers (dermis and epidermis) work together to synthesize sunlight, protect against infection, and insulate warmth. In deference to the fact that they spend more time outside than we do, and don't use sun block, horses have more sebum in their coats—an oily substance that is water-repellent and makes the coat shine. A horse with a dull coat isn't just neglected, but possibly sick, or amazingly, depressed, since some recent research has indicated that neurotransmitters move through all areas of the body.

Coats of Many Colors

You've been secretly wondering what "bay" meant when it's not in a stew recipe. And is "chestnut" brown, or red? Here's a quick horse palette for you:

- **Bay.** At its classiest, a mahogany brown rather like milk chocolate, but also comes in reddish brown and paler shades. All bays have black points—black mane, tail, and legs, although white markings can sometimes obscure them.

- **Black.** Authors Walter Farley and Anna Sewell gave this shade a great push, but it's rarer than other coloration, and incredibly dramatic when pure and not faded out.

- **Brown.** Basically, brown is brown—any color between black and red, but with absolutely no red in it—sometimes with lighter or darker "points," disparagingly called "mealy," as if the horse had been gobbling something that stayed stuck to his muzzle.

- **Buckskin and dun.** Sometimes these terms are used interchangeably, but all these horses are some shade of yellow.

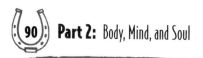

The horses with black points are called dun. If primitive marks (see Chapter 3) are present, they are called zebra dun, but all fall within the Buckskin color group.

- **Champagne.** What it sounds like, a sort of creamy beige, usually with chocolate points.

- **Chestnut and sorrel.** Any shade of red: copper, flaxen, golden, or liver (a dark chocolate shade) with manes and tails also any shade of chestnut or sorrel. The light-colored flaxen manes and tails are particularly stunning. The designation "chestnut" or "sorrel" depends upon the breed, with sorrel used more commonly by Quarter Horse and draft breeders.

- **Cream** or **cremello.** Light, almost white coat, with blue eyes. A genetic anomaly, this is fairly rare.

- **Gray.** A variety of shades from white to pale silver to deep gray are known by this term; they are also defined by such patterns as dapples or small flecks on brown (flea bitten). The skin is black.

- **Palomino, Paint, Pinto, Appaloosa:** See "Color Breeds" in Chapter 3.

- **Roan.** A particularly lovely effect in which white hairs are mixed in with a base color, like stippling in interior decorating. Roans come in blue, red, strawberry, and frosty, which make them sound like milkshake flavors.

- **White.** Grays are really variations on white, but real white is almost as startling as real black. Albinos, whose skin is pink, are the only true white horses.

It's All in the Details

In addition to basic coat shades, horses, like dogs and cats, also come with "points" (the shadings around areas like the muzzle, lower limbs, and mane and tail) and a variety of white markings with more variations than a Jackson Pollack painting.

If all horses of the same color look alike to you, stop for a moment and compare their white markings. No two sets of marks are exactly alike. These markings are important for identifying horses, and they are recorded in detail in words and exact drawings on a horse's registration papers and on veterinary certificates. For Pintos, drawing exact markings can prove tricky, so three photographs (one of either side and one of the face) are attached to the registration papers. Now, what exactly are these marks and how are they classified?

The white markings on a horse's legs are described as follows:

- A **sock** (also called an anklet) is a white leg up that extends over the fetlock.

- A **half stocking** means white partway between fetlock and knee.

- A **stocking** is a white leg up to the knee.

- A **pastern** looks like a sock, but it stops short of the fetlock.

- A **coronet** is a narrow white ring of hair just above the hoof.

- A **heel spot** is exactly what it sounds like, a white patch on the heel.

- **Ermine spots** are dark spots on white leg markings.

The white markings on a horse's face are described as follows:

- The **star** is a white spot (any shape or size) on the forehead.

- The **strip** is a narrow stripe down the entire face.

- The **snip** is a white spot on the muzzle.

- The **blaze** is a wide stripe down the entire face.

- The **bald face** means that white hair covers the entire face and may even extend and envelope at least one eye.

The star, strip, and snip can all be present, or they can combine in any order to produce a variety of white facial markings. It's not uncommon to see a horse with just one of these features or any

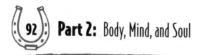

combination of them, and they provide vivid "punctuation marks" to a horse's appearance.

The Vision Thing

The most dramatic thing about horses' sight is the one it's easiest to see—their panoramic view of the world. A prey animal, it was important that they develop a comprehensive field of vision in case anything planned to sneak up on them.

Horses can see pretty well all around them with the exception of a six-degree blind spot at the very back and at the very front. (This becomes important to remember in jumping, because a horse can't actually see a fence at the moment he is going over it—how's that for a leap of faith?!) But like a video screen, the view is flat, with only about 30 percent depth of field. It's as if they are looking at a painting in which the objects keep moving.

Horses are born with bifocals. They can focus on near and far objects, but only by moving their heads. One of the most important recent discoveries about how horses process visual information is that the information from their three fields of vision (to either side and just in front of them) are processed separately by the brain. If the left eye doesn't see what the right eye has seen, as far as they're concerned it's a completely new tree/barn/flapping bag/car. Over the years, this has led to a lot of human/equine misunderstanding, and the false belief that horses are stupid.

Some other points to bear in mind about equine vision:

- Horses with thinner faces have better forward vision than horses with wide foreheads.

- A grazing horse can see in all directions without moving his head.

- A horse must raise and lower his head to be able to "focus" clearly on an object in front of him.

- Horses must raise their heads to see at a distance and lower them to see close and below them.

- Horses operate both eyes independently and are able to see behind themselves, but they can't do both at the same time.

- Horses are able to see behind because their eyes are placed on the sides of their heads, but when they are facing directly forward, they are unable to see someone coming from directly behind. Hence, never walk up directly behind a horse.

- Horses cannot see the tips of their own noses or what lies beyond in that direction.

- The ears and eyes operate together—when ears are pricked and pointed forward the eyes also look in the same direction.

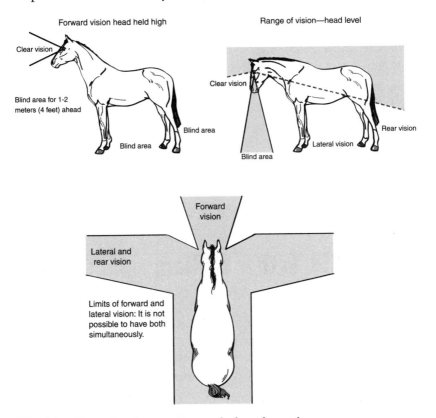

The vision thing: where horses can see, and where they can't.

 Whoa! _____

> Equine eyes work independently of each other. This means that if your horse spooks at an object, turn him around and go past it again so that he sees it with the other eye as well. He'll probably spook at it again, so be ready.

Fix the Antenna: Hearing

When we ride, we are looking between our horse's ears, and sometimes this can look like riding behind a TV antennae, because they are constantly flicking, twitching, and shifting. Really, they're more like satellite dishes, picking up (independent of one another) frequencies too high or soft for us to hear. Humans can hear sounds in the range of 100 to 15,000 hertz. Horses can hear sounds at a much higher frequency, up to 25,000 hertz. As with their vision, as prey animals they needed to know much sooner that we, the predators, were advancing with our clubs. And as with the way they see, this is another reason a horse might seem spooky, or suddenly freeze when he's being ridden—he's heard a sound that it will take you much longer to process.

 Horse Sense _____

> Horses have 10 muscles attached to each ear. One of these is also linked to his tongue! It is dangerous to casually try to shift a horse's tongue (to examine his teeth, for example). Pulled roughly, it can cause disorienting inner-ear problems.

You Are Old, Father William

While horses in the wild rarely live beyond 16 years, possibly because of untreated dental problems that eventually make eating impossible, today's domesticated horse, like today's active senior, has a much longer life expectancy. As little as 20 years ago, a horse of 20 was usually a retiree, and horses of 30 something for the record books. But better care, advanced nutrition, and an affluent society focusing as much on the sustained health and well-being of its companion animals as it is on itself has made active horses in their 20s commonplace. Different horse breeds also mature and age at different rates— Thoroughbreds are trained and racing at two in this country (though some believe this is eventually harmful to their still-forming legs), while the more stolid warmbloods sometimes don't come into their own until they are five or six.

Horse Ages and Stages

Age	Stage
0 to 11 months	foal
1 year	yearling
2 to 3 years	adolescent
3 to 5 years	young horse
6 to 15 years	mature horse
15+	older/senior

How Big Do They Get? And How Small?

Remember the hand (four inches)? Well, at their biggest (Percheron and Shire draft breeds), horses can measure up to 19 hands. And how small? In the United States, with the exception of some horse breeds that run smallish, under 14.3 is officially a pony, and over that height would be ineligible for pony classes. Minis, of course, are the exception to all kinds of rules, and are considered horses despite their diminutive size (34 to 38 inches).

How Much Do They Weigh?

Horses weigh between 800 and 1,500 pounds, although again, this can vary tremendously by breed, with the big draft horses sometimes weighing more than a ton, and mini foals somewhere around the terrier class. This matters, as we'll see, because feed and dosage of medication is often calculated by weight, and some forms of

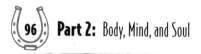

transportation can be dangerous if the horse is too big. But unlike the devotees of Weight Watchers, you rarely wind up weighing your horse constantly, although the use of a weight tape to establish an initial base is useful. Instead, you wind up with a sense of what the healthy weight is for your animal depending on his breed, age, workload, and metabolism.

Why Should You Care About This Stuff?

Someday, maybe in a chapter or two, you will be looking for a horse of your own. Then, all these arcane data will be a crucial part of your shopping list. You may be drawn to him because his flashy raised head makes him look commanding, but did you know that it is a sign of an "upside-down" neck? What about those elegant pasterns (ankles to you)? The slope often means speed and a smooth ride, but can also indicate weakness and a tendency to injury. Like that gleaming white coat? Did you think about sunburn? What do all those poets mean by "a liquid eye"?

The horse's body is a map, and especially when you're shopping for one, it's a map of a territory you'll want to get to know.

The Least You Need to Know

- The way a horse is built influences how comfortable he will be to ride, the type of work he can do, the discipline he will excel in, and how sound he will be during his life.

- Horses come with a variety of (usually white) markings on their faces and legs; these are used to help identify them, and all have specific names.

- The four gaits of a horse are walk, trot, canter, and gallop.

- The way horses react to their environment is partly affected by their unique peripheral vision, developed from their history as prey animals.

- The foot is the most important part of the horse; as the old horseman's adage has it, "no foot, no horse."

Chapter 6

And It Eats Like a Horse: Nutrition

In This Chapter

- Teeth and their importance in feeding and training
- The equine digestive system
- How horses eat, and how to feed them
- Types of feed and their effects

Before we can even consider the tricky business of equine nutrition, we should look first at the gatekeepers of nutrition, the teeth. While clearly a part of the body, we want to look at them in this chapter because without healthy, well-maintained teeth a horse cannot process efficiently the nutrition we urge on him.

The teeth are the gateway to a complicated digestive system that is essentially a prehistoric model operating in the modern world. Understanding how horses process food is essential to making intelligent feeding choices. And what of those choices? They have never been broader, owing to new nutritional research and a booming

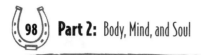

industry. But sometimes, as we'll see, the good old-fashioned approach is still the right one.

Ring Cycles: Teeth

A horse's teeth are like the rings around an oak—an indicator of age and wear, as well as being fine tools for tearing and grinding, the two tasks nature expects of a grazing animal. Like us, horses have two types of teeth, incisors for tearing and molars for grinding.

The jaw is constructed very symmetrically, with six pairs of incisors and six pairs of molars (upper and lower). In addition to these, many horses have an extra upper tooth called a "wolf" tooth, probably a prehistoric leftover, like our wisdom teeth. Also, right behind the lower incisors, the boys often have a tooth called a tusk. This is famous for catching on things and causing dental problems, but might once have been a fighting tool, since mares rarely have them.

Don't Look a Gift Horse ...

Admit it: You've always wondered what that expression was all about. And the answer is that, up to a point, a horse's teeth can be read like a map, with the shape and patterns of wear fairly accurate indicators of age. A horse's permanent teeth grow in under the temporary ones, which form a kind of enamel cap. As these caps wear down, the dark "cups" at the center of the teeth disappear, exposing the pulp, which is known as the "dental star." In addition, the general shape of the teeth goes from being roughly oval to more acutely triangular. The angle of the teeth also changes, becoming more prominent and acute (and, like ours, discolored, even without a lifetime of cigarettes and coffee!).

But the biggest "trick" in telling a horse's age is a line that grows on the outside of the corner incisors, beginning at about the age of 10 and growing steadily downward until it reaches the bottom of the tooth at about age 20. Then it begins to disappear from the top, and is usually gone completely by the time a horse reaches 30. (Don't worry; there are plenty of other ways to tell whether your horse is 9 or 31!). The line is called Galvayne's groove, after the nineteenth-century Scottish veterinarian who invented this technique for aging horses.

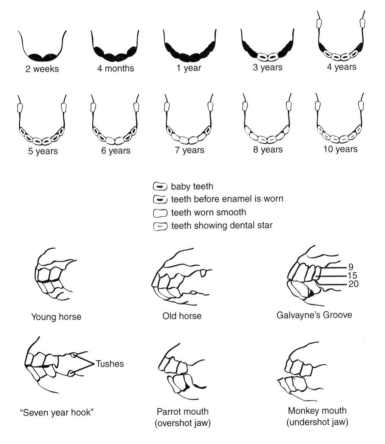

Long in the tooth: Wear on the surfaces is an indicator of a horse's age.

Tooth Maintenance

A grazing horse eats up to 16 hours a day, and even a stabled horse should be feeding constantly on hay in between his grain rations. This means a lot more regular wear on the teeth than we experience, and horses' teeth are designed to wear away gradually. Because, as in

humans, the upper jaw is larger than the lower, this can eventually cause problems as the uneven wear creates sharp edges at the outer edge of the molars. Untreated, these can cause severe abrasions inside the mouth, making it painful for the horse to eat. When the pain is really extreme, we usually get a clue in the form of "quidding"—the horse will grasp his food as usual with his incisors, but, unable to grind it properly, will wind up rolling it into small pellets and spitting it out, like an old-timer with chewing tobacco. But sharp teeth may be causing pain and inefficient digestion way before this, so regular dental checkups should be routine for horses, as for us.

When teeth need to be leveled, this is done with a large alarming-looking file called a rasp, and the operation of recontouring the teeth is known as *floating*. This should be done at least once a year, but some experts feel it should happen even more often, and the teeth of young horses, which are still coming in and setting, should be checked every three months for irregularities. Accidents or biting problems may well cause abscesses or fractures as well, and sudden behavior problems have often been tracked to tooth problems.

> **From the Horse's Mouth**
>
> **Floating** is the term used for the procedure vets or equine dentists use to file down the sharp edges of a horse's teeth. Floating should be done at least once a year for all horses, and more often for young horses, seniors, and performance horses.

Horses Prefer Dim Sum: Digestion

The Golden Age for horses was probably sometime not long after the Ice Age, when, fully developed as Equus, they roamed an earth lush in grass, even if they had to keep looking over their shoulders for predators. Horses were, and are, designed for constant grazing and roaming, and domestication has taken a considerable toll on their digestive systems. An old horseman's adage used to be "feed little and often," and this was a way of trying to replicate the state of nature from which we have deprived them. Today's busy barns and riders have had to create feeding schedules that more closely approximate our own, although it is usual to feed at least two or three times a day to accommodate horses' smaller stomachs, which cannot process large amounts of food at a time.

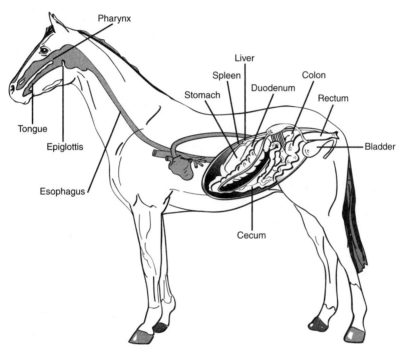

Complicated plumbing: the digestive system.

How Horses Eat

For all the time and money horse owners lavish on grain feed, a horse's greatest bliss is fresh forage. They were designed as grazing animals, and their digestive systems are able to extract and process nutrition from a wide range of grasses and plants, and, with domestication, from grains and "combination" or "complete" feeds. This process begins at the first bite—horses' saliva helps to break down the food, and to help this along they roll it around in their mouths,

which is one reason many horses' feed tubs look like babies' high chairs, liberally adorned with this morning's breakfast. (This is also a sign of a greedy feeder.)

One other distinct feature of a horse's digestive system is that they cannot vomit. This means that there is no quick (if messy) solution to intestinal disorders, which often result in more serious symptoms such as colic or choking (see Chapter 7).

How Much?

On average, an adult horse in moderate work should be eating between 1½ to 3 percent of his body weight. Of that, at least half should be forage (and usually more—70 to 80 percent unless the horse is in heavy work), 8 to 11 percent protein, and the rest carbohydrates. (Note that minerals and vitamins are usually contained or extracted from the feed, although sometimes are fed as supplements, usually in modest daily doses.)

Feeding Chart (per Hundred Pounds of Body Weight)

Work	Grain (Pounds per Hour of Activity)
Light	0.5 to 1.5
Moderate	2 to 3
Heavy	4 or more

Light work: 1 to 3 hours
Moderate work: 3 to 5 hours
Heavy work: 5 to 8 hours

In addition, feed 1.5 to 1.75 pounds/100 pounds body weight daily of average or better quality roughage. Adjust the amount fed as necessary to maintain optimum body weight and condition. The basic maxim is, "Feed according to the work done." And of course, no table is a substitute for close observation of your particular horse.

The Menu

The "restaurant" in this instance is collaboration between nature and commercial feed suppliers, and quality and availability will vary according to region and circumstance. Here are the basics, so you can keep in mind what to look for when you are ordering up yourself, or are in discussion with the barn that is responsible for your horse's care.

Fat of the Land: Forage

Forage is derived from pasture land, and comes in two forms: (1) legumes, which are mineral-rich plants such as alfalfa and clover that contain high levels of calcium, phosphorus, and beta-carotene; and (2) grasses, such as timothy and bluegrass (these vary from region to region, although fields cultivated for hay will often have been seeded with the most common and approved mixtures). Alfalfa should be fed cautiously, however, as it is very rich (like too much cream and butter for us).

Dandelions Are Dandy

One pasture plant that horses love is the dandelion. If your horse eagerly gobbles dandelions, yellow flowers and all, let him enjoy them. Dandelion roots and leaves are rich in potassium (a mineral horses lose through sweating). Because these plants also contain calcium and magnesium, they also function as a natural electrolyte.

Just Because It's Green Doesn't Mean It's Good for a Horse to Eat

Horses generally can distinguish between what is good for them to eat (after all, they were around for millions of years in the wild—long before they ever got sweet feed) and what isn't, as long as pasture conditions are good. But just to make sure your horse remains safe, here

is a list of some plants that can be toxic to horses. Learn how to distinguish poisonous plants and banish them from your pasture.

Azalea	Mustard plants
Black Walnut	Poinsettia
Buckeye and Horse Chestnut	Poison and Water Hemlock
Bulbs	Pokeweed
Buttercups	Potato and tomato plants
Catnip	Red Maple
Easter Lily	Rhododendron
English Ivy	Rhubarb
Ergot	St. John's wort
Jack-in-the-Pulpit	Tansy
Lupin	Tobacco
Marijuana	Yew

 Whoa!

Look at what is growing in your horse's pasture; some plants are harmful to horses, and some can even be fatal. Many poisons are fast-acting, so be on the lookout for these symptoms and call your vet if your horse …

- Stays off by itself.
- Seems weak with an unsteady gait.
- Struggles with rapid breathing and pulse.
- Suffers from diarrhea or frequently urinates.
- Foams at mouth.
- Collapses.

Hay Is For …

Hay is what happens to forage. It is cultivated pasture in its dried and concentrated form, and usually contains a similar balance between legumes and grasses, though some mixtures, such as alfalfa, are very rich, and should only be fed in limited quantities. Good-quality hay is crucial to a horse's nutritional well-being, and it is very vulnerable to damp, mold, and dustiness, so storage becomes as important an issue as quality. Hay should be constantly available to stabled horses, and to horses in pastures that have been worn or eaten down. Not only does it satisfy important feeding requirements, but it helps to prime the horse's antique digestive system and to keep boredom at bay.

"It's in There": Mixed Grains and Feeds

We often seem to be caught between the rival appeal of "do-it-yourself" and "all purpose," and this is certainly true in the horse-feeding business. With time, money and research staffs on their side, commercial food manufacturers have worked hard, and for the most part responsibly, to create combination feeds that are nutritionally "complete," balanced grain mixtures with a variety of supplemental nutrients and an astonishing range of product lines (much as has happened with commercial dog food) for every horse lifestyle.

A "typical" mixed grain might contain oats, corn, and molasses. (Molasses helps to tamp down the dust on grains, but is also very fragrant and yummy.) In addition, it will probably be supplemented with linseed (another good fat source that also helps keep the coat sleek and healthy), alfalfa, and vitamins and minerals. They are designed to

Horse Lore _____

Horses are prone to hay belly, the equine equivalent of the beer belly, but it's now thought the cause is bad hay, rather than too much. So if your horse has that one-too-many look, check the quality of your hay.

Horse Sense _____

Horses can actually store energy in their muscles, and the old sayings about a horse "feeling his oats" or "being fresh" are exactly what they sound like. If your horse isn't in hard work, or is off for a few days, you should decrease the grain ration accordingly.

supply the right balance of crude protein (8 to 16 percent), energy-producing carbohydrates, and vital minerals such as calcium and phosphorus. These feeds are also available in pellet form—which, frankly, looks like rabbit food. These feeds should be supplemented with hay to provide sufficient roughage. There are complete feed lines, meant to meet all of a horse's daily nutritional needs. These should contain at least 26 percent crude fiber. If the horse is stabled indoors, it's often still a good idea to feed a little hay to stave off boredom.

Horse Sense

Complete or sweet feeds are commercially manufactured feeds that combine various grains and supplements to offer a nutritionally complete product that works well as a base diet for many horses.

Blinded by Science: Supplements

Baby boomers are determined not to "go gentle into that good night," and many human health, exercise, and diet regimes are designed to stave off anything vaguely resembling old age or infirmity as long as possible. This health consciousness has fueled an entire industry of "health" foods and an increasingly sophisticated focus on vitamin and mineral supplementation.

Invariably, the movement has spread outward to encompass our animals, meeting up with better research into animal biochemistry and physiology. The result is a deluge of products: multivitamins; individual doses of B, C, or E, calcium and phosphorous; joint supplements (the same glucosamine/chondroitin combination awaiting your cranky knee at the health food store); hoof supplements; and salt. Some barns also add a small amount of corn oil to increase the amount of fat in the diet.

As with our own diets, some reinforcement in the form of concentrated supplements—especially for horses in heavy work, pregnant mares, seniors, or those with inadequate access to pasture—may be helpful. However, because most commercial feeds also contain supplements, it is possible to overdo it and wind up with toxic levels of some elements, or with one group canceling out the good effects of another.

Horse Sense

In the horse world, you can have too much of a good thing. Be sure to read the label of your commercial feed carefully if you are planning to feed supplements, to insure that you are not double-dosing your horse, because many have already added essential nutrients. In some cases, too much of a supplement can lead to toxic amounts in the bloodstream. This is the case with selenium, for example. In other cases, excess quantities of one vitamin or mineral will interfere with the beneficial actions of another. This is the case with the two most prevalent minerals in a horse's body, calcium and phosphorus, which are largely present in bones and teeth. The ratio between the two should be at least one part calcium to one part phosphorus. More calcium is usually not harmful, but if there is too much phosphorus, it begins to impede the absorption of the calcium.

Regularity: Fiber

Bran mashes used to be considered chicken soup for horses. This sweet, soothing mush, made from pouring boiling water over wheat bran and adding a little salt and a "sweetener" like linseed jelly or molasses, has been used for decades after hard work, to relieve colds, and as a laxative. Modern nutritional studies have suggested, however, that there might be excessive amounts of phosphorus in wheat bran, which can affect bone growth, and that beet pulp may be the better source of fiber. Nevertheless, this is a sentimental favorite, and fed judiciously, is as close to mothering (or chicken soup for the soul) as you're likely to get.

Have an Apple: Treats

Don't think it begins or ends with apples and carrots. Horses also enjoy pears, peppermint, and licorice, and won't say no to a jelly

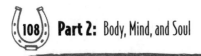

doughnut, although this isn't any better for them than for us. And those canny manufacturers haven't missed a trick (or treat)—there are plenty of horse cookies and stud muffins (we kid you not) on the market, mostly grain and molasses based.

Horse Cookies

These homemade horse treats are easy to make and they're a hit at our barn.

1½ cups wheat bran

1 cup barley

4 cups regular rolled oats (not the quick-cook kind)

1 cup bulgar wheat

1 cup cornmeal

½ tsp. salt

⅓ cup honey

1 cup molasses

2 TB. brown sugar

1 large carrot, coarsely grated

1½ cups hot water

1 egg white

Mix wheat bran, barley, oats, bulgar wheat, cornmeal, and salt together in large bowl. Add honey, molasses, brown sugar, grated carrot, and hot water; mix well; cover; and let sit for at least 30 minutes. Mix in egg white. Mixture should stick together.

Drop with tablespoon (these cookies will not "spread," so you can get a lot on one pan) onto an ungreased, nonstick cookie sheet. Flatten and bake at 275°F for 30 minutes, then turn each one over and bake an additional 45 minutes. Cool on rack (they get harder as they cool) and store in an air-tight container. Use within three weeks, or put them in the freezer where they'll keep for a very long time.

If you don't have honey, substitute corn syrup or maple syrup.

Bake two pans at once to save time.

You should get between 80 to 100 cookies (depending on size).

Give treats sparingly and only when they're earned, and, if possible, put them in the feed bucket. If you must hand-feed, stretch your hand so the skin on the palm of the feeding hand is taut and extend your thumb as far as you possibly can away from your hand. Horses have big teeth and strong jaws and you don't want your fingers accidentally consumed with the treat.

If you like cooking for your animals, and/or are thrifty, homemade treats are easy to create. We've included our favorite recipe here, and you'll probably be able to think of variations.

Whoa!

Don't create a monster by feeding treats. Too many treats and the horse will be looking for them, and if he doesn't find one he could get nippy.

Horse Sense

Drinking enough water keeps a horse healthy (and the average 1,000-pound horse needs 10 gallons every day) so it's important that every horse has access to fresh, clean water at all times. A salt block should be available, too, because salt helps horses retain water, especially during hot weather.

Water with Everything

Clean, fresh water is vital for the well-being of your horse. An average 1,000-pound horse will drink about 10 gallons a day, but this can vary with the amount of work he is doing, and with the seasons. If he is outside much of the day, the paddock should be supplied with water tubs, and these should be checked regularly for insects, scum, and debris. A stabled horse should have at least one, and ideally two buckets of water available at all times, and these, too, should be checked several times a day. Some horses drink more often than others indoors, while others like to wash their food in their buckets and in warm weather; the result is an unhealthy fermented sludge.

Horse Sense _____

Some horses, believe it or not, won't drink "strange water" when away from home. If you own one of these fussy equines, you'd better start looking for ways to carry along some H₂O from home. You can pick up handy water carriers available at camping stores, or if you'll be away for a few days at a show, you should check out a few catalogs for the water carrier that doubles as a saddle rack.

The Least You Need to Know

- A horse's teeth are an indication of his age, and proper maintenance will aid his digestion, keep him pain-free, and make him a more tractable mount.

- Horses are essentially grazing animals, and feeding programs should be keyed to their eating habits and digestive systems.

- An ideal diet depends on a horse's age, weight, and work, but on average he should be getting at least $1\frac{1}{2}$ to 3 percent of his body weight in food, and at least half of that should be forage or hay—vital for contributing fiber to the diet, stimulating the digestive system, and alleviating boredom.

- Supplements have become as fashionable and available in the horse world as in the human one, but should be used judiciously.

- Be sure to provide plenty of clean, fresh water for your horse.

Chapter

7

Sounding a Little Ho(a)rse: Common Ailments

In This Chapter

- Common ailments and their causes, symptoms, and treatment
- Vital signs: body temperature, pulse, respiration rate
- When to call the vet immediately
- Home made fly preparations
- Alternative therapies

We know why you wanted a horse—beauty, power, romance, the gentle pleasure of the trail, the thrill of the chase, yada yada. But sometimes it's going to feel as if you've acquired a large child with four legs and a tail. Horses, like children, are prone to cuts and scrapes, tummy aches and stubbed toes. The difference is that, in some cases, these things can go from being a minor discomfort to a

recurring problem to a major crisis, so it helps to be able to recognize some of the most common syndromes and symptoms, and to know what to do quickly.

Most of the ailments that plague horses on a regular basis have their origins in the still perpetual conflict between the lives they were physically designed to lead and the ones we require of them, and in the sometimes punishing amount of work we ask of them. And, it has to be said, the problem is sometimes human ignorance, error, or carelessness, so you'll want to know how to prevent problems as well as how to solve them.

Tummy Troubles

That digestive system we learned so much about in Chapter 6, and a horse's basic eating habits, can lead to more than weight problems.

Colic

This catch-all term probably originated around the time all human colds were being called "the grippe," and has about as much specificity. It really applies to a whole range of intestinal/abdominal pains, like our stomach ache. And because horses can't vomit, gas and fluid get trapped. At its mildest, it's like indigestion, with the same causes—and at its most extreme, it can indicate intestinal blockage or a twisted gut, which is often fatal, although surgical intervention can help.

Common causes include the following:

- Bad hay

- Rich food

- Eating too soon after hard work or while the horse is hot

- Eating too quickly (bolting)

- Sudden changes in the diet

- Toxic substances

- Stress

- Parasites

Symptoms:

- Restlessness—pawing the ground and pacing

- Looking at the belly

- Rolling

- Groaning or yawning

- Sudden sweating

- Lack of appetite

Horse Sense

Colic, the leading killer of horses even in today's nutritionally correct age, is still mostly a man-made problem. Here's how to help prevent it:

- Never work a horse right after he's eaten.
- Never feed a horse right after he's been worked—if he's thirsty, offer sips of water and cool him off before letting him drink his fill or eat.
- Stick to the same feeding schedule—every day.
- Don't make radical sudden changes in his diet or in the amount of feed.
- Make sure clean water is always available to stabled and pastured horses.
- Provide free-choice hay. Horses are built to graze all day and a hungry horse is more likely to bolt down his food.

What to do: Call the vet—even mild symptoms can suddenly escalate, and you'll want guidance. Take away any leftover food and water. If he will lie quietly, leave him, otherwise try to walk him

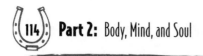

around until he seems more comfortable, then put him back in a freshly bedded stall. Check on him every half hour until he seems settled. Once symptoms have cleared up, feed a small bran mash. If symptoms do not clear up within the hour, have your vet come out.

Parasites

Because horses eat from limited pastureland and/or from the floor of the stalls, they are usually in close proximity to manure and fly larvae looking for a good home. The guests include red and white worms, seat or whip worms, and the opportunistic tapeworm. Left to run riot in your horse's digestive system, these can cause colic, allergies, and general debilitation, since the mission of any parasite is to siphon off nutrients for its own benefit.

Common causes:

- Exposure to larvae
- Poor stabling hygiene, which increases exposure

Symptoms:

- Poor condition
- In severe cases, intestinal bleeding and colic are likely

What to do:

- Keep stalls as clean as possible.
- Rotate pastureland as much as possible.
- Consult with your vet and/or barn manager about an appropriate worming program—these are medicinal preparations, usually in paste or powder form, that are mixed in with the horse's feed to cleanse out the system or, if fed daily, to arrest larvae development.

"No Foot, No Horse"

The most significant bit of horse lore there is revolves around the crucial importance of good feet. A horse's legs are both strong and delicate, and the complicated structure of the foot, as well as the concessive work we ask of them, makes them vulnerable to a variety of bruises and strains, as well as to two severe and potentially fatal conditions: laminitis and navicular disease.

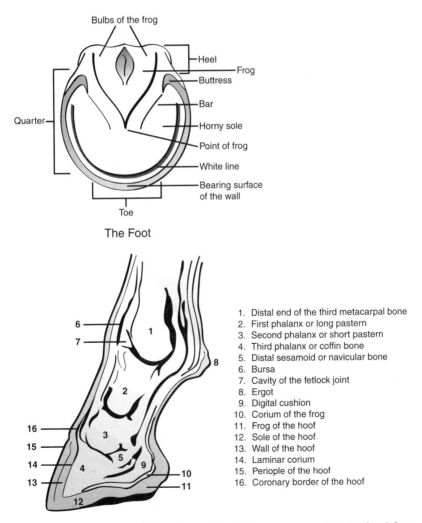

The Foot

1. Distal end of the third metacarpal bone
2. First phalanx or long pastern
3. Second phalanx or short pastern
4. Third phalanx or coffin bone
5. Distal sesamoid or navicular bone
6. Bursa
7. Cavity of the fetlock joint
8. Ergot
9. Digital cushion
10. Corium of the frog
11. Frog of the hoof
12. Sole of the hoof
13. Wall of the hoof
14. Laminar corium
15. Periople of the hoof
16. Coronary border of the hoof

The most important part of the horse. The delicate structure of the hoof and foot is weight-bearing, but vulnerable.

Bruised Soles

The sensitive underside of the hoof is bruised.

Common causes:

- Hard ground
- Stones

Symptoms:

- Horse might seem "off" (lame), especially on hard ground
- Bruise might be visible, in the form of a pink spot
- Untreated bruises sometimes abscess, and will eventually rupture and drain

What to do:

Be sure that horses who work on hard or rocky ground are shod. This will usually prevent bruised soles, but if it doesn't …

- Remove shoe on the injured hoof.
- Stop work for several days.
- Apply a poultice—if bruise is going to abscess, this will encourage it and relieve the horse sooner.

Laminitis and Founder

This acute condition is one of the first recognized consistently by horsemen, probably because of its dramatic onset and potentially devastating effects. Essentially a "fever" in the foot, it is caused by blood vessels in the hoof area congesting—at its most extreme, it causes the small, triangular coffin bone to separate from the inner hoof wall. At this point the condition is officially known by its traditional name, "founder," almost always signaling chronic, irreversible degrees of lameness.

Common causes:

- Overeating of rich food, especially large amounts of grain and fresh spring grass

- Obesity

- Trauma to the hoof, particularly hard work on hard ground

- Drinking cold water when excessively hot

- Stress of illness, pregnancy and partuition (giving birth), shipping long distances

Symptoms (laminitis is a progressive disease, so these will vary):

- Unfortunately, in the early stages of laminitis, circulation blockage prevents the horse from feeling anything, and you often don't notice a problem until he is in the more acute stage

- Hoof walls are hot to the touch

- Horse is in great pain and may even moan

- Horse lays down more than usual

- "Sawhorse stance"—legs stretched out unnaturally in an attempt to relieve weight on front feet

- Misshapen hooves

- Loss of appetite

What to do: Call the vet if you suspect your horse has been exposed to any of the potential causes of laminitis or you see even the faintest symptoms. This is a potentially crippling disease.

Navicular

One of the most common ailments in horses, this arthritic condition abrades the navicular bone in the foot, bruising the attached tendon.

Common causes:

- 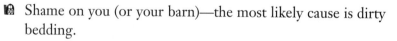 Old age

- Progressive arthritis

- Faulty conformation

- Bad shoeing

- Hard surfaces

Symptoms:

- Heat in the hoof

- Signs of lameness, especially early on in a ride

- "Pointing" the foot when standing

What to do: Consult your vet. Treatments include drug thera-pies, special shoeing, increased turnout, light work, and, as a last resort, "nerving"—cutting the nerve in the heel so that the horse does not feel the pain.

Thrush

The athlete's foot of the horse world. The fleshy underside of the horse's hoof, the frog, becomes infected, emitting a really nasty smell.

Common causes:

- Shame on you (or your barn)—the most likely cause is dirty bedding.

- Shame on you (or your barn)—the next most likely cause is not picking your horse's feet out properly (we know, we haven't told you about that yet).

- Predisposition—some horses seem to be more vulnerable than others to thrush.

Symptoms:

- Strong cheesy smell—believe us, you'll know!

- Black discharge (in untreated cases)

What to do: Clean up the feet, and your act. Treat with one of several over-the-counter topical remedies.

Windpuffs or Windgalls

Sounds like an exotic plant, but is actually a puffy swelling just above the fetlock joint. Caused by concussion, standing in a stall after hard work. They are common in horses that have been "used" during their lifetime and more common in older horses. Windpuffs usually aren't painful and don't cause any problems, but have them checked out by your vet just to be sure the swelling isn't an indication of stress on the legs and tendons that could lead to more serious symptoms.

What to do: Some competitive riders wrap their horses' legs to prevent these, and a related temporary condition called "stocking up" where the horse's legs fill with fluid when they are inactive, such as being stalled overnight, but the swelling goes down shortly after the horse begins to walk around. For the most part, rinsing with cold water and treating with a cooling gel will help relieve the strain; but some horses, especially those in repetitive heavy work, get windpuffs for good.

Whoa!
Get out the sunscreen. Horses with pink skin sunburn and peel just like us. Slather those velvety noses with a high-number SPF sunscreen and keep light-colored horses indoors or provide shaded areas for them to hang out on sunny days.

Skin Deep: Skin Ailments

They may not look as if they need to worry about their complexions, but horses have delicate skin and are prone to cuts, scrapes, bruises, and various skin disorders.

Cuts, Scrapes, and Bruises

This is where the inner child really comes to the fore. Outside, horses' idea of playtime resembles the Stanley Cup playoffs, and occasional cuts and bruises are inevitable. Indoors, although we hope your stalls are free from protruding edges and splinters, horses often catch themselves on their own shoes when lying down.

Symptoms:

- Bleeding or rawness in the case of cuts; swelling or soreness in the case of bruising

- If unnoticed, signs of infection may become present

What to do: Use your common sense. Wash the area with warm water and an antiseptic soap. Don't use hydrogen peroxide—it actually kills skin cells. Most cuts don't require bandaging (horses aren't really the bandaid set anyway); instead, there are a range of antiseptic ointments and aerosol sprays you can use to prevent infection and keep the wound clean. If it has already become infected, poultices and antibiotic ointments are helpful. In the case of bruising, running cold water over the area can be soothing, and if the skin isn't broken, try a cooling gel or witch hazel. Bruises are especially important to monitor, because if they occurred anywhere near a joint or tendon, the injury may be deeper than it first appears.

Saddle Sores

Sort of a cross between bedsores and blisters, usually caused by ill-fitting saddles, persistent rubbing, or poor grooming.

What to do: As for cuts, cleanse and apply antibiotic ointment. Most important, try to keep off the horse's back until the wound has healed, and get rid of, or adjust, the guilty piece of tack. Continued pressure can cause deep tissue damage that can affect your horse's way of going.

Rain Rot (Greasy Heel, Rain Scald)

Hard to believe in an animal that's designed to live outdoors, but persistently damp coats, especially during a warm, wet winter and spring, sometimes invite a micro-organism that causes hair to fall out in tufts, angry red skin, and nasty scabs on the back, belly, and lower limbs.

What to do: Brush horse frequently to keep coat and skin as clean as possible. Be sure coats and extremities are thoroughly dried off; if symptoms appear, wash affected area with Betadine, apply a topical antibiotic to ward off a secondary infection, and keep the area dry.

Scratches (Cracked Heel, Mud Fever)

Not those scratches—the other scratches. This somewhat archaic name describes a viral inflammation in the heel area, caused by damp conditions.

The symptoms are painful inflammation of the skin on the back of the pastern, resulting in oozing, scabs, and horizontal cracks in the skin. The constant motion of walking causes the cracks to gap and become painful, which in turn can lead to lameness or allow bacteria to enter, causing severe infection.

What to do: Consult with your vet. Scratches are a chronic condition and some horses, particularly draft horses, with their feathered lower legs, are prone to getting it. Treatment involves washing the area well with Betadine and then smearing with antibiotic ointment to stop any secondary infection. Above all, keep the area dry! When the cracks heal, keep the skin supple with a lanoline-based ointment that also works to provide a water barrier.

Ears

Horses' ears are coated with a fine layer of hair, which helps to keep out dirt and debris, but this area is usually kept trimmed for tidiness and sometimes this invites invasion. Ear mites and insect bites are

common, and ears should be checked regularly for signs of soreness or infection. Even if you don't spot something right away, your horse may let you know by suddenly becoming head shy or difficult to bridle and by shaking his head.

Eyes

Our problem, children of the TV housekeeping generation as many of us are, is that nature looks messy to us, and we're always rushing in to tidy up things that might have a function. In both horses and dogs, moisture in the corners of the eyes helps to keep them clear and to capture debris; once it has, it should only very gently be cleared away with warm water. Keep an "eye" out for redness, swelling, discharge, or sensitivity to light. Eye injuries and corneal abrasions are common. Sometimes, though, red eyes may only be a sign of allergens (his stall may be too dusty), but to be safe, call the vet. If vision is failing slowly, horses actually adapt better than we do, but uncharacteristic clumsiness or elevated head posture might be a sign of compensation.

Whoa!

One serious eye infection, called "moon blindness" (Equine Recurrent Uveitis), is a recurrent inflammation that causes acute pain, cloudiness of the cornea and extreme sensitivity to light in one or both eyes. If treated early enough the complete blindness that is the inevitable outcome of this disease can be delayed. Call the vet at the first sign of any eye problems.

Flies

If there is a grand plan in nature, it is hard to figure out where the fly fits in, though there's probably an entomologist out there to tell us. Maybe it's why horses have tails. From a horse's-eye view, however, flies are a plague upon the land, a constant irritation, sometimes literally to the point of madness—inflicting bites, sucking blood, and fostering the spread of larvae, which equals worms.

Flies happen. They are more prevalent at certain times of year, of course (August is an especially miserable month in many regions), and species vary from place to place. Common types include the basic housefly, which seems to be eager to leave the house in summer; deer flies, which look like small Stealth bombers; and the vast, repulsive horseflies known as "bombers."

What to do: The range of insect repellents on the market probably rivals the cosmetics lines by now. Read the labels and instructions carefully, since different products work best for different conditions—short lessons, long rides, turnout, etc. There are spray-ons for the whole body, roll-ons for the face, gels, and repellents especially for healing wounds. "Green" products are increasingly available, too, though cynics (and we are among them) admit that those nasty monosyllables (Deet) and polysyllables (cypermethrin) really do seem tougher. While you're at it, buy a human insect repellant for yourself—flies bite people, too!

As an additional measure, a shoo-fly or fly swisher can provide some relief. The shoo-fly is attached to the bridle's throatlatch or curb strap, and its motion while you're riding keeps flies away from a horse's neck and jaw. An alternative is a fly swisher, which is like a miniature horse tail (using real horse hair) on a stick, to be carried on the trail or while walking your horse. That way he can take care of the back, and you can take care of the front.

Heat Stress

Sure, there's no such thing as global warming. Tell it to your horse. Record temperatures in recent years have really put a strain on our equine athletes, and during hard work, even normal summer heat will take its toll if you're not careful. Of course horses get hot, and have natural cooling mechanisms, just as we do, but you should be able to recognize the signs of something more serious, and know how to treat your horse safely and humanely in warmer weather.

Horse Sense _____

If you're afraid of putting too many chemicals on your horse, make your own chemical-free fly spray at home. It's also cheaper.

Home Made Fly Spray I

$1/4$ cup Epsom salts (dissolved in hot water)
$1/2$ cup hot water
$1/2$ cup cider vinegar
$1/4$ cup Avon's Skin-So-Soft

Dissolve Epsom salts in the water, then add vinegar and Skin-So-Soft. Mix well before filling spray bottle, and shake well before each use.

If you live in an area where biting insects are a real problem and you need extra protection, try mixing up a batch of the following spray for the real nasties:

Home Made Fly Spray II

$4^1/2$ gallons water
6 oz. Blue Dawn dishwashing detergent
1 oz. Permectrin (available through catalogs)
16 oz. Avon's Skin-So-Soft
$2/3$ cup citronella oil
4 oz. mineral oil

Mix ingredients in a five-gallon bucket. Stir well before filling spray bottles, and shake well before each use.

 Horse Sense _____

It's good to know your horse's "normal pulse range" so you can make a quick diagnosis in case of illness. To get this, take his pulse (under the jaw or behind the pastern) only when he is relaxed several times a day over a period of two to three days and then average the total.

Symptoms of heat stress include the following:

- Panting—a normal breath rate in hot weather would be 10 to 30 breaths a minute. Forty or above is dangerously elevated.

- Elevated heart rate (normal is 28 to 49 beats per minute)—take the pulse under the jaw or behind the pastern.

- Profuse sweating—or no sweating, a sign that the horse's system is breaking down and heat is trapped inside.

- Dehydration—a simple test is to pinch a loose flap of skin on the shoulder or the cheek. If the skin remains puckered and doesn't immediately go back to its normal state, the horse is in serious need of water.

- Sluggishness—heat is drawing blood away from the brain and other vital organs.

- Dark or bloody gums or mucous membranes in the nose.

What to do:

- Walk your horse for 10 or 15 minutes after vigorous exercise; this helps restore the circulation to normal.

- Run cool water over the horse, or apply with a sponge or towels, but don't leave towels on, as these will hold in heat. Scrape water off as it warms up, and continue to apply until horse's skin is cool to the touch.

- Allow him free access to water once he's been walked for a few minutes, but be sure water is not ice cold.

- Don't feed him until he has fully cooled down.

Monitor him constantly, and call your vet, who may administer electrolytes.

Horse Sense

It used to be a byword that you shouldn't let a hot horse drink, but research done in preparation for the Olympic Games in Atlanta demonstrated that horses should in fact be allowed to drink as much as they like when they're hot. While normally you'd walk them out a little first, in extreme heat preventing dehydration and loss of vital minerals is key. Washing them with cold water was also thought to spasm muscles, but this turned out to be another old horsewive's tale.

Colds

Horses suffer from a variety of cold-related ailments, most treated, like ours, with a combination of rest, warmth, mild diets, and antibiotics. It is important to treat these "sniffles" attentively, however, because colds in horses can lead to chronic respiratory problems that can literally take the wind out of their sails.

Alternative Therapies

In between the Ibuprofen and the dental floss, you've got a bottle of St. John's wort. Your aunt swears her chiropractor has saved her life. Your boss could never run in those marathons without seeing his acupuncturist. Trends that are moving into the consumer mainstream for humans have also trickled increasingly into the equine world. Why? More research suggesting that finding ways to stimulate the body's ability to heal itself may benefit the horse in a more sustained way than it does with humans. We know, for instance, that many performance problems in horses stem from musculoskeletal irregularities that can be corrected with acupuncture, massage, and spinal manipulation. These days it's common to find holistic veterinarians who may also practice homeopathy, naturopathy, chiropractic, acupuncture, aromatherapy, electrical stimulation, and magnetic and laser therapy (see Appendix B).

> **From the Horse's Mouth**
>
> In **holistic** medicine, the aim is to treat, not a symptom, not even a single disease, but the whole entity as a complex interconnected organism.

> **Whoa!**
>
> Many alternative techniques have not been fully explained or researched. If you are considering an alternative therapy, talk to your own vet or call an association like the American Holistic Veterinary Association (see Appendix B) for a referral.

As Healthy as a Horse Should Be

When you work out, you check your pulse rate to make sure that you're not overdoing it. Can you monitor your horse's vital signs as well as you can your own? If you haven't a clue, read on.

- A healthy horse has a normal temperature of 99 to 100.5°F (37 to 38°C).

- A healthy foal has a normal temperature of 101.5°F (38.6°C).

- A healthy horse breathes 8 to 12 times a minute.

- A healthy horse has a pulse of approximately 44 beats per minute. Pulse will be faster if the horse is excited or has just been worked.

 Horse Sense _____

A first-aid kit for the barn:

Vet wrap	Scissors
Vaseline	Lubricant
Dose syringes	Mortar and pestle (or a hammer) for pulverizing pills
Disinfectant	
Antibacterial soap	Betadine scrub
Aloe cream (great for minor scrapes and scratches)	Towels (terry cloth and paper)
Liniment	Boric acid powder
Rubbing alcohol	Rolls of cotton and gauze
Epsom salts	Thermometer
Tweezers	Adhesive tape

When to Call the Vet

Except for minor wounds, you probably want to consult your vet about most issues, since small problems have a way of escalating

into big ones, and intervention at an early stage can prevent many problems later. Veterinary medicine—and the tools of the trade—have become infinitely more subtle and sophisticated. But even if you're thrifty, or independent, you absolutely must call your vet if your horse is showing signs of any of the following:

- Acute pain

- Persistent loss of appetite—almost always, if a horse fails to eat his grain, it is sick and needs diagnosis

- Acute or persistent lameness

- Heat prostration

- Symptoms of poisoning—panting, drooling, spasms

- Impaction—a clean stall after a night in and his usual meal is not good news

- Acute injuries of any kind involving deep cuts, tissue, profuse bleeding, etc.

- Violent coughing, shivering, or sweating

- Dramatic changes in vital signs such as pulse, respiratory rate, or temperature—for example, if a horse's temperature exceeds 101.5°F (38°C) or falls below 100°F (37.7°C)

The Least You Need to Know

- Colic, the leading killer of horses, is a blanket term for intestinal distress and should be treated promptly.

- Internal parasites are a fact of life with horses, but should be managed to prevent damage to his digestive system.

- Heat can be a real killer. Learn to ride safely in warm weather, and to recognize a meltdown.

- An increasing range of alternative therapies, from massage to magnets, is available for horses. Shop wisely.

Chapter

8

Born to Run (and Jump and Rein and Trail): Maintaining Fitness

In This Chapter

- Fitness regimes for horses
- Monitoring vital signs
- Nailing shoeing

You may be in good general health, able to walk up a flight of stairs without puffing, and not too embarrassed in your swimwear, but that doesn't mean you're ready to run a marathon. The same is true for the equine athlete; he may be bright-eyed and bushy-tailed, but if you are expecting to do serious work with him, or even just enjoy long trail rides, you need to slowly condition him to sustained effort. This means reducing excess fat and increasing muscle, strengthening those muscles, both in the legs and all over the body, and improving his wind.

Fat vs. Fit

No riding horse should be overweight and undermuscled, but different disciplines require different levels of fitness—racing, eventing, and endurance horses have the most demands made on their systems, and are much more aggressively conditioned than, say, show hunters or trail horses. As you become familiar with the discipline of your choice, you will become more fully acquainted with its standards, and with special techniques developed by experts in each field.

Where to Begin

We'll assume that your horse (or the horse you'll be working with) has had the winter off. Maybe (if you're hardy, or in a temperate climate) you've ridden a little, but most of the time your horse has slowly been turning into a soft, flabby plush toy. This is the time to begin daily grooming, have him worked, check his teeth and feet, and measure his vital signs—pulse, respiration, and body temperature. These aren't only important baselines to alert us to health problems—as with human athletes, you'll be looking to improve these rates, and to monitor recovery times from strenuous exercise for your horse. (Think of this as a horse stress test.) Don't rush to increase his feed—this should be done gradually as you move into really demanding work.

Horse Sense

To check a horse's respiratory rate, watch his flank, and count each inhalation over a 15-second period. Then, multiply by four for the rate per minute.

Now that your partner has had his annual physical, it's time to begin your routine.

How Long/How Often?

It takes approximately six weeks to two months to condition the average horse, but this will vary depending on your horse's age, weight, breed, metabolism, temperament (there are Type A personalities in the horse world, too), previous fitness levels, and, most important, how much time you are able to put into your regime. The ideal riding program, as recommended by many professionals, assumes that you are working your horse six days a week, for about an hour to an hour and a half each day.

> **Whoa!**
>
> If you are riding your horse only on weekends, accept the fact that it is going to take longer (three months, rather than two, at least) to get him fit. Don't try to compensate for your schedule by accelerating your training either. Forcing a horse into work for which he is not ready will simply result in stress and injury.

"Stretch and Bend and Touch Your Toes ..."

What actually goes into a fitness regime for horses? There are no stretch aerobics classes, but putting them "through their paces" has the same effect over time. These exercises can be done by riding and/or from the ground, by lungeing the horse on a long line. If your horse is just coming back into work after the winter, you'll want to begin with lots of long walks, including hills if you have access to them, and slowly work up to trot and canter work as his muscles get toned.

> **Horse Sense**
>
> Who needs Richard Simmons? In addition to mini-massage, one good way to begin conditioning a horse from the ground is by making him work for his treats. If you're offering a carrot, stud muffin or horse cookie, hold it back by the horse's shoulder and make him stretch his neck around to reach for it. Do this in both directions (two treats—we promise he won't complain!).

If you are competing with your horse, you will probably need a more strenuous and specific regime, and the resources devoted to each discipline will outline the best course for its particular challenges.

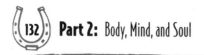

The Unbroken Circle: Ring Work

Although much conditioning work is done outside the ring when possible, basic ring work, riding and lungeing, is also an important part of any fitness regime. Taking your horse through a variety of school movements such as circles and changes of direction helps to create flexibility, balance, and obedience.

Another useful tool is the cavalletti (another thing we owe the Italians, along with Caprilli's forward seat!). This is simply a long wooden rail, placed on the ground (singly or in groups) to improve a horse's balance, help him to use his back and leg muscles more efficiently, and prepare him—and you—for more advanced schooling.

Everything Old Is New Again: Interval Training

Remember Kikkuli (1345 B.C.E.), the Hittite Horsemaster? He is probably the first professional horseman to use interval training, in which short intense periods of stressful work are punctuated by brief "intervals" of rest. Kikkuli's system was lost, except to scholars, until recently, but interval training made its way back into the horse world by way of cross-pollination with other sports. The system, which is thought to help prime the heart, lungs, and muscles, is used by competitive runners and swimmers. Like doing exercises in sets of a fixed number of repetitions, it involves clusters of paces, such as three five-minute trots followed by two four-minute canters.

> **Horse Sense**
> Be sure to vary your workouts, balancing serious school work with nice long walks, drilling movements with some leg stretching canters and gallops (when the horse is fit enough). Horses get just as bored with routine and mindless repetition as we do.

> **From the Horse's Mouth**
> Not all the work of conditioning a horse takes place on his back. One common technique involves **lungeing:** exercising a horse, from the ground, on the end of a long rein. This improves balance, coordination, and muscle tone without the horse having to cope with the weight of a rider.

How to Tell if It's Working

Is your fitness regime working? Here are some clues that it is:

- 🐴 The horse will be flab-free, with visible, toned muscles.

- 🐴 The coat will be shed out and shiny (if it is spring or summer).

- 🐴 After stressful exercise, the recovery rate for vital signs will improve. The horse's pulse rate should recover within 10 minutes of rest to a pulse of no more than 68. This is the most important rule of thumb to determine if the horse is fit and prepared for the work it is doing.

- 🐴 The horse's sweat will be clear and liquid, not filmy and sticky.

- 🐴 He will be able to undertake strenuous workouts without being winded or showing signs of lethargy and fatigue.

Horse Lore

The first horseshoes were introduced by the Romans (second century C.E.) and were known as hippo-sandals (you can imagine today's marketing campaign). These iron shoes were tied to the horses' feet with leather thongs. Next came shoes that were nailed onto the horses' feet.

Why Not Footloose and Fancy-Free?

Horses' hooves were designed for grazing on open, semi-arid pastureland, and if this was all they did, they'd be happy waggling their one toe freely in the breeze. But domestication brought with it burdens—cartloads and humans, rough roads, long journeys, and the varying rigors of competition. All of this threatens to tear up the hoof, causing soreness, and to produce uneven patterns of wear that eventually affect the alignment of the whole body.

In addition to simple protection against wear, today's *farriers* are able help correct conformation flaws, change ways of going, and complement the wide range of equestrian activities.

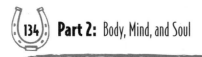

From the Horse's Mouth _____

Around the Middle Ages, blacksmithing was becoming a specialized profession, with smiths starting to use ready-made shoes, and in the sixteenth century, its practitioners were given their more formal name, **farrier,** from the Latin *ferrum* and French *fer,* the words for "iron." This reflected the most common material used for shoes.

Hot and Cold Running Shoes

Blacksmiths use one of two methods to fit shoes—"hot" or "cold" shoeing.

- Hot shoeing involves the forging of a new shoe especially fitted to the horse, and was the traditional method for many years.

- Cold shoeing involves altering a ready-made shoe, with a hammer and anvil, to approximately correspond to the horse's hoof.

Air Jordans for Horses

You think you know what the basic horseshoe looks like, that vaguely oval symbol of good luck and backyard games. But these days there are almost as many types of shoe as there are horses, and if you look at them closely you will see many minute variations on the classic shape.

The basic ready-made shoe is called a keg and is usually made of iron, steel, or some composite. It encircles about three quarters of the hoof, leaving the heel area open, comes grooved or ungrooved, and has nail holes. In addition, grooved shoes with more grip and custom tapering are used in a variety of disciplines such as hunting and reining to allow a horse to move at speed and stop suddenly, while racehorses, like today's swimmers in their microfiber suits, wear very light aluminum or plastic shoes.

And the high-tech athletic footwear craze has made it into the realm of horseshoeing. Today's performance horses may be getting the extra support they need from "sneakers" for horses, or from enhanced footwear with names like Flex-Steps, Glu-Strider, and Level-It.

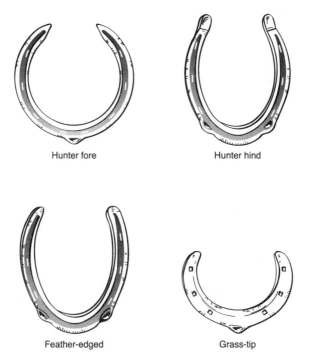

Horseshoes—something for every season.

A Little Lift: Corrective Shoeing

The fields of blacksmithing and veterinary medicine have come much closer over the years, and as a result a wide variety of sophisticated corrective shoes are available. These range from bar shoes—raised shoes that usually cover the whole hoof—used to treat dramatic foot problems such as chronic navicular, to variously tapered shoes designed to minimize injury in horses who strike themselves while in motion, to shoes fashioned longer at the back to correct one of the most common foot problems in horses—a long toe and contracted heel. Basically, the aim of a corrective shoe is to return the foot as much as possible to its most efficient form—level and bearing weight evenly.

Low Tech/High Tech: Materials

Horseshoes now come in classic iron, lightweight aluminum, titanium, stainless steel, and plastic, and can be glued, as well as nailed on, for horses with severely compromised hoof walls.

Your Farrier: What's He/She Doing?

One fascinating way to spend your afternoon is to observe your farrier at work. Here are the basic steps he or she takes to reshoe your horse:

- **Removal.** Cutting the clenches (top side of the protruding nails) and gently prying the shoe off.

- **Preparation.** This is the basic manicure, involving cutting away excess growth, trimming the foot, paring the ragged edges of the wall and frog, and rasping the whole into an even shape.

- **Forging or fitting.** With forging (hot shoeing), a template is fired and then placed on the sole of the foot for sizing (this does not hurt, though it produces a sensational sizzling sound); with fitting (cold shoeing), a ready-made shoe is compared to the shaped hoof and beaten into the appropriate shape. Any disparity is usually modified over time as the foot begins to conform to the shoe.

- **Nailing on.** This might also be accompanied by fitting pads, often with pine tar or clay packing to preserve moisture in the foot. The nails are hammered into the outer perimeter of the hoof, where there are no nerve endings, and twisted off. The usual number is three nails on the inside and four on the outside.

🐎 **Finishing.** The clenches are rasped smooth and tapped into a small bed in the hoof. Clips and caulks are tapped into place, and the whole hoof is rasped once around for smoothness.

A horse in work should be shod every four to eight weeks, depending on the condition of his feet, the type of work you are doing, the climate, and the rate of hoof growth. Even shoeless joes—horses who are off work or ponies with tough hooves—need regular trimming and checkups to be sure the feet aren't splintering or cracking. Horses that are ridden infrequently on soft, non-rocky ground, do not really *require* shoeing, but do need to be trimmed regularly.

Horse Sense

Six thousand years ago horses in the Far East wore protective boots made of hide or plant matter. Today, the horseman's friend is the Easy Boot, a slip-on shoe substitute to be used for shipping, in emergencies (when your horse casts a shoe on the trail or hunt course), for applying medication, and for ceremonial occasions where more support might be needed. A tub-shaped plastic, they are rather like galoshes for horses, and clip into place like ski boots. They should be standard equipment in the barn and in the field.

The Least You Need to Know

🐎 It takes six to eight weeks (more if you're a weekend rider) to condition a horse for strenuous work.

🐎 Fitness programs are designed to strengthen and tone the horse's muscles, limbs, and heart and lungs.

🐎 A horse should be exercised both from the saddle and from the ground for optimal results.

🐎 Good shoeing is key to a horse's soundness and ability to perform, and this age-old profession has a new high-tech face, offering solutions that not only protect, but correct and enhance.

Chapter 9

The Three Horse Genders: Mares, Stallions, and Geldings

In This Chapter

- The three horse genders and how they behave
- Why stallions are not for beginners
- Mares and that girl thing
- The best choice for you

Generations of riders had their first imaginary horse experience through the pages of Walter Farley's romantic adventure story, *The Black Stallion*, first published in 1941. Others may have been touched by Mary O'Hara's story of a passionate filly, *My Friend Flicka*, which came out a year earlier. And readers and filmgoers thrilled to the unlikely moment when Velvet Brown, the butcher's daughter, rides in England's greatest steeplechase, The Grand National, on The Pie, a carthorse with extraordinary gifts.

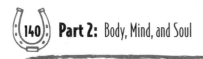

All three of these stories present the best—and most traditional—view of the three horse genders: stallion, mare, and gelding: bold, willful, and willing. As a horse rider—or owner—today, you'll want to be able to separate fact from fiction so you can successfully bond with the beauty, or friend, of your choice.

(© Pete Siegel)

Grand old man. The last triple crown winner, Affirmed, at 25. This celebrated thoroughbred was unbeaten on the track, and other honors include being named horse of the year twice.

Male and Female He Created Them: Hormones

You know about *hormones*—a subject almost as common as toothpaste in today's health-conscious world. Hormones regulate your biological clock, drive the reproduction instinct, and alter your body chemistry in accordance with rhythms that have been around longer than the word that describes them.

The word comes from the Greek *horman*, "to urge on," and that's exactly what they do. In equine terms, that principally translates to the urge to breed, and both stallions (intact males) and mares are influenced by this to a degree that affects the way they relate to us and to each other. Domesticated though they may be, these instincts are much closer to the surface than they are in the average suburbanite (except maybe in a John Updike novel).

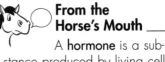

From the Horse's Mouth

A **hormone** is a substance produced by living cells that is transported as by blood or sap, and stimulates other cells by means of chemical action.

Boys Town

Of course stallions are romantic. They have magnificent proud heads held high on shapely necks (thick neck muscles are one sign of an intact male horse), they plunge and snort, and in general answer our barely acknowledged fantasies of what pure masculine power represents. And it would be an injustice to portray them as unmanageable bundles of testosterone (you know, what makes Arnold, Arnold). While mares were the preferred war horse in the East, stallions were commonly ridden in battle, and used for hunting, in Europe. And today, they are still shown under saddle in breed shows, are the traditional mounts at the Spanish Riding School in Vienna, and are featured at many ceremonial occasions.

Nevertheless, they are volatile and extremely powerful, and do not make good mounts for inexperienced riders. Nor are they glamorous pets—even model citizens can become uncontrollable Casanovas around mares in heat.

Horse Whispers

A fine little smooth horse colt should move a man as much as doth a son.
—Thomas Kyd

Stallions are not pets. And unless you are a very experienced horseman or horsewoman, they are not your mount of choice. Under that glamour package of flashing eyes, dilated nostrils, and bulging muscles are raging hormones. Trust us—if you want a man in your (horse) life, get a gelding.

When Is a Boy Not a Boy?

The very fact that the word *gelding* comes from the Old Norse *gelding* suggests how long it has been since it became clear that many animals would have more productive—and less destructive—working lives if they were not dominated by drives that it was no longer practical to satisfy. Aside from the need to create safe, tractable mounts, the growing trends in selective breeding in all horse-oriented cultures must have influenced decisions to restrict mating to animals whose traits were desirable.

Gelding is a simple surgical procedure usually performed before a horse is 2 years old (11 months is common), and involving nothing more complicated than a local anesthetic—in other words, it's an outpatient procedure. We know what we lose (in case you were out that day in high school biology, testicles are what produce testosterone and without them there is no sperm production), but what do we gain? While it would be an exaggeration to say that we gain a perfect gentleman, more often than not a gelding will retain the strength, authority, and sang froid ("What's that?" you say? Read about mares in the following sections) qualities of the male, while losing the uneven temperament and threat of aggression.

Sometimes you even get more than that. As with eunuchs and *castrati*—the human equivalents fashionable at various periods in history as either "safe" companions for women or as performers—gelding does not in fact deprive a gentleman of his instincts, and *your* gelding, especially in spring or around a flirtatious mare, may suddenly begin to strut his manly stuff, get a bit lively in the ring, and feel competitive with other males (this is especially true of horses who were gelded late; one sign is a very thick neck). This rarely causes serious problems in work, so if "in the spring a young man's fancy fondly turns to thoughts of love"—let it.

Girl Talk

Feminists, beware. Every prejudice you thought you eradicated in the early 1970s is alive and well in the horse world: Mares are considered picky, cranky, touchy, erratic, moody, and just plain impossible at that time of the month, which happens every three to four weeks during their season. And the bad news is, some of this is true.

There are two reasons for this combination of truth and horse lore: Mares' position in the equine social hierarchy, and their reproductive cycles. Unlike stallions, with their eyes on the horizon and their harem, mares in a herd are part of a complex social hierarchy, and are destined to become fiercely protective mothers. In feral herds, they are also often the decision-makers. This makes them more alert to power struggles, criticism, slights, and what they perceive as disorder. They don't trust easily, but once their trust is won, they are loyal and affectionate.

Horse Whispers

Mares, she said, had not been altered, in them the blood flowed freely, their life cycles had not been tampered with, their natures were completely their own. The mare usually had more energy than the gelding, could be as temperamental as the stallion and was, in fact, its superior.

—John Hawke, *Whistlejacket*

And how they respond to you, and to the work you demand, will depend in part on where they are in the pecking order (or where they are temperamentally in the pecking order—some of this is preprogrammed by nature, so even if your mare hasn't really been socialized in a herd, she will have some innate predispositions). Alpha mares will either give you their all or fight for supremacy;

lower-ranking girls will need you to prove you're in charge or view your riding time as their chance to rule the roost—after all, if they can move up a notch, they've got a better chance of being bred.

PMS: It's a Mare Thing

Back to high school again. Estrogen levels spike during a mare's heat cycle, and are at their peak just before ovulation. At the same time, the complementary hormone progesterone, which suppresses ovulation (readying her for pregnancy), drops. Simply put, her body, and sometimes her mind, are on sex, and the visible symptoms can range from mild to nightmarish (and you wondered where that word came from!). They include the following:

- Inability to concentrate

- Crankiness and stubbornness

- Girthyness (protesting when the girth is tightened)

- Physical aggressiveness: pinned back ears, swishing tail, bared teeth, nipping, bucking

- Touchy over the back and loin areas

- Flipping her tail to one side

- Constant urinating in small amounts

Treated sensibly and sensitively, most mares can work normally during their heats, but in more severe cases of equine PMS, and for performance horses where even the slightest deviation in behavior can count heavily in the show ring, veterinarians and trainers have started using synthetic progesterone (Regumate is the most popular brand) to suppress heats and extreme behaviors.

There Is No Mare Menopause

A female horse usually has her first heat cycle at 18 months of age, and after that she comes into heat pretty much every month for three to five days throughout her life. Ovulation is governed in part by sunlight, so during the dark winter months mares have a period of anestrus and most do not show heat at all during that time.

Horse Sense

What to do when it's that time of the month:

- Be aware that your mare might be distracted.
- Keep lessons simple, and try to steer clear of stressful performance situations.
- Stallions in your neighborhood? Steer clear!
- If she's really impossible to work with, or seems potentially dangerous (cranky mares have bucked off their owners and returned to the stable to check the personal ads), call your vet, who may prescribe Regumate.
- A mare can be spayed, though this rarely is done.

Baby Talk

A Foal is a baby (colt or filly) at birth and up to January 1 (the official universal horse birthday for most breeds).

A Filly is a young female (up to three years of age).

A Colt is a young male (up to three years of age).

There are no gelding foals. Geldings are made, not born.

Keep these in mind when you're looking at horse ads, and you won't be as confused as one author's doctor husband, who was sure "M" was a mistake on her mare's registration papers!

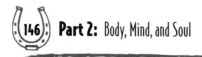

Horse Lore

Mares have long been known for their courage and willingness to go the extra mile for the right rider. In addition to their
prowess as war horses, they have proven to be spectacular
performance horses. One of the most famous show jumping partnerships of the 1950s and 1960s was the German national
team member Hans-Gunter Winkler and his small mare Falla,
and in 1984 *Sports Illustrated* awarded its prestigious "Woman
Athlete of the Year" award to U.S. team member Joe Fargis's
mare Touch of Class, who had carried him to an individual gold
medal in show jumping.

The Better Sex?

There isn't one. With the exception of stallions, who are problematic for the reasons we mentioned earlier, it all becomes a matter of
personal preference and mutual temperaments. Talk to gelding owners and you'll hear that they are even-tempered, perfect gentlemen,
and who wants to deal with moody females? Talk to mare owners
and you'll hear tales of loyalty, affection (once they decide you
belong to them, mares will nuzzle and "speak" to you), and determi-
nation, and who wants to ride a boring old gelding?!

The Least You Need to Know

- There are three horse genders, two natural—stallion and
  mare—and one man-made, the gelding.

- Stallions are romantic, but are not usually safe or sensible
  choices for amateur riders or owners.

- Geldings are traditionally more even-tempered, but have
  plenty of panache.

- Mares have a reputation for moodiness, brought on by their
  place in the pecking order and their heat cycles, but most are
  rewarding to work with.

- For more extreme cases of mare PMS, a synthetic hormone
  called Regumate is being used successfully to alter behavior.

Chapter 10

Saber-Tooth Tigers Are Stalking Your Horse: The Power of Instinct

In This Chapter

- ▣ The power of instinct
- ▣ How horses think and how they learn
- ▣ How training combines nature and nurture
- ▣ Stable vices and what to do about them

As numerous self-help books on relationships can tell us, human beings have enough trouble understanding one another, so imagine the challenge of trying to see the world through the eyes and brains of our horses.

How Their Minds Work

Horses' behavior is guided by two powerful instincts, for survival and for community. And compared to other domestic animals,

horses were domesticated more recently and are closer to their prehistoric counterparts. They were prey animals, so their map of the world is still likely to be filled with potential predators and the instinct to flee them. And the best protection against assault was a strong and stable community—the herd. Understanding these two underlying compulsions is the key to understanding, and training, your horse.

Run for Your Life!

If you've been around horses at all you've probably seen it—that sudden leap sideways (sometimes propelling the rider off in the other direction) in reaction to something no one else registers. The catalyst can be as obvious as a big truck, or as seemingly innocuous as a stool, but it evokes the same response: "This could be dangerous, and I'm outta here." Horses are pattern-oriented animals—something we take advantage of when we train them—and anything that upsets that pattern triggers their alarms. It's the equine equivalent of that old thriller cliché: "It was quiet, too quiet."

> **From the Horse's Mouth**
> **Habituation** means learning by repeated exposure that an act has no negative consequences and an object means no harm.

One key to overcoming horses' natural timidity is called *habituation*. If your horse spooks at something (like a plastic bag or a bicycle) that you'll definitely encounter again and again, you should desensitize him through habituation. It will be a good strategy for you in the long run and may keep you both safe.

Here's how (using the plastic bag and bicycle as examples):

- **Plastic bags.** When you're back in his home territory, rub him with plastic bags, pour his feed out of a plastic bag, take treats out of plastic bags, hang them from his saddle, tie them to the fence—you get the idea. Pretty soon plastic bags will become a nonissue. Don't forget that the bag blowing down the driveway may startle him, but it won't be the bag, it will be the sudden movement of an object. It may even startle you, too!

Bicycles. Bicycles are particularly frightening to horses. They don't make any noise, but people are moving toward them. This is clearly witchcraft. We've found that horses who show are less likely to react badly when encountering a bicycle on a trail, because so many people use bicycles to get around show grounds (although some equine veterans still don't know what to make of scooters!). So show him how the trick works: let him look at a standing bicycle, have people walk with bicycles, ride one around the barn—eventually he'll get the idea.

Whoa!

Any inanimate object can cause a horse to spook. Come to think of it, anything a horse is not familiar with can cause him to spook. When riding, be alert for those potential saber-tooth tigers!

Horse Lore

PJ's bombproof mare was ridden by a friend for security duty at the Pocono 500 Nascar Race. While on parking-lot duty patrolling the campers and tailgaters, a plastic bag, propelled by the wind, blew into the mare's legs and startled her. She gave a tiny buck that de-hatted her rider (who managed to catch it with one hand and place it back on her head immediately—to a round of applause from the crowd). If this horse hadn't known about plastic bags, the results would not have been so inconsequential, or amusing.

Joining the Crowd: Herd Instinct

When people hear the word *herd*, they tend to think of a moving clump of animals, but a horse herd is as complicated a social organism as your average cocktail party. There are leaders and followers, hangers-on and social climbers, bright young things, and many long-time companions. In addition to the basic framework in which a stallion guards his mares, there are sometimes numerous subdivisions within herds that include both friendships and rivalries. The "pecking order" is rarely fixed, but often, as in our world, depends

Whoa! _____

There is a downside to herd instinct. Some horses, known as "herd bound," get agitated if separated from other horses. This also means they are hard to ride alone, and that when on a trail ride, or even in a field, if they get too far away from the group, they will plunge anxiously—and sometimes dangerously—back toward the herd.

on context—the milquetoast at work might be a tyrant at home (or vice versa!). And for those afraid to turn their horses out—establishing dominance in the herd is in fact a way to avoid conflict. Although they should be, many stabled riding horses aren't exposed to the dynamics of a herd, but they still retain many of these instincts. Given a chance, they will form close bonds with other horses—and, in their absence, with you.

E[quine] = MC²: How Bright Are They?

There has been a lot of contradictory information over the years about horse intelligence, ranging from the belief that they are fearful and stupid to the idea that they are mystically intuitive. As usual, the truth lies somewhere in between. Recent research has suggested that they have much higher levels of reasoning than was previously assumed—associative learning rather than simple "conditioning," but it is also true that some of their intelligence is "kinesthetic," working through the body, not just the brain. Horses can literally "think on their feet."

Horse Whispers _____

When I hear somebody talk about a horse or a cow being stupid, I figure it's a sure sign that animal has outfoxed them.

—Tom Dorance

Because of this, some intelligence tests in which they compare poorly to other animals may (like school tests for children) be skewed. Horses have relatively large brains for their size, but much of it is "hardwiring" for complex physical functions. All the things we take for granted—their gaits, their ability to travel safely over uneven ground, their speed and balance—actually require a lot of neurons. (Think how "stupid" you feel when you're learning to dance or ice skate.)

ABCs: How Horses Learn

Many researchers (and trainers, even if they don't know it) make use of a system outlined by Roger Thomas, called the hierarchy of learning, which describes eight levels of learning ability. The lowest are habituation, classic conditioning (the old Pavlovian ring-a-bell, get-a-biscuit sort), and "operant" conditioning, which involves learning to do things better and faster. At the higher levels, you are looking at distinctions and decisions based on context. We don't need to be blinded by science here—the important thing to remember is that learning is progressive, and that one part of it involves "learning to learn"—taking less and less time to respond to a cue.

Research has also taught that these "cues" aren't necessarily the ones we thought we were using, which is why people often encounter problems in training and riding. Horses respond simultaneously, and equally well, to visual, auditory, and tactile messages, so if the commands you are giving are contradictory (you want your horse to move forward, but you're unconsciously tightening your grip on the reins) you will not get the result you were looking for.

Going Against Nature

One challenge we face in training horses is that we are often asking them to go against their nature—teaching them to stay when they want to flee, or turn away from the herd, or go backward when they want to go forward. It is easy to teach a horse something when the desired behavior comes instinctively, harder when it goes against his instincts. This is where operant training comes in, getting the horse to focus on the way a particular response will produce a particular reward ("If you move forward, I'll stop kicking," for example).

+/-: Negative vs. Positive Reinforcement

One reigning controversy in training has been whether negative or positive reinforcement works better to elicit the right response from a horse. At its most extreme, there are situations where people attempt to brutalize their horses into submission, but most of the time the distinction is subtler, and again relates to the way horses are hardwired. Learning is still related to survival for them, so the absence of disagreeable stimuli is often a powerful incentive. The most common example used relates to pressure on the bit—if the horse relaxes his head, which is what we want, the pressure should go away.

Horse Sense

It is possible to overtrain a horse. Once the horse "gets" what you've been trying to teach him, reward him by moving on to something else or stopping for the day. Think about it: If there is no reward for doing something right, why should the horse bother?

The more the behavior called for goes against nature, the more likely it is that you will want to use positive reinforcement with your horse—to substitute the range of associations you create (praise, treats) for the prehistoric ones already lodged in his brain. And don't rush things—he needs time to process the information.

Memory: The Double-Edge Sword

Everyone involved with horses, from grizzled old cowhands to Ph.D.s, can tell you that horses have phenomenal memories, for the good and the bad. They can remember cues and commands up to a year after they've learned them, and they can remember that the last time they went past that red barn something scared them. Because of this, repetition is the key to training, and bad habits are hard for them to unlearn. In fact, sometimes trying to correct a problem turns out to reinforce it, because your very insistence tends to fix the subject in their brains, which either reinforces the "bad" behavior or makes them worry so much about what response you want that they get confused.

Horse Lore _____

Sometimes a horse's phenomenal physical memory produces odd quirks. We met a young girl recently at a horse show whose first pony had an earlier career giving pony rides around a circle and only to the right for so long he would never turn left!

Finding Their Way Home

One aspect of horse "memory" that's been much touted is their ability to find their way home. Not much research, other than anecdotal, has been done on this, but this "homing instinct" is probably left over from a migratory way of life; they develop "mental maps" of physical environments. Their strong social skills are also a factor: They can follow their own tracks or those of other horses they know. The cues are mostly visual, but they have been observed sniffing the ground, "casting" like a hunting dog for lost tracks, or sniffing the wind to get a whiff of the barn.

Mommy, I'm Bored!

Horses suffer from boredom as much as we do, both in the stable and in the ring. While training involves repetition of cues, commands, and demands, too much "sours" your horse, making him either dead to the cue (you've done it so much, and he's gotten so little in the way of reward, that he just doesn't pay attention any more) or nervous and resistant. Vary your work in the ring and on the trail, and consider shorter intense sessions with longer down time in between—another good reason for interval training.

Where's My Prozac?: Stress

You're not the only one feeling the pressure. Your horse, whether he is a hardworking school horse or your show hunter, is every bit as much a victim of modern life as you are—and in fact, you may be part of the problem! The more you interfere with his instinctual

rhythms, the more likely your horse is to feel stressed out. If you don't want a stressed-out horse:

- Feed him frequently and in small amounts to mimic his natural grazing behavior.

- Keep him with his horse buddies—horses need to be part of a herd. If he's stabled indoors, be sure he can at least see a horse friend from his stall.

- Be aware that horses—like people—get stage fright.

- Be tolerant of the horse who has been ill or injured, is nervous about trailering, or is upset or anxious about a change in his environment. Take your time.

- Turn him out to pasture regularly—recess helps horses as well as kids to relieve boredom and get rid of excess energy

- Keep daily care and training on a regular schedule—horses are creatures of habit.

So is he stressed? Here are some common symptoms:

- Ulcers

- Stiffness and tightness

- Anxiety and disobedience in work

- Vices (see the following section)

Trouble Right Here in River City: Vices

No, not smoking, drinking, or gambling. In the stable, bored or stressed horses sometimes exhibit a range of behaviors that are similar to human obsessive/compulsive disorders. In other words, they are natural behaviors like eating, breathing, and walking taken to unnatural extremes. Common vices include the following:

- Weaving—standing in the stall moving constantly from side to side

- Cribbing—chewing on wood, iron bars, or any other stationary object within reach

- Wind sucking—grabbing a surface, such as the rim of the stall door, and gulping in air; some horses can do this anywhere, even without a surface to grab

- Pacing constantly

Vices are destructive and debilitating, and are linked to colic, lameness, and the number of times you have to replace your stall doors! They are also extremely difficult to "cure" once they become established. But absolutely the best way to cure them (and to prevent them from occurring in the first place) is to provide lots of turn-out time and exercise. Exercise is one of the horse's most primary needs, and the more natural his life, the happier and less anxious he is. If you can't change all your barn management routines to accomplish this, or have little influence over those who do, try to alleviate the major causes, and give your horse something to play with in his stall—this exercises his mind and his body. (And you might know it—boys like toys more than girls. Alas, there's no horse Nintendo. For restless girls, try walking her out.)

Toy Story

There are many great commercially available stall toys—huge inflatable balls with handles that the horse can toss around (in his stall or outdoors)—but you can also make your own. It's not that hard to come up with things that will keep your horse amused, and sometimes the homemade ones do just as good a job.

- **Empty gallon milk jug** (minus the cap). Hang these from the ceiling or from a chain on the wall. Like a kitten chasing a bit of cardboard at the end of a string, the horse will bat this jug

around. It makes noise, too, all the better it seems. To make even more noise, toss in a couple pebbles.

- **Traffic cones.** No, you shouldn't steal them, but if any fall off a truck in front of your house and no one comes back to claim them, I guess they're yours. You can also buy them in catalogs. Horses love these. They toss them around (one stallion even managed to heave his large cone over his stall wall on a regular basis). When they're not being used for toys, you can use them as markers when you're riding.

The Least You Need to Know

- Horses are guided, but not necessarily ruled, by instinct, and the key to dealing with them is finding a balance between "natural" and conditioned behavior.

- Horses aren't stupid—their intelligence works differently than ours and we need to learn to understand it and appreciate it.

- Horses have good memories and learn from repetition, but these traits can backfire if we unintentionally teach them bad habits or bore them.

- Bored and stressed horses are prone to stable vices that are difficult to cure. Try to spot the triggers and be sure your horse has some relief in the form of recreation, toys, and friends. (Yes, this is your child.)

11

Every Horse Is a Mr. Ed: Communicating

In This Chapter

- Learning to speak horse
- Horse whisperers and what they're saying
- Horse body language
- Horses and companionship

The 1960s television series that gives this chapter its title, the intellectual race of horses in *Gulliver's Travels* called the Houyhnhnms (pronounced *whinnims*—get it?), and numerous children's books and films have treated us to talking horses and mules.

Clearly, this idea is fundamentally appealing to us—why, oh why can't they speak to us? The answer is, we've got it the wrong way around—they are speaking, all the time—to themselves and to us—in a language fully developed while we were still trying to master that standing upright thing. Often we're just not listening—or more to the point, looking.

Berlitz Course: Speaking *Equus*

Training horses used to be (and in many places still is) a matter of subduing, or "breaking" them. This can be done brutally and inhumanely with whips and hobbles, or slowly and incrementally through what's known as "progressive desensitization" where the trainer introduces the new element (bridle, saddle, bit, water, etc.) bit by scary bit. But in either case the underlying premise was, "This is our world, welcome to it." Recently, with innovative work originating in the West through the observation of wild Mustang herds, but now practiced by a wide range of trainers, we're learning to speak *horse*.

Talking Back: What the Whisperers Are Saying

A veritable fountain of books, videos, and courses—not to mention Nicholas Evans's book and Robert Redford's film—has made "horse whispering" fashionable currency, and made cult figures of these mysterious beings who "talk" to horses. But the whisperers themselves will say that there's no big mystery to what they do. By observing herd behavior, they have fashioned techniques based on how horses actually interact with one another, instead of how we wished they interacted with us.

A simple, key example was the discovery that you can get a horse to bond with you more quickly by first chasing it away (this is usually done in a round pen). In the language of *Equus*, this threatens isolation from the herd, which is disastrous, and rather than face it, the horse will eventually seek ways to approach you. Once the bond is formed, the horse views the trainer as his trusted guide to the unknown. Horse trainers who work this way are often able to do far more, and far more quickly, than with traditional methods.

One Touch at a Time

Although horses in the wild have many conversations without touching, and we'll review some basic body language soon, they are still very sensual creatures, and whole systems of both training and physical therapy (which recognize the links between them) are based around the idea of reprogramming the nervous system, and breaking down resistance, through touch. Once again, horse society provided the clues: Mutual grooming probably began as a helpful way to get rid of those pesky parasites, but it also strengthens bonds and is as relaxing as a massage. In training regimes like those created by Linda Tellington-Jones (called, alliteratively, TTouch), various acupuncture points around the body are stimulated to make the horse more relaxed and aware. Touch also signals trust to a horse, and trusting you on the ground eventually leads to trusting you in the saddle.

I'm irritated

I'm feeling great

Bye

Well, "Hello"

You'd better think twice before petting me

I can only listen to one thing at a time

Huh?

Horse Sense _____

Mutual grooming is a sign of affection, and has useful side effects. The most popular site, the area around the withers, is near a major nerve in the autonomic nervous system, and stimulation of this area has been found to lower horses' heart rates. Remember this when you're told to reward your horse during a ride: Those hearty slaps on the neck are the equivalent of guys punching each other on the arm; speak horse instead, and rub or scratch gently.

Baby Steps

Even before formal training begins, foals should be handled and accustomed to human touch. This allows for *imprinting*. It makes it easier to introduce them to basic rituals such as being groomed and led, and to speak *Equus* to them later. This is another delicate balance between our two worlds—horses who are not handled sufficiently as youngsters are often either bad-mannered or skittish. But sometimes imprinting can go too far, and you wind up with a teenage colt who would like to take you for a drive in his car, or a filly who wants to prove that anything you can do, she can do bigger.

From the Horse's Mouth _____

Imprinting is psychologist Konrad Lorenz's term for the process of attachment that occurs when animal babies transfer some of their instinctual responses to humans. In the horse world, veterinarian Robert Miller has continued the exploration of this phenomenon in his work with foals.

Alpha(bets): Who's the Boss?

Regardless of what training system they espouse, all trainers agree on one thing—in your equine partnership (and this is what we urge you to strive for), you still have to be the leader. If you want to get your horse to listen to your commands, you must get your horse to believe that you are higher in the pecking order of your herd of two than he is. This means, as we've seen, that you must act like a horse. For example, don't let him crowd you, or rub on you. Maintain your personal space and push him out of the way in the same way his horse buddies do. If you are too afraid to train him in good stable manners, hire a trainer, but show no fear (he's sizing you up, too, and he's bigger and better at this body language thing than you are) or he will take advantage of the situation. Just as trust on the ground translates to trust on the ride, so does respect.

Horse Whispers

What the colt learns in youth he continues in old age.

—French proverb

Whoa!

It's cute when dogs and cats rub their heads against you; it's dangerous when a horse does it—you don't need a creature 10 times your size using you as a scratching post. (Not to mention th ffect on your clothes.) Do not encourage your horse to rub   you for any reason (many do this when they're swe   ' make a big deal of it; tell him to "quit it" an   If he's got sweat running down his   it off with a towel or damp   needs it. Then you'll both be happy.

Bou

So we're learni   *Equus*, and it's time to master some basic vocabulary. The mo   ou learn about horses and riding, the more complex your horse vocabulary will become, but imagine the words you spell out with big block letters. Some of this behavior is natural in a paddock with other horses, but at home with you it can present a problem.

- **Pardon my rump.** Horses swinging their rumps around are engaging in passive aggression, warning that they might kick if the intruder/rival doesn't move off.

- **Ears.** Pinned back means "Back off." Pricked forward means "You've got my full attention."

- **Tail wringing** (this is when the tail turns into a propeller). The horse is not swishing flies, he is annoyed. This is not a winning move in the show ring, and in the barn could precede a kick.

- **Foot stamping.** The horse hissy fit. It's another move that means "I'm annoyed," "I'm bored," "Get me out of these cross ties," "I don't want to be fussed with."

- **Giving you lip (and teeth).** This can be a threatening move, a playful act between pasture mates, a reprimand if it's a mare nipping her foal, or an act of aggression for a stallion defending his mares and territory. If it happens over a stall door, don't assume he's kidding. Move on.

- **Kicking.** While sometimes playful in the pasture, it is also the other side of the flight response—a horse will kick if he feels trapped or threatened, and an aggressive horse may need no reason. Sometimes, however, as with other stable vices, genuine instincts become meaningless ticks, and a bored or impatient horse may kick his stall.

Horse Whispers

The ears never lie.

—Don Burt

- **Head and eyelids drooping** (usually standing on three feet)—like, totally relaxed.

Body Blows

There is no right end to a really aggressive and bad-mannered horse, and it's a good idea to know what to do about kicking and biting (maybe some of these guys are ex-boxers) in case it occurs.

I Get a Kick Out of You

For most horses, biting or kicking at a pasture mate is normal behavior that helps to establish or maintain pecking order, wards off aggressive behavior, or is a playful bit of *joie de vivre* (as in "kicking your heels up"). However, excessive kicking means either an overly aggressive, or overly fearful, horse who is a potential danger to stablemates and humans alike, and kicking around humans should always be considered an aggressive act.

It is with horses like this, often the victims of either abusive or idiotically permissive training, that horse whisperers and touch therapists have had some of their greatest successes.

If your normally placid horse begins to kick out unexpectedly, look for obvious causes before assuming a personality disorder. Mares sometimes kick in season, and many horses respond to stinging fly bites with dazzling rodeolike displays.

Love Bites

As with kicking, some biting behaviors are natural to horses and are used in play and courtship. And of course, biting is a prelude to eating, and we often unintentionally train horses to bite the hand feeding them treats. To humans, feeding is intimacy; to a horse, it's function, and he'll begin to treat you like a dispensing machine. The instinct to reward is strong, and very much part of communicating with your animal, but touch is more potent than treats (which can still go in the feed bin).

Most of the time a biting can be stopped (within three seconds of the threat) with a loud reprimand and a quick *light* smack on the neck or nose (never hit a horse in the face—it's unacceptably brutal, and could make him head shy).

Horse Sense _____

If you do not correct a bad action instantly (literally, within a couple seconds), forget about doing it because the horse will not be able to associate the punishment with the crime. Once reinforced, however, that marvelous horse memory comes into play, and you should be able to teach your horse good manners.

Work as Play

Edutainment is a trendy byword of early education, but has recently come to the fore in the horse world as well. Some researchers believe that domestication has preserved a horse's inner child, and that games help to stimulate his intelligence and maintain interest in his work. In fact, one school of thinking believes that this is the reason good performance horses approach their demanding work with zest: It may be the jumper finals to you, but it's one big game to them. Running, jumping, zigzagging through those barrels—what could be more fun? Bear this in mind when you train—variety and challenge will consistently reward your horse *during* work, not just afterward.

What's That You're Saying?: Horse Talk

In addition to body language, horses do vocalize, and while you're never going to hear yours ask you what's in the morning paper, here's what you might hear:

- **Snorting.** Usually a danger signal, or a challenge to an aggressor (like the combatants' cries in martial arts).

- **Blowing.** Same apparatus, different meaning. When a horse blows gently through his nose, it signals relaxation, and is one of the most encouraging signs you can get when riding on the flat, because it means that the horse is relaxing through his entire body. Some horses, especially Thoroughbreds, blow rhythmically through their noses when running, also.

- **Squealing.** In boys, this means "one more step and I'll shoot" and can often be heard during fights and mock fights. In girls, it's often that old "let them chase you until you catch them" thing, a flirtatious move designed to keep them guessing. (In mares who are still nursing, it sometimes indicates tender teats.)

- **Neighing.** Here is where our translation skills break down. Horses neigh constantly to each other, especially stable or pasture mates who are being separated. As in many collective animal societies, it is probably a form of reassurance, reaffirming the bond, but for all we know, they might be saying, "I think she's going to make me do the water jump again."

🐎 **Nicker.** The kinder, gentler side of neighing, used by horses greeting one another, mothers to their children, courting horse couples, hungry horses reminding you that it's dinnertime, and, if you're really lucky, your horse talking to you.

Horse Sense _____

Some backyard horses don't have the privilege of horse companions because of space considerations. This can be a problem because horses are herd animals and they need companionship to thrive—so to solve this problem, many horses have pets. We've read (and seen firsthand) horses who live with pigs, camels, llamas, chickens, sheep, a wild duck, and even a parrot. Every match is not made in heaven, however. If the arrangement doesn't work out, instigate a divorce and get someone new.

You Gotta Have Friends

Everything we've told you must make it clear that horses crave companionship. Ideally, this should include friends of their own species (minis are a good investment, rather like giving a doll or an action figure to your child), but if a horse is isolated for some reason, or seems especially fretful when indoors, consider getting him a pet. Goats and dogs are traditional companions, but horses have proved to be very cosmopolitan in their tastes.

Quality Time

Of course, we really hope your horse's best friend will be you. And even if you're just taking lessons, you may have the chance to form a bond with a favorite school horse. Aside from all the training and obedience issues, just take time getting to know your horse.

Horse Whispers _____
To ride a horse well, you have to know it as well as you know your best friend.

—Katie Monahan

Take him for a walk, scratch those good places, and talk to him. (One woman we know says the best part of grooming is *smelling* her horse!) The more time you spend together, the more this unique partnership will thrive.

The Least You Need to Know

- Horse whisperers have popularized revolutionary training methods based on observing horses in nature and learning to speak their language. Some of these incorporate touch therapy.

- Horses have a range of common body signals for fear and aggression you'll want to recognize.

- You want your horse to be a friend and partner, but you still need to be the Alpha in your herd of two.

- Companionship is key to a happy horse, and quality time spent with yours will be infinitely rewarding.

Part  Preparing to Ride the Beast: Grooming and Saddling

Here comes the real fun: becoming a horseman. Your mind may be leaping ahead to the picture of you sitting tall in the saddle, but there are some important first steps, like learning to work safely around a horse on the ground. And oh yes—cleaning him!

Then there's horse clothing, which is more complicated than you might have imagined. We'll take you on a historical tour of tack (that's what saddles and bridles and all the other accessories are called collectively) and explain why different riding traditions call for different equipment. We'll also tell you how to choose it, put it on safely and correctly, and how to shop for it.

Now that you're all dressed up (we'll tell about that, too, including the all-important safety helmet), you're ready to go, and we'll take you through proper mounting and dismounting techniques. (Forget what you've seen in those Westerns!)

Appaloosa Sugar's Domino, owned by Tina Veder, shows why sometimes wishes are horses.

(© Lori Steffensen)

12

Get Off My Foot! Safety on the Ground

In This Chapter

- 🏚 Ground rules—do's and don'ts
- 🏚 Tying a horse—crucial tips
- 🏚 How to dress for the barn

We hate to be the ones to tell you, but there's likely to be a little pain mixed in with your pleasure. As we've seen, horses are rarely vicious, but they are big and volatile, and sooner or later you're bound to get a bump or two. The aim of this chapter is to keep those bumps to a minimum, and to alert you to some of the horse-size safety risks involved in simply being around horses.

Surprisingly, more than one third of fatal accidents involving horses happen on the ground, so you can imagine how many minor ones are waiting around the corner. Most of them have to do with having left your common sense at the barn door, and with forgetting that, as Olive Oyl said of Bluto, "He's LARGE."

Right Between the Eyes: Approaching the Horse

This is a no-brainer, right? You already know that horses have a blind spot directly in front of them and at the extreme rear, and need to process information from both sides of the brain. They are also sensitive to abrupt movements and sounds, and nervous of strangers until they are proven friends. So we know you're not going to gallop up to your new acquaintance, scream hello in his ear, and bang him on the rump.

What you are going to do is approach softly, usually from the left (traditionally training leaves most horses left-oriented), watch to see how he is responding to you (which should be calmly—we're assuming that you are likely to be meeting a trained school horse for the first time, not a neurotic), and stroke him on the shoulder, while introducing yourself and saying his name. Then, move over to the right side and introduce yourself again (this is not an elaborate ritual—you are likely to be grooming this horse, so moving around him will be your first communication anyway).

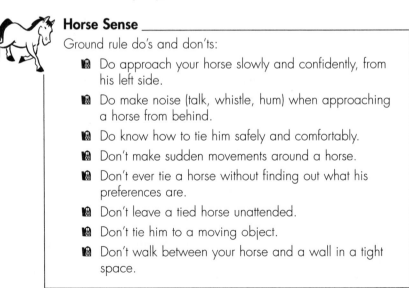

Horse Sense

Ground rule do's and don'ts:

- 🐴 Do approach your horse slowly and confidently, from his left side.
- 🐴 Do make noise (talk, whistle, hum) when approaching a horse from behind.
- 🐴 Do know how to tie him safely and comfortably.
- 🐴 Don't make sudden movements around a horse.
- 🐴 Don't ever tie a horse without finding out what his preferences are.
- 🐴 Don't leave a tied horse unattended.
- 🐴 Don't tie him to a moving object.
- 🐴 Don't walk between your horse and a wall in a tight space.

Remember that softly does not mean timidly. There is nothing that induces wariness faster in an animal than a suggestion of fear. Whether it's body chemistry or body language, they pick right up on it, and go on the alert—the last thing you want.

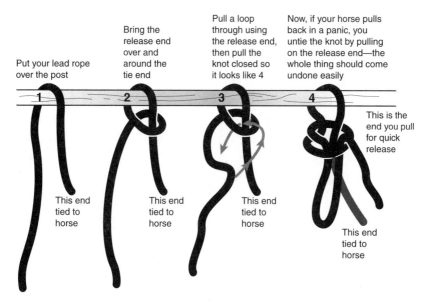

The quick release knot, also known as the slip knot.

Personal Space: Where Are You?

There are several common scenarios for meeting a horse, and these dictate some of the most basic safety precautions. By far the most common (if you are a riding student, for example) is that you will meet your horse at his barn. If you are a complete novice, a staff person will probably have groomed and tacked your horse for you, but once you begin a regime of lessons (as we'll discuss in Chapter 13) you will probably be expected to groom your own horse, and then you will either work with him in his stall or put him on *cross-ties*.

From the Horse's Mouth

Cross-ties are long suspended lines, usually of canvas or nylon, that hold the horse in place in the aisle. They are attached to each side of the halter rings at the horse's muzzle.

Your first crucial safety tip is to *ask* what grooming position your horse prefers. Some horses are tense and aggressive in their stalls, but docile in the open; others have had a bad experience with cross-ties and panic at the very sight of them. Remember, to a horse, a perceived danger is just as scary as the real thing.

Room Service: The Stall

Approach quietly, open and quickly (but not *too* quickly) close the door (many barns have rubber guards in place during the day, and these just need to be ducked under). Check to see whether the horse is *haltered*; if not, put it on (see the following section). While in the stall, be sure that you are not hemmed in near a wall—it takes only a sudden shift of body weight to turn you into paste.

Barns that prefer horses to be groomed in the stall, or have horses that prefer to be groomed in the stall, will usually have attached a ring to tie him (with the nifty quick-release knot we just showed you) somewhere at the center of the stall wall. In a pinch, you can tie him to the bars of the stall, but again, don't do this without checking that he is not upset when tied, and be sure to leave very little slack in the rope. The horse should be loose enough to move his head comfortably, but tight enough that he can't get his head below his chest level.

> **From the Horse's Mouth**
>
> A **halter** is a loose-fitting head harness that looks a lot like a bridle without the bit. Usually made of nylon or leather, it has rings at the cheeks and under the chin, for attaching a lead rope, lunge line, or cross-ties. This is what a horse wears when you need to lead, tie, or groom him.

Always tie a horse before beginning to work with him. Otherwise, he has no way of knowing it's time to begin his working day, and it is both unsafe and inconvenient to be following him around in an enclosed space.

Appaloosa Navajets Storm, a chestnut with blanket and spots, being ridden Western Pleasure, by his owner Dawn Sweeney.

PJ and her Half-Arabian Bay Tobiano Pinto mare, LH Endless Luv, in a Western Pleasure class. (Note the difference in the favored styles of Western riding between Arabian and Appaloosa, the preceding photo.)

A Gray Arabian in native costume. Ridden and owned by Cynthia Goldsmith.

*Amy Barkely Carey shows
fine barrel-racing form
on Quarterhorse Monte
Doc Bar.*

Born to Boogie, a National Champion Morgan Stallion, doing what Morgans do best in high-stepping style. Driven by Lynn Peeples and owned by Bryna Watson, Honeytree Farm, Rye Brook, New York.

Handsome gray Shire driving.

Fred and Agnes Boberg's matched team of Belgians (Kit and Willy) pull a century-old bandwagon of performing musicians in parades throughout New York and Pennsylvania when they aren't working on the Boberg's Maple Sugar Farm in Delevan, New York. They even pull a sleigh in the winter.

Palominos come in all different breeds. Here, a handsome Palomino Saddlebred is bringing home a blue ribbon.

The National Show Horse is a flashy horse that attracts attention in any color, but this gorgeous Chestnut Tobiano is hard to miss as he shows off the riding talent of his young rider, Melissa Milligan.

Nineteen-inch-high Solar Wind Savannah's Echo at three weeks old, getting acquainted with Heidi. (See mom, Persia, in Chapter 4.) Owned and bred by Solar Wind Miniature Horses, Perkasie, Pennsylvania.

Born to run. Diego, a Thoroughbred, shows what makes this a heart-stopping breed.

Welsh pony = Pony Power. A lighthearted moment for TangwylltSweet 'n Low and Maureen Datti.

Nothin' but a Warmblood: Adam Gershberg rides Elvin in dressage competition.

Robert Hooper exhibits Peruvian Paso HDP Reno.

Standardbred racing at The Red Mile in Lexington, Kentucky.

KC Carlson demonstrates why they're called "sporthorses" on Thoroughbred/ Connemara cross, Garron.

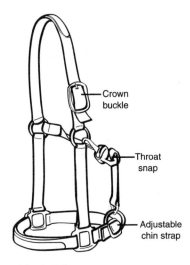

Crown
buckle

Throat
snap

Adjustable
chin strap

A basic halter.

Neutral Territory: Cross-Ties

This simple device should rank somewhere near the coat hanger as a contribution to society (at least *our* society). The simple process of anchoring a horse outside his stall makes the act of grooming both more efficient and safer because it's easier to move around the horse. That, however, doesn't mean that cross-tying a horse is inherently safe (even if the horse is totally relaxed about the whole process). The one thing you never want to do is to leave a cross-tied horse unattended. Some are clever enough to untie themselves and can be found wandering down the road the minute your back is turned; others get fretful and start trying to knock the nails out of their shoes, or begin shouting for friends. And PJ's mellow mare, now a Golden Girl, dozed off in her cross-ties one day and fell down, when PJ was only a few feet away looking for her bridle. Happily, people were on hand to operate the quick release and no harm was done, but you don't want your horse to try this at home!

> **Whoa!**
>
> Cross-ties can be very dangerous to the novice. Beginners should be supervised for a long period of time before being allowed to cross-tie a horse themselves because any number of things can go wrong. Beginners can easily forget where to correctly hook cross-ties and if the horse fights the ties at all, it can get *very* dangerous *very* fast. Horses can flip over backward, break snaps, or lunge forward and turn around quickly. To compound this situation, a beginner's first response is to try to control the horse, which is impossible under these circumstances. We recommend that you avoid working with a cross-tied horse until your instructor feels you're experienced enough to safely handle a horse in a variety of situations.

Cross-ties—often the best place to hang your horse when grooming.

Open Air

Horses in a pasture tend to gravitate toward people (you might be a source of food), but bear in mind that you are very much in their territory here, and might wind up in the middle of a fight or frolic, even if it's your own horse you're greeting. Best to get him inside before catching up on all the gossip.

You Can Lead a Horse to Water ...

But only if he knows how. Horses need to be taught to lead correctly, otherwise it becomes a pulling and pushing contest—and you'll lose.

The first stage involves haltering the horse (assuming you'll have an experienced horse, not one to whom halters are a novelty). If you are new to this, ask someone in the barn to show you how, but basically a halter is designed to be either unbuckled at the crown, or unlatched at the cheek (some have both options); open either one to allow you to slip the halter easily over the horse's head. You approach him, as for most initial operations, from his left side, and keep your right arm over his neck so he has the impression that he's secured before it's even happened (this doesn't work with all old-timers, but it's worth a try!). When you halter your horse outside of his stall, make sure your lead rope is attached to the halter just in case he changes his mind about being caught.

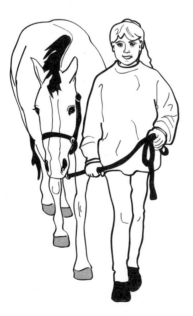

The safest way to lead a horse—first recommended more than 2,000 years ago by the Greek general Xenophon.

Once secured, the important thing to remember is that you're setting the pace. A horse should walk quietly by your side. You should be positioned halfway between his head and shoulder and close enough to have a secure grip on the lead line with your right hand, near his head, but far enough to avoid being stepped on. An arm's length away is the general rule, depending on how the horse is behaving. Your left hand carries the excess lead so it's not dragging on the ground. A horse that tries to charge ahead should be jerked up firmly, and sometimes a light slap against the chest with the lead line is all that's needed.

Horse Whispers

If horses knew their strength we should not ride anymore.

—Mark Twain

There are also sluggards, of course, and the last thing you want to be doing is dragging half a ton of horseflesh up a hill. Instead, go to the horse's side, and inch him forward a few steps at a time, maintaining your position at his shoulder. Tap the horse lightly with the end of the lead to keep him moving forward. Never turn around and look him in the eye—this is an aggressive stance, and will probably keep him from wanting to go anywhere, but also positions you as a ninepin should he suddenly surge forward.

In truth, there's a limit to how much of this can be conveyed in the two-dimensional universe of a book. Leading horses is really like dancing—you get a feel for each other's bodies in space.

Whoa!

Never wrap anything around your hand that is attached to a horse—this means reins, lead line, or lunge line. If the horse bolts you won't be able to let go quickly, and could wind up being dragged or losing a finger or two. Always loop excess line into a figure-eight and hold it together in your hand.

Don't Tie Me Down

Well, actually, we have to. As we've said, it's not really safe to work around a horse who is wandering about in his stall. Horses should be secured by their halters only, *never* by their bridles. Halters have rings at both the sides (for cross-ties) and under the chin. Cross-ties are usually commercially manufactured, and the best ones have quick-release snaps so that if a horse panics he can get free easily (just make sure the quick-release snaps are on the end that attaches to the wall, and avoid elasticized ties, as these can snap back and hurt your horse). If you are tying a horse up, use a quick-release knot and tie him only with a rope or his lead if it is made of rope, as other materials (leads often come in various synthetics, or leather) will not release quickly enough. Check yours out in a trial run before you use it to tie your horse.

Why Not by the Bridle?

For one thing, it's in his mouth, and a frightened horse will be that much more alarmed by jabbing pains in his mouth if he starts pulling. And if it begins to shift, he could be injured by the buckles or caught up in the reins. At the worst, he could be seriously injured; at the least, you've probably lost a valuable piece of equipment and rattled your animal. (See Chapter 14 for information on bridles.)

If you must tie a horse up while bridled (you're on your way out and forget to get your gloves or something), slip the halter over the bridle, being sure that the reins are well back on the neck, and then secure him by the halter.

Clutter = Catastrophe: Barn Safety

In addition to working safely around your horse (you'll hear more in our grooming chapter), the greatest perils are all around you, in the barn itself. While you may not always be the person responsible, you should still know what to do to keep the barn safe:

- Aisles should be clear of buckets, rakes, pitchforks, hoses, tack, sharp objects, and anything else a horse could step on or into.

- Stalls should be similarly clutter-free, and if your horse is fed with a hay net, be sure that it is far enough off the ground so the horse doesn't step in it (hay nets deflate once the stuffing is eaten!) and injure himself. Hang it at or above the horse's head.

- Be sure all food is secured, ideally in a locked room, but at least in bins with tight lids. More horses have been lost (to colic and founder) to midnight dormitory binges than any single accident.

- Be sure medications are secured and clearly labeled. You've probably brushed your teeth with your hand cream occasionally; imagine this scenario with a welter of similar-looking over-the-counter horse remedies.

- Be sure all electrical wires are properly insulated and not lying on the ground or in or near the horse's stall. Make sure, too, your horse can't reach the barn radio cord, or he'll bite it or step on it. Metal shoes conduct electricity.

- Beware of protruding hooks, nails, saddle racks, or anything else that could catch on you, your horse, or your tack.

Horse Sense

Assume that if there is an accident waiting to happen, your horse will find his way to it. Your job is to keep those accidents to a minimum, and to insure that when things go wrong (like a panicky or loose horse), they go wrong as "safely" as possible. Often it is safer to allow flight than to prevent it—a frightened horse who cannot free himself might plunge until he hurts himself or someone else, but calm down if he perceives himself to be free.

Dress for Success

We're not talking about your smart riding togs, but the casual clothes you might wear to and around the barn. Forget for a moment that it is a picturesque horse hotel, and think of it instead as a jungle of pointy, prickly, furry things waiting to get you. Even the best-run establishments have their share of nails and splintery wood, and dust and hay permeate the very air. Not to mention that grooming, as you'll see, is a grubby business.

To work safely and comfortably, don't think along the lines of a Ralph Lauren advertisement. Unless the weather is stupefyingly hot, wear long pants and a long shirt (if you come to the barn dressed for your lesson, carry a work shirt with you that you can put over your riding shirt), a cap or bandanna of some kind, or something to keep your hair up and out of your eyes (and free from dust) if it's long.

Leave your bangle jewelry, hoop earrings, and rings at home. Many people have lost fingers to rings that have gotten caught in halters and other things around the barn. Most important, wear sturdy boots or shoes—not sandals, flip-flops, or mules. There is no quicker way to trip or lose a toe.

Whoa!
Coming to the barn? Leave those fashionable open-toed sandals at home. Sturdy footwear that protects and supports the whole foot is crucial for safety both on the ground and in the saddle.

Familiarity Breeds Accidents

The worst mistake you can make in working around horses is to assume that if you know the animal, the rules don't matter anymore. Although it is true that a horse who knows you is less likely to spook at the sight of you, he is still prey to the alarms and instincts of his kind, and when frightened, or just distracted, is just as capable of hurting you without meaning to.

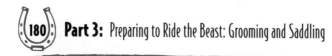

The Least You Need to Know

- To approach a horse safely, be calm, confident, and slow, and remember where his blind spots are.

- Horses must be tied safely, using ropes or cross-ties with quick-release mechanisms.

- A cluttered barn is a dangerous barn.

- Cowboys don't wear shorts: Dress safely and appropriately for barn work.

Chapter 13

How Do They Get So Dirty? Grooming Basics

In This Chapter

- Hands-on communication
- Why horses need grooming and you do, too
- The right tool for the job
- Brushing up your technique

Good grooming makes the difference between a real horse person and a wannabe—and the horses definitely appreciate it. Horses like getting dirty, and spiffing them back up requires elbow grease and a sense of humor. But grooming is more than just a chore: We've seen how horses groom each other as a social convention.

The Importance of Grooming

Eliminating every vestige of natural oil, or even dirt, isn't what grooming is all about. Grooming is communication, massage, and amateur medical examination all rolled into one calm and friendly activity. You want to cultivate a good rhythm, firm strokes, and sensitivity in your touch. That's how horses get shiny coats—not with soap and water, but with good old-fashioned brushing.

Horse Sense _____

Horses hate surprises. Talk to them when you're grooming. And always make sure they know where you're going if you have to walk around them.

As we said in Chapter 12, knowing how and where (and even whether) to tie a horse is a vital safety issue. There are horses that simply can't be cross-tied, and horses that can't be tied at all but are perfectly angelic in the field or stall. You've got to know what you're working with.

Here's the Rub

Wild Mustangs can roll in sand and dirt to rid themselves of parasites and dead hair. They never have to contend with wearing saddles and bridles that trap dirt, mix it with perspiration, and cause trouble.

Domestic horses who aren't groomed regularly tend to show it. Their coats can be dull, and frequently don't lie flat. That's because there's been no brushing to distribute the oil throughout the hair, and no way for the horses to work it out themselves.

Horse Whispers _____

If you don't have time to groom, you don't have time to ride.

—Old horseman's adage

Whoa! _____

If you're short, find a sturdy box to stand on while you're grooming. Don't use buckets or ladders.

Putting a saddle, harness, or bridle on a dirty horse is asking for trouble. Particles of foreign matter rub and cause sores, to say nothing of what they do to leather. One ill-fitting or tight piece of tack, particularly on a hot day, can put a horse out of commission for weeks.

Grooming is the best way to check on the health of a horse. You'll notice any new nicks, scratches, changes in the way the horse stands and holds himself, and how well he's keeping weight on (or off). You'd never believe how many serious problems have been averted by an alert groom running her fingers down a horse's leg, or accidentally discovering an area that's become mysteriously sore. You might feel a bump, or something wet, or hot. You've just detected a wound before it's had time to get infected, or a stress injury before it's been aggravated by exercise.

Hair Today ...

A horse that's slick as a seal in summer may get as hairy as a grizzly bear when winter rolls around. The old-fashioned approach was to leave off the deep currying and simply brush off the visible dirt. "Scurf," or greasy dandruff, keeps horses warmer if there's no protection from wind and rain. But most horses in regular work wear blankets in below-freezing weather. They need vigorous brushing to aerate their skin.

Springtime is murder. There's just no way to avoid being covered with sloughed-off winter hair every time you groom. If winter has been cold, there'll be buckets of pesky shed hair in April and May, and it will all end up on you.

Horse Sense
Don't wash mud off horses' legs, especially in cool weather. Wait until they're dry and brush them instead.

Horse Sense
Allergies or asthma? Shedding season could be a problem. A few suggestions:

- 🐴 Make sure your inhalers are fresh and full.
- 🐴 Get someone else to do the brushing.
- 🐴 Invest in a horse vacuum.
- 🐴 Wear a mask.

Late spring is heaven for grooming. The horses have finished shedding out all their winter hair, and it's not hot enough yet to have to deal with flies and sweat.

In summer, they get sweaty even before you ride. That's what towels are for: rub dry first, then brush. And leave time for a bath when you're through. (For him, silly.)

Fall is hard work time as the winter coat starts to grow. You have to make sure the horse isn't getting so furry that he's soaked with sweat every time he's ridden. Wet, salty winter coats are very hard to dry, and expose a horse to risk of pneumonia and chills.

Horse Sense

If it's already freezing out, it's too late to clip. Even with a blanket, your horse will shiver like a nudist on a ski slope.

To Clip or Not to Clip?

Clipping can be a lifesaver for horses who need to work during the cold months. But if you do clip, he will almost certainly need to wear a blanket.

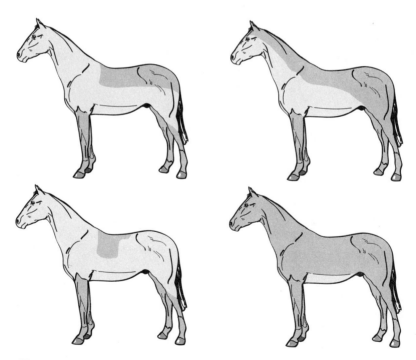

Horse hairdos: Partial hunter and trace clips keep horses insulated but cool for winter riding.

Don't try to clip a horse yourself unless you have professional help. That's how you wind up with the shaved-rat look—and a very cold horse.

Tools of the Trade: Equipping Your Grooming Box

The most important grooming supplies you'll ever own are a hoofpick and a soft rubber curry comb with flexible cones or "fingers." These are great for massage as well as loosening dirt and mud. Hoofpicks come in many different shapes and sizes. The simplest ones are fine.

The very least you'll need include the following:

- A rubber curry. The one you use depends on the thickness of the horse's coat and sensitivity of his skin. Choose the wrong one and you'll find out soon enough.

From the Horse's Mouth

Curry is something you do, not serve, in the horse world. Originally from the French *cuir*, for "hide" (as in skin), it developed a range of meanings from tanning to flattery, and eventually came to apply to both the action of rubbing dirt loose from your horse, and the nubbly combs with which to do it. Want to curry favor with him? Then curry him.

- A dandy (stiff) brush, for removing mud and heavy dirt. Plastic bristles are fine. These come in bright colors, and small, easy-to-hold sizes.

- A medium body brush. Natural or synthetic.

- A hoofpick.

- A mane and tail comb—people ones are good.

Some important extras include the following:

- Fly spray

- Scissors

🐎 A soft body brush

🐎 A pulling comb or Mane Tamer (more on this later)

🐎 Hoof dressing

🐎 Towels

Niceties:

🐎 Coat-polishing spray (Show Sheen or similar)

And always:

🐎 A Vaselinelike wound ointment for small cuts and scabs

You'll have to wash the contents of your grooming box every month or so. Otherwise, you're just redistributing the dirt.

Grooming, the Real Fat Burner

The sequence is simple:

1. Loosen the dirt.

2. Remove it.

3. Comb mane and tail.

4. Clean the feet.

Starting on the horse's shoulder, take your curry comb, and with a steady, circular motion, begin to work the dirt and dead hair out. Every five to ten strokes, whack the curry on a flat surface to clean it. Keeping the curry in contact with the horse's skin, work your way up his neck, back down, and toward his back. Don't curry legs or bony spots. Be careful in tender areas such as the belly and inguinal area (flank). End with the rump. Walk around him carefully, letting him know where you are, and do the other side.

Tired? You should be. This is one activity where it doesn't pay to be delicate. Don't attack the horse, but don't dab at him either.

Put your back into it. It's hard to stimulate the skin circulation on an animal this big without using a considerable amount of muscle. You'll find that after a couple months of doing this well, you'll have upper arms an exercise instructor would envy. Switch arms when you curry. Think of it as bathing suit training.

Whoa!

Squat, don't kneel, while you're grooming. You won't be able to get out of the way fast enough if Seabiscuit decides to kick at a fly.

Next, take up your dandy brush. Look for mud and heavy dirt, and brush it off. Bear down on the brush in long, sweeping strokes. You may choose to do the legs now with the dandy brush, or even the entire horse if he is very hairy (except the face—no dandy brushes on faces). Otherwise, it's time for the medium-softness body brush, starting at the neck and working backward. Don't ignore the legs—this is where the injuries show up.

Now look at your horse. Does he look relatively clean? He should. Now pat him on the rump. Do you see a cloud of dust? Brush the trouble spots again. If he still looks dusty, go at him with the soft body brush, the one you use for faces. If that still doesn't do the trick, go get a damp towel and rub.

Brush out the mane and tail. Don't be too thorough—the point is to make everything hang nice and straight without ripping all the hair out. The key to maintaining a nice, full tail is to brush it regularly, but don't try to remove every kink. You may want to spray it with a coat-slicking product, like Show Sheen. Once or twice a week with these products is plenty because they dry out the hair if used too frequently.

Horse Sense

Remember boarding school? Gym class? Or camp? *Label everything.* Everybody's grooming supplies look alike.

Whoa!

Don't spray silicon coat-slicking products on the saddle area. Your tack could slide right off. And keep them out of the horse's mane, too.

Amazing Feet

Want a truckload of heartache? Neglect your horse's feet. Stones cause bruises, and compacted manure causes thrush, a smelly fungal disease that can make horses lame.

Here's how to pick a horse's foot: Stand by the horse's shoulder facing toward the rear, slide the hand closest to the horse down its leg, and when you get down between the knee and fetlock (ankle), squeeze. He should pick up his foot. If he doesn't, take it from the top, and this time lean on his shoulder. Now cradle the foot with the hand closest to the horse, and, holding the hoofpick in the other, remove the manure, pebbles, and dirt from the concave undersurface of the hoof. Don't poke at the frog (the triangular, fleshy pad in the center of the hoof). Just work the hoofpick gently but firmly down into the cleft on either side of the triangle, and flick out what's there. Move toward the rear end of the horse, and repeat the process at his rump for his hind feet. Do this with supervision and instruction at first. There's an art to holding the feet to avoid getting stepped on or pulled, and some horses like to lean on you while you're working.

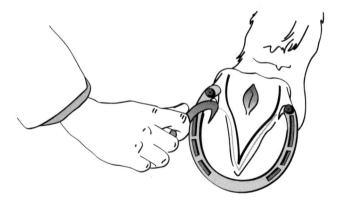

Picking out the feet.

Now you can tack up your clean, calm companion, and take him for a spin.

Once Is Not Enough: Groom Before *and* After the Ride

After you've properly cooled out your mount and removed his tack, assess the situation. If he's relatively dry, do a "turnback," an abbreviated version of the grooming you did before you got on. You'll notice when you brush him after exercise that everything's much cleaner and softer. Pick his feet again; he may have jammed a rock or two into his hooves while you were riding. Skip doing the mane and tail again. Chances are he looks great now, unless he's wet with sweat, in which case you'll have to go to plan B, for Bath.

For a finishing touch, apply hoof dressing (to keep the feet from becoming dry and cracked). Pine tar hoof dressing is cheap, and is as good as any other kind.

Bubble, Bubble ...

How do you bathe a horse? It depends on whether you want to get him clean. Don't laugh. Sometimes in summertime you just want to cool him and dissolve his sweat marks. Horses rarely need to be shampooed like dogs, though it's a good idea to start off the warm-weather riding season with a good, soapy scrub.

You need the following:

- A bucket (or two, or even three, if the water that comes out of your hose is too cold to use)
- A giant sponge
- A sweat scraper or horse squeegee
- Two big old towels
- Horse shampoo (optional)

A sponge bath is nothing more than a refresher after a sweaty ride. Use warm or room-temperature water, and gently remove his sweat marks, zipping off extra water with a sweat scraper or a rubber squeegee (made specially for horses) so he doesn't drip for hours and either acquire a fungus infection or a cold. Don't forget to sponge around his eyes and nostrils. A real horseman will have a special sponge to freshen his dock, that tender triangle of skin under his tail.

If you really need to get him clean, first make sure that it's 65°F out or warmer, and that he won't be standing in a cool breeze either during or after the bath. Wet him all over first, either with water that's warmed in the sun, or hose water that's not icy cold. (Warm is always best.) Dissolve some shampoo in water in another bucket, and sponge it on. You may not get much of a lather; that doesn't matter. Dab a bit of soapy water on his face, if he'll tolerate it. You'll have to rinse it off with a sponge, not a hose.

Whoa! _____

Don't use people shampoos on horses! They irritate the skin and dry the hair.

Horse Sense _____

Buy at least one black bucket. You can fill it with water before you ride and leave it in the sun—for a nice and warm sponge-bath later.

Whoa! _____

Never let a horse roll with his tack on. Yell, clap your hands, smack him on the butt—do anything to prevent him from hitting the dirt with a saddle on his back or a bridle on his head.

To wash his tail, take a bucket about halfway full, put shampoo in it, hoist the bucket up behind him, and stuff his tail into the water. Get the top of his tail with a sponge. Rinse the same way.

Color-enhancing shampoos for horses may not work, but "blueing" shampoos for white horses do. Wash them out well, though, or you'll end up with a purple horse.

Dry with a towel. You'll see whether you did a good job or not.

Down and Dirty

After the bath, take him grazing in a favorite grassy spot, and hang on to his leadrope until he's dry. You may need to put a cooler—a loose, light blanket—on him if the sun isn't strong.

You can put him in his nice, clean stall if it's warm enough. Stick him back in his paddock, and he's going to roll. He's wet, and he wants to be dry. He'll think it's hilarious.

Neatness Counts

The best-looking horses are the ones with no extra-long hairs any-where. Trim all extra-long hairs, unless it's freezing out.

The Mane Event

Horses' manes should never be cut—they look awful that way. Shorten-ing them involves a process called "pulling," in which the longest hairs are wrapped around a short metal comb and yanked out. Ouch! Some horses don't mind this, some hate it. (Arabians, Morgans, and Minis, along with some other breeds, are always shown with their manes in a natural state and never have to tolerate mane pulling—lucky them.) Some breeds' manes can be "roached" or shaved off (Quarter Horses/ Appaloosas). For the sensitive types, buy a tool called a Mane Tamer. It's essentially a razor inside a plastic comb. It's expensive, but worth it.

A Delicate Subject

The famous equipment on male horses can cause problems. Yep, it's your duty to clean his "sheath" every six months on the average. Buy Tea Tree sheath cleaner (available at tack stores), get a good pair of latex gloves, put on some romantic music, and follow the directions on the label. If the horse doesn't like what you do, you're being too rough. Some boys are real "gentlemen" about this, but make sure that the horse is not going to kick. Some geldings will not tolerate having their sheath cleaned, and for tough cases you can have your veterinar-ian do it in the spring or fall with the horse mildly tranquilized.

The Least You Need to Know

- 🐴 Grooming is a great way to establish trust with a horse.
- 🐴 Clean and shiny means healthy.
- 🐴 Curry hard, brush carefully.
- 🐴 Never neglect the feet.
- 🐴 Don't ignore the dirty jobs—they may come back to bite you.

Best-Dressed List: Tacking Up

In This Chapter

- Tack and how it got that way
- The basic types of saddles and bridles
- How to buy it, and how to put it on
- Clothes horses: accessories

"Beware of any enterprise that requires new clothes," cautioned antisocial Henry David Thoreau; assuming that his horse was of the same mind, both would have been horrified by the amount of gear to be considered by the average rider today. Whether you're just tacking up (what's that word?) for your weekly lesson or are ready to outfit a horse of your own, you'll need to know what all this stuff is for, and how to put it on.

A (Tack)ful History

Only Centaurs are able to ride without some assistance. For the most part, however, the task of "persuading" a large animal to do one's bidding requires a tool or two. In the earliest period of domestication, which involved mostly work in harness, horses, as we saw in Chapter 1, were the Johnny Come Latelys, and were outfitted uncomfortably in equipment designed for oxen—talk about hand-me-downs! Refinements in harnessing were responsible for some of the first concepts in saddlery, such as bits, nosebands, and reins, but the first documented evidence of men riding horses in a bridle comes from the tomb of the Egyptian Pharoah Horenhab, in the fourteenth century B.C.E.

Saddle Clothes to Sedan Chairs

Riding bareback looks romantic in travel brochures, but can be sweaty and itchy, so real men did wear saddle clothes and saddle pads, which slowly evolved into the structured saddles we know today. Over time, saddles have become the perfect example of form following function; the elevated pommel and cantle that gave saddles a chairlike character were popularized by the cavalry and continues in the Western tradition, while the need for speed in hunting and racing gave rise to the flatter, sleeker English saddles.

Oh, My Aching Feet: Stirrups

This modest invention changed the history of horsemanship, providing stability and security for the rider that allowed for longer distances and a far wider range of maneuvers, and the ability to wield a sword in battle. These originated in China in the third century C.E., and were probably first used just for mounting. The popularity of the paired riding stirrups grew quickly, however, and is credited in part to the raids of Attila the Hun (and we thought he was such a bad guy).

Horse Lore

A pottery horse discovered in a tomb near Nanjing, China, dating from 322 C.E., is wearing the first known representation of riding stirrups. Judging from other finds, they were probably forged of bronze or iron. This simple invention changed the nature of riding.

Best-Dressed List: What Horses Are Wearing Today

A combination of fashion and function dominates the huge array of *tack* available to the rider today. There are saddles for every discipline, available often in both leather and synthetics, and a similar array of bridles, and dozens of different kinds of bits.

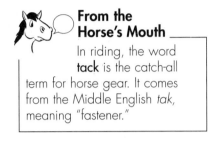

From the Horse's Mouth

In riding, the word **tack** is the catch-all term for horse gear. It comes from the Middle English *tak*, meaning "fastener."

Giddy Up: The Western Saddle

Western saddles are the descendants of medieval Spanish war saddles, with deep seats to provide security over long distances. They have retained the Spanish decorative tradition, also, and are often (especially show saddles) intricately carved and ornamented in silver.

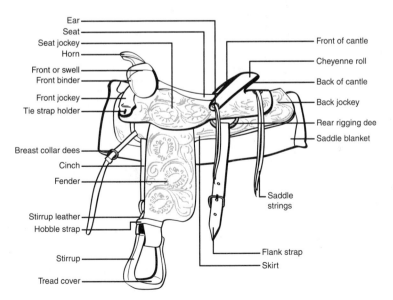

Parts of the Western saddle.

Tally Ho!: The English Saddle

A generic term that is used to define everything else, English saddles derived from the lightweight hunting and racing saddles of the seventeenth and eighteenth centuries. They have many variations in shape to accommodate different riding traditions and disciplines.

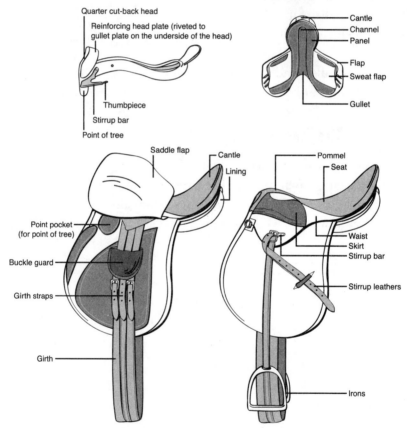

Parts of the English saddle.

Choose Your Seat

To the novice, English and Western are the two types of saddles and, except for color, all of the saddles in each type may look alike. But there are various types of saddles for each, depending on the discipline.

Western saddles include the following:

- Pleasure
- Cutting and reining
- Roping
- Barrel racing
- Trail

English saddles include the following:

- All purpose
- Hunt seat (hunting, jumping, polo)
- Dressage
- Saddleseat

Specialty saddles look like a cross between English and Western saddles and are designed to be comfortable for long hours of riding. They include the following:

- Australian stock
- Endurance

Unbridled

The basic structure of bridles hasn't changed since the first horsemen began to experiment with them. They come in five basic types and are defined in part by the nature of the bit attached to them:

- The snaffle bit is a bar—straight or, more commonly, jointed— that acts on the corners of the horse's mouth and sometimes on the tongue, depending on the breaking action of the joint. Its action is also affected by the nature of the cheek pieces it's attached to.

- The curb bit, which often has a raised middle called a port, acts on the bars and tongue, and makes the horse bend from the top of his head, or poll. In Western bits, the shanks that extend from the bar itself can be as long as eight inches. The longer the shank, the more severe the bit.

- The double bridle combines the curb with a lightweight snaffle bit called a bradoon, and allows for more refined leverage in the hands of an experienced rider.

- The Pelham is a single bit designed to combine the actions of a snaffle and a curb, and is sometimes known as "the poor man's double bridle"; it's useful if you want a little more control, and some horses prefer them.

- The hackamore—a bitless bridle, another relic of the seventh- and eighth-century Moorish traditions that were transformed by the American West—puts pressure on the sensitive nerves down the side of the horse's face and around his nose.

Bridles themselves are made up of only a few common elements, but just try taking one apart! Most have a browband, noseband, throatlatch (a thin piece of leather that goes between the horse's cheeks and neck to keep the bridle from slipping off), cheek pieces, and reins. Again, the various traditions that have come down to us reflect the shape and style of these, with classic English bridles being plain rich leather, all one color.

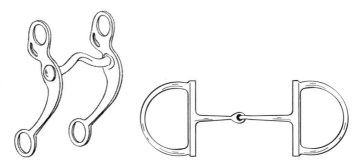

Two of the most common bits: the curb (left) and the snaffle (right).

A Western sliding ear show bridle with curb bit.

A hunter bridle with D-ring snaffle.

A Weymouth double bridle with bradoon.

In saddleseat classes, the browbands are often colored, and white browbands are popular in the upper levels of dressage. As with Western saddles, Western bridles are much dressier (at least for show), often with beautiful silver ornamentation. Western bridles

may or may not have a browband, noseband, or throatlatch, although the traditional Western headstall consists of cheek pieces with one earpiece. Hackamores (and their bosal nosebands) are made of rope, leather, and horsehair. Reins come in a variety of materials including leather, rope, and rubber, and of patterns, including plain, plaited, and laced.

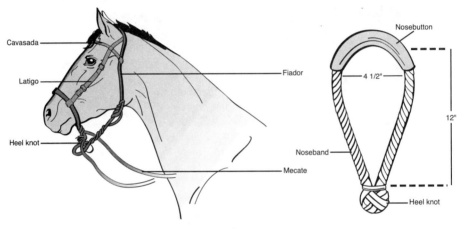

Hackamore bridle and bosal.

Clothes Make the Horse

Not in the sense in which they make the man—as an enhancement of looks and social status—but as something that affects a horse's comfort and performance. It is crucial (but not easy) to fit saddles correctly, and to choose bridles and bits appropriate for your horse, your discipline, and your level as a rider.

Saddle Fit

Imagine your suit jacket coming with 150 pounds of lead inserted in it, and you can imagine the way the horse feels in his saddle. In the first place, it lies along his spine, and then we get into it and bounce around. Basically, good saddle fit is designed to minimize those two problems by evenly distributing the weight of the gear and allowing for the correct and effective movement of the rider. While English and Western saddles "sit" differently on horses, and therefore have different pressure point problems, here are some basic guidelines for a proper saddle fit:

- The saddle should not press down on the horse's spine, and should fit snugly along his ribs.

- The pommel should clear the withers.

- The saddle should allow for free movement of the shoulder.

- The saddle should not move from side to side when the horse moves.

- The saddle must fit you and your horse; always arrange to try it on him before you buy.

Seat length is measured from the back of the *pommel* to the front of the *cantle*. Ready-made youth saddles range from 12- to 14-inch seats and adult seats range from 15 on up. The average adult saddle is 15 to 17 inches, and most trainers recommend that you get a saddle that gives you a clear inch behind—so swallow your pride and figure out how much behind there is … behind.

From the Horse's Mouth

The **pommel** is the saddle's raised front part (on a Western saddle, it's called the horn) and the **cantle** is the raised back section. The gentle arch they form helps to keep the rider in place.

Just Like Real—or Not

For many professionals, leather is still best when it comes to buying tack, though the market for synthetics is growing. Inexpensive, lightweight, and durable, synthetics are favored for kids, cash-strapped schools, and thrifty endurance riders, but some models have seats that don't "breathe." That means on a long trail ride on a warm day you could experience a very wet behind from sweat that cannot evaporate, and they don't age handsomely.

Homemade to High-Tech: Padding

Saddles evolved from the clothes and felt pads that ancient riders first put on their horses, but these were not rendered obsolete. Once the saddle became the dominant accessory, pads of various kinds remained, originally to keep the saddle clean, and more recently, to help protect the horse and to wick away sweat. Pads come in a variety of materials, from quilted cotton to fleece to wool to felt to microfiber, and a variety of sizes to complement various disciplines. And there's a shade and pattern for every taste, from pristine white, to fuchsia and leopard print.

In addition to the decorator colors, pads now come in a range of therapeutic applications—gel packs and various "shock-absorbing" brands claim to relieve pressure and help redistribute the rider's weight. And as with shoes, a variety of foam-rubber inserts, called "lift pads" or shims (in Western riding) are available to tweak an awkward fit.

 Whoa!

There is no such thing as a perfect saddle fit, and many people compensate by using extra pads under it. However, unless this is carefully done, you can often inadvertently cause more problems than you solve. Horses with really challenging conformation issues (very high, bony withers, for example) may have to have their saddles custom fitted, just like very tall men have to have their suits made to order.

Bits and Bridles

On the subject of bits, there are as many opinions as there are horse professionals, which is the reason the bit sections of tack stores and catalogs would give Tiffany's a run for its money. The basic fit of the bridle, however, is less in dispute:

- The bridle should fit snugly, but allow about a two-fingers' distance between the noseband and the cheek bone.

🐴 The bit should rest gently on the bars of the mouth, and be suspended just enough to create a little artificial smile at the corners of the horse's mouth.

🐴 The throatlatch should allow four fingers under it, so the horse can flex his neck freely.

Horse Sense

Used tack is a good option. Many tack stores have consignment sections these days, and there are used tack sites on the Internet. Just be sure to thoroughly "vet" your purchase—check that the leather is in good condition (dry, cracked leather leads to breakage and falls from the horse as the rider goes off with the saddle), the stitching is not frayed, the tree of the saddle is not twisted or the padding lumpy, and all the fixtures are secure. And as with new saddles, ask for a test drive.

The Horse Valet: How to Tack Him Up

So you've finally got the gear of your choice, or you're about to start riding lessons and want to be a little bit ahead of the curve. First, be sure your horse is clean; dirt mixed with sweat under the surface of a saddle or bridle can irritate your horse's skin. If you've been grooming your horse, he's already secured in his stall or cross-ties—never try to tack up a loose horse.

How to Saddle a Horse

Follow these steps to saddle your horse:

1. Put the saddle pad on first, being sure that it (or they if you've got Princess and the Pea–like layers, as many riders do these days) is evenly distributed on both sides and there are no wrinkles or bumps. Start several inches forward of where you want it to be, then smooth it back in the direction the horse's coat grows.

2. Next, lift the saddle straight up, so that it clears your horse's back and can be set gently down. Unless you are tall (we're both shrimps), we recommend doing this with steps. Humping a

saddle onto a horse may do a lot for your machismo, but it is no good for your back or his.

3. Be sure that he can see you—some horses spook at the sight of a strange flying object on its way to their back!

4. As with the fitting guidelines, the saddle should sit comfortably just behind the withers, with the front flaps clear of the shoulder. It should rest evenly on both sides, so be sure your horse isn't slouching when you adjust it.

5. Next, tighten the girth, and be sure to check it several times before mounting, as many horses distend their bellies while being girthed or cinched.

Horse Balloons

Some horses (and lots of ponies) play a game where they inhale (when they see you're ready to place the saddle onto their back) and hold their breath for what seems like forever. Then they exhale after you think you've got the girth tightened. Get the picture? This is why a rider checks and rechecks his girth. This behavior, to be fair to the horse, probably began at an early age when someone cinched him too tightly or too quickly, turning him into what is called girthy, cinch-bound, or girth-bound. You can't really cure a horse of this vice, but you can work around it so that you are safe and he stays comfortable and no one gets hurt. Here's how:

Whoa!
Never try to knee, tickle, or scare a horse into exhaling—this is painful and dangerous.

1. At first, tighten the cinch only as much as your horse-balloon allows—resist the temptation to try for "one more hole" on the girth.

2. Walk the horse around and continue to tighten until the cinch is secure enough for you to safely mount up. Ride at a walk and keep checking the cinch until you're sure that the horse is totally

deflated. Watch, though—some horses have honed this skill to a fine art and don't totally deflate until they are in a canter!

A girthy horse can be danger-ous if you cinch him too quickly or are too rough. A horse in this predicament can react violently by rearing, kicking, or trying to get away. If a horse is prone to this behavior, it's best not to tie him when you're saddling up.

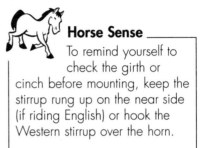

Horse Sense

To remind yourself to check the girth or cinch before mounting, keep the stirrup rung up on the near side (if riding English) or hook the Western stirrup over the horn.

Bridling Made Simple

Here are some tips on bridling your horse:

1. Begin by untying the horse, or removing the cross-ties, and then removing the halter and repositioning it around your horse's neck, so you have something to grab if he starts to wander away from you.

2. Hold the bridle by the top of the headstall in your right hand, and draw it up the length of the face so that the bit (rested in your left hand) comes in contact with the lips of the horse's mouth.

3. Slip your finger (it's safe, we promise) into the corner of the horse's mouth, where the bars are—most horses who are accus-tomed to being bridled will open their mouths right up at this point. Pull the bit gently into the mouth, which will also allow you to position the headstall over the ears.

4. Secure the noseband and throatlatch (or the curb chain on a Western headstall).

5. Check both sides to be sure everything is properly buckled and that the ends of the leathers are in their keepers.

6. Check that the horse's mane and forelock are clear of the brow-band (many horses have a "bridle path" shaved just behind the forelock to make this easier).

Horse Sense

Bridling can be a chore if the horse is head shy, doesn't like his ears touched, or has dental problems that make biting painful. As with any problem, make sure that there isn't a physical cause, and if there is, have it attended to promptly for his comfort and your safety. Otherwise, try putting a little honey on the bit, or warm it with your hand before inserting it.

Accessorize

In addition to the basics—saddle and bridle—there are almost as many accessories for horses these days as for people. These come in three basic categories: schooling, safety, and comfort.

Schooling

Schooling aids, designed to help teach a horse about such basics as pace, rhythm, and head position, include the following:

- **Lunge lines.** Long lines of leather, nylon, or canvas, that allow the trainer to work the horse in a circle.

- **Cavessons.** A type of noseband with a ring fitted at the center, so the horse can easily be lunged in both directions.

- **Draw reins.** An extra pair of reins attached to the bit and running under the girth to adjust the horse's head position.

- **Long reins.** The same idea as Draw reins, but long enough to control the horse from the ground without mounting.

Safety

Safety accessories include the following:

- **Halter.** A simple headpiece that goes over the nose and ears to make your horse easy to catch and tie. Halters come in leather, nylon, rope, and various synthetics.

- **Martingale.** Strips of leather extended from a circular piece that goes around the horse's neck and are designed to check a horse whose head rises above the angle of control when ridden.

- **Breast plates.** Accessories that have endured since medieval times, and are serving the same function, to keep the saddle from slipping backward during vigorous exercise.

Support and Protection

With the increasing demands on today's performance horse, there is a greater possibility of injury in the field, and of work that exacerbates movement problems that might cause injuries. To combat these, there is an impressive array of horse battle gear to protect their hooves and legs, including protective boots for both legs and hooves. In fact, the average sport horse, fully rigged out, doesn't look much different from his great-grandsire on a battlefield in the Middle Ages!

Keep It Clean

No matter what bargains you find, you will wind up investing a considerable amount in your tack, and it will be worth your while to keep it in good condition. Well-cared-for tack lasts longer, is better for your horse, makes you look nice in public and in the show ring, and, if you've got a futures trader mentality, has much greater resale value. Your local tack shop or favorite catalog will have a wide range of up-to-the-minute leather cleaners and conditioners. After each ride, be sure to at least wipe your tack down, even if you save the big cleanup for a rainy day. Run water through your bit to keep saliva (and any grass your horse has snatched up when you weren't looking) from encrusting the bit, and wipe off your stirrups.

Horse Sense

Wipe down your tack after every ride. Pre-moistened leather wipes (available in catalogs and variety stores—you'll find them in the auto section because they're also used to clean leather car seats) are inexpensive and do a good job. This doesn't mean that you should let these quick wipedowns substitute for giving your tack a good cleaning at least once a month.

Mold Happens

Those hot, wet summer days, even those balmy days in spring and fall, can start mold growing on any piece of leather tack faster than a horse running back to the barn. Mold can kill leather, so it's important to kill it first. You can buy commercial preparations or use that good old mold-killer, vinegar (any flavor or color).

1. First, remove the mold with fine-gauge steel wool or an old rough rag. Old terry cloth works well, too.

2. Next, wipe the saddle with a cloth dampened (not dripping) with the vinegar, and make sure to get into those grooves around the stitching, and under the fenders or flaps. Let it sit for four to six hours. Then clean and condition as you usually do.

3. At the first sign of any new mold, wipe it off with cloth dampened with vinegar.

The Least You Need to Know

- The first bits may have existed as long as 6,000 years ago.

- Choose a saddle and bridle appropriate for you, your horse, and your discipline.

- Dress (your horse) for success—if the tack doesn't fit, or isn't right for the job, your horse can't do his best for you.

- Keep your tack clean to keep it longer.

Chapter 15

All Aboard!
Rules of the Road

In This Chapter

- What real riders wear
- How to get on and off a horse—whether you planned to or not
- Rules for riding in populated places
- The chops you need to carry it off

Before you actually get on that beast and make some tracks, you have to be geared up properly. You don't want your tender parts getting pinched, rubbed, banged around, or dragged—all of which could happen if you don't play your cards right. Lack of the right stuff can change your life forever. So here's a list of the bare-bones necessities for mounting up:

- An ASTM-approved helmet
- Sturdy pants that go all the way down to your ankles
- Boots, at least ankle-high, with a good one-inch heel on them

Boots and pants specifically designed to ride in are best, but you can improvise if your horse trip is a one-time thing. Some people can get away with regular jeans, though most find they rub, but you can buy jeans with knee patches made specifically for riding. You're wearing a helmet. Don't argue. Head injuries top the list of horse-related accidents, so all real horse people love their helmets. People who want to ride without them are losers.

> **Whoa!**
>
> Wear a real riding helmet when you're riding. Not a bike helmet. Not a skateboard helmet. When you're sitting on top of a horse, your head is at least 12 feet from the ground. Drop anything fragile from that height and see what happens to it. It's also a good idea to have kids wear their helmets when grooming or leading horses

Hard-Headed: The Only Real Helmet Is an ASTM-Approved Helmet

The American Society for Testing and Materials (ASTM) is the only approving body for helmet safety, and you should regard any helmet that's not ASTM-approved as having the efficacy of a hollowed-out half-grapefruit. Legislation is currently pending in Congress to tighten requirements for equestrian helmets in the United States.

> **Whoa!**
> Some horses are deathly afraid of rustly noises they can't see. Don't wear crinkly rain gear on horseback. And watch it if you need to unzip something—the sound can make horses freak out.

Thanks to the ASTM, helmets now have thicker shells but are lighter and easier to wear. And the fasteners are better, too. In the old days, those old elastic bands that held "hunt caps" on would just begin to give way at the precise moment a horse started to buck.

Here's a bonus: A zip-up vest made of enclosed-cell foam can make a difference between a rib-cracking injury and one that just makes you feel a little sore. They're comfortable, too. If you ride alone, particularly if you jump, get one.

You might want to wear gloves and sunscreen. You're definitely wearing a shirt that isn't a tube top. You're not going near a horse in big dangly earrings, scarves, or bangles. Your wallet is in a safe hiding place (not in your pocket), ditto your car keys and glasses case. Your jeans, or whatever trousers you've selected, are just loose enough so you can bend your knee and swing your leg a bit. So now, helmet securely fastened, let's get on.

Mounting Terror

A depressing number of people "come to grief" (an old foxhunting euphemism for getting flung into the dirt) trying to just get on. Mounting is a skill that should be cultivated. If you do it wrong, you may never have that ride you were planning on. Here's the drill:

1. Check your girth so you know your saddle won't slip.
2. Lead the horse up to a mounting block, making sure it's to the left of the horse.
3. Step quietly onto the block, take the reins in your left hand so they're even and slightly taut, and grab either the horse's withers (that bump at the base of his neck) or a chunk of mane with that same hand.
4. Face the horse's rump. Now grasp the cantle (back) of the saddle with your right hand.
5. Put your left foot into the stirrup and step up onto that foot, pulling your body close to the horse with your right hand. Now your entire weight is in the left stirrup.
6. Swing your right leg carefully over the cantle, letting go with your right hand.
7. Ease your rear end tactfully into the saddle.
8. *Sit still.*

Not everything makes a good mounting block. Car bumpers, ladders, most overturned buckets, and almost all farm equipment are treacherous. Big rocks or logs are lovely. Getting on from fences isn't easy, but it can be done. Actual structures designed as mounting blocks are best. It's physically possible, and sometimes necessary, to mount from the ground, but it torques the horse's back and wrenches the saddle out of place. If you get a "leg up" from someone, make sure they don't toss you right over the other side.

In order to get through this in one piece, you need a horse that stands still. If there's too much traffic where you are, get someone to hold him, or retreat to a quieter place. If he won't stand still then, he needs either further training or a brain transplant, and you're better off going out for pizza.

Chaos Reins

The first thing you do once you're in the saddle (you're going to get sick of hearing this) is adjust everything so it's right and tight. Check your girth again. Chances are it's shockingly loose: The way a saddle fits changes a lot once somebody's sitting in it. Now do your stirrups: Let your legs dangle. The stirrup should hit you at the level of your ankle. Sometimes you'll want them shorter, but this is a good place to start.

The reins are your brakes and steering. You need to be able to hold them just in front of the withers, about six inches up from the horse's neck and about eight inches apart with your palms facing inward. If they're too short, the horse can pull you right out of the saddle; if they're too long, you have no control. So shorten them enough to get a light feel of the horse's mouth. And don't budge until you do.

Forward, March

Now you're ready to explore the wilderness, or the inside of a nice, calm arena. First, decide where you want to go, and look at that spot. Then stretch up (always the operative movement in getting horses going), keep your butt in the saddle, and squeeze with your legs, giving the horse's head and neck a little room by letting him move your hands slightly forward. Presto! Locomotion.

Heads Up, Heels Down

The minute you leave the safety of the barn, you encounter civilization in its many forms. This means lawns, roads, dogs, bicycles, blowing garbage, broken glass, rusty nails, loud noises (frequently made by other riders), and—gasp—traffic. You need to be able to deal with all these hazards.

As you already know, horses are scared of everything. Being able to ride confidently, with an understanding of what makes horses comfortable, is crucial. Minimally, it means being able to control your upper body so it stays erect and still, and so you can keep your hands still, too. If the horse starts going too fast, sit down on him. Keep that butt in the saddle. Draw back both hands, nice and low, and hold them there. If he won't stop, turn him in a circle.

Says one Pony Club official, "Riding is like doing yoga on the deck of a rolling ship." You're trying to get all the big parts of your body acting independently, while not letting your compromised balance change the way you sit and move. Meanwhile, there's about a thousand pounds of raw power churning slowly around under you.

> **Horse Sense**
>
> A good leg position means a safe seat. Sit up straight (a saddle is not an easy chair) and maintain an imaginary line from your shoulder straight down past your hip to your heel. Keep those heels down (toes up).

Out to Launch

So let's say your riding teacher has certified you ready to take a spin around yonder field. Everything is copasetic, and suddenly a huge dog jumps out of a hedge. Your horse scoots sideways like a pat of

butter on a sizzling grill, and you are airborne. Let's rewind the video and see what went wrong.

Well, possibly nothing. Everybody takes a spill now and then. But there are a number of things you can do to avoid it.

- Sit in the middle of the horse, with your weight as far down in your (nice and flexible) legs as possible.

- Look where you're going, and sit up straight.

- Don't let your horse rubberneck.

- Don't go any faster than you know how to.

- Be alert for signs your horse is about to go AWOL.

How do you know trouble's brewing? The horse's head suddenly goes up, like he's doing a llama imitation. His ears are pointed forward so hard you could spear salmon with them. He feels stiff. He may even stop and snort.

Of course, he may not give you any warning at all; he may simply become fearful. Keep him moving straight. Sit in the middle of his back. Don't scream. Insist that he face what's scaring him. Never whack a terrified horse.

Horse Whispers

We have almost forgotten how strange a thing it is that so huge and powerful and intelligent an animal as a horse should allow another, and far more feeble animal, to ride upon its back.

—Peter Gray

Falling Down

Of course, the worst-case scenario might happen, in which case, try to relax. You want to land rolling on your shoulder or the fleshy part of your hip. You have a second or two to say "roll" to yourself on the way down. It helps.

What next? You should get right back on, right? Not if you feel dizzy, or nauseated, or just not one hundred percent. There are always other days and other horses.

(© Sterling Photography)

Agony …

(© Sterling Photography)

… and ecstasy. A game rider carries on after an awkward spill at a hunter pace.

Horse Sense

Knowing how to ride well isn't only for the show ring. It helps you maximize the horse's potential and style (this is the fun part) so injury is minimal for both of you (the practical part).

Road Warriors: The Rules of the (Urban) Road

Motorists these days are demonstrating less and less of a sense of how animals feel about cars. They tend to regard equestrians as intrusions on their precious racecourses, i.e., public roadways. You're going to encounter some of these lovely people sooner or later, if only to get across a county one-lane to a quiet field.

You're stuck on a road and hear a vehicle approaching, fast. What to do? Turn your horse so the driver can see you, and get his or her attention. Give the "slow down" hand signal—palm down, pressing your hand earthward like a plunger. The driver may notice and comply. Or he may not, which leaves you with another problem: Sometimes horses shy toward the thing that scares them, which is a drag if that thing is a car.

If the car or truck doesn't slow down, get your horse into somebody's driveway if possible, or at least as far off the road as you can, with your horse obliquely facing what's scaring him. (In the country, there may be barbed wire at the edge of the road, so be very careful.) He may dance and prance, but he must not edge back into the road. This is where a good seat and legs are vital.

Of course, the drivers may be polite folk who hop on the brakes, in which case you can continue

Whoa! _____

During deer hunting season, if you must ride, get a blaze orange vest. Some hunters trespass and will shoot anything that moves. Check dates for seasons in your area. Bow hunters are less likely to try to make a meal out of your horse, but you never know.

Whoa! _____

Never leave one or more horses tied in a public place unattended. Leave one or two people from your group to watch them, or better yet, hold them. If they get loose, it's trouble à la carte. Amish farmers drive to town all the time because they have to. Their horses are saintly. Yours—trust us—isn't.

clip-clopping and not have to turn at all. Wave and smile at these people. Blow them kisses. (Often you'll find they grew up on farms.) As for those lice in human form who "buzz" you with their cars, research is inconclusive on whether flipping them the bird furthers the cause of road safety. What they're doing is, in most states, illegal. But they don't care.

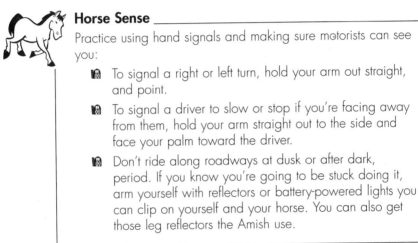

Horse Sense

Practice using hand signals and making sure motorists can see you:

- To signal a right or left turn, hold your arm out straight, and point.

- To signal a driver to slow or stop if you're facing away from them, hold your arm straight out to the side and face your palm toward the driver.

- Don't ride along roadways at dusk or after dark, period. If you know you're going to be stuck doing it, arm yourself with reflectors or battery-powered lights you can clip on yourself and your horse. You can also get those leg reflectors the Amish use.

Home on the Range

Naturally, you'll want to trail ride with a group, a situation that's ripe with anxious possibilities unless everyone knows the rules and follows them.

- The group must keep to the pace of the slowest rider.

- Nobody passes without permission, or rushes up on anyone.

- Permission is obtained to ride on private land.

- Everyone rides with the traffic on paved roads, unless local laws say differently, and stays near the curb or shoulder.

- Everybody knows the hand signals.

- You close every gate you open. You stand still and wait for anyone who has had to dismount for any reason.

Nobody clucks to their horses. All the other horses will speed up.

 Nobody tailgates!

 Horses that are known to kick wear red ribbons in their tails, but it's still their riders' responsibility to keep accidents from happening.

Beam Me Up, Scottie

Take your cell phone trail riding, but for goodness' sake make sure you can get service where you're going—and attach the cell phone to you and not your horse. Or get a two-way radio. The newer ones have a range of five miles, cost under $200, and are getting cheaper all the time.

The Right Tool for the Job: Your Body

Posture and flexibility are everything in riding. Strength is useful, but really not the most important element. After a couple of hours in the saddle, the things that hurt the most will be (you may shuffle the order):

 Your seat

 Your lower back

 Your hips

 Your thighs

If you're totally out of shape, you can expect a goodly amount of pain in all four. But why let that happen? There are plenty of things you can do to help you be fit to ride:

1. Swim

2. Bike

3. Do yoga or pilates

4. Walk

5. Stretch your legs and back

The secret for comfortable, efficient riding is a flexible back and good abs; you can't control a horse if you can't sit straight. So get with those crunches! You'll look better, anyway. Even rather round people can be "light riders" if they're graceful and balanced, but weight can be a problem if you're not in control of which way it's moving. You're sitting on an animal's spinal cord; you owe it to him or her to make the burden light as you can.

Good-Bye Old Paint

Eventually, you're going to want to get off this lovely animal. Do it right, by finding a nice quiet place to stop. Then …

- Kick *both* legs out of the stirrups.

- Take both reins in your left hand and rest it on the withers.

- Put your right hand on the saddle flap on the horse's right side, somewhere above your knee.

- Lean forward slightly and lift your right leg over the cantle of the saddle.

- Let your body slide down the horse's barrel slowly, and you'll be standing on unsprained ankles, holding the reins, when you land. Ta da!

The Least You Need to Know

- Safe gear is everything.

- Maximize the possibilities that nothing bad will happen while you're mounting.

- In a fight between a car and a horse, the car's going to win.
- Strength isn't everything in riding; flexibility and balance are.

Part

School Days: Learning to Ride or Drive

Knowledge is pleasure, as well as power, and this section is where we'll tell you about the various horse-related disciplines—their histories, what makes them exciting, and what kinds of training, and horse, you might need to participate. The good news is that lots of sports are democratic, and don't require you to run out and purchase an expensive animal. But all require focus, dedication, and hard work. We'll talk about some activities out of the saddle, too, like driving and working with miniature horses.

How are you going to learn to do this? By choosing the right school and instructor—we'll give you some tips on what to look for and what to ask.

Standardbred: Former racer Bold Lady (still looking pretty bold) is owned by Andy Card of Black Walnut Farm.

(© Rusty Perrin)

Chapter 16

Seat in the Saddle or Two Feet on the Ground: Choosing a Style

In This Chapter

- ⚉ The major riding traditions and their basic form
- ⚉ Related disciplines—from trail riding to polo
- ⚉ What you can do off the back of a horse

Well, you've cleaned him off, tacked him up, and you're about to get on. So what are you doing up there? We've said that there's never been a better time to be a horse, but the truth is, there's really never been a better time to be a rider. There's a style of riding for every taste and temperament (if not every bank account), and if you love the idea of horses but aren't sure you want to see the world from the back of one, there's something for you, too.

In this chapter, we'll look at the major traditions of English and Western riding and their offshoots—riding disciplines that cover everything from genteel pleasure riding to extreme sports like eventing

and endurance. Overachievers that we are, many disciplines are defined in terms of competition, so we'll be looking at them in this context, but we won't neglect the softer side of trail and pleasure riding.

A Seat Is a Seat Is a Seat

The appearance of the rider and the outline of the horse can vary dramatically in Western and English riding, and among the various disciplines, but these differences are more cultural than physical, and there's one thing they all have in common. What is known as the "basic seat" is the same for all types of riding. It calls for the rider to sit lightly over the horse's center of gravity; to move with the horse when the horse goes forward and when the center of gravity shifts (as in jumping); to use the legs, seat, and back in conjunction with one another to apply aids (a.k.a., commands to the horse); and to use the reins for guidance. Each riding discipline interprets these basic guidelines a little differently, in terms of the depth of the seat, position of the hands, and whether the rider is behind or ahead of the vertical, because each is looking for a different combination of carriage and pace from the horse. Easy, right?

From the Horse's Mouth

It's all in the **seat.** The three basic riding styles are Western (sometimes known as "stock" seat), hunt seat, and saddleseat (the latter derives from the English tradition), and each varies the basic seat to suit. Saddleseat riders sit farther back on the saddle to enhance (raise) the forehand of their horse; hunt seat riders sit forward to facilitate jumping fences; and Western riders sit deep in the center of their saddles with a long leg.

Howdy, Pardner: The Western Tradition

When the Spanish conquistadors came over in the fifteenth century, they brought not only the first horses to touch the North American continent in 8,000 years, but the cattle ranching traditions that formed the American West. Everyone is familiar with the archetypal cowboy—a lean, unflappable guy in a Stetson, gazing into the sunset atop his trusty cow pony. The style of riding that goes with this image embraces two extremes: slow and easy, and fast and hard, both coming out of the realities of day-to-day ranch life—long rides moving cattle (stock) from pasture to market, and short intense bursts of energy to round them up (hence the term stock seat, which is used in competition).

In the various types of Western competition, you get the moves of the ranch transported to the show ring; in the Western Pleasure classes, you're walking the walk, only without any "stock" (i.e., cows) on your conscience, but some events, like roping and team penning, require cattle. When a curb bit is used, the reins are usually held in one hand (so you've got a free hand to lasso any cow you might encounter), so Western horses are trained to "neck rein"—respond to pressure against the side of the neck (required in the show ring). Outside the show ring, many Western horses are ridden in a snaffle with two hands on the reins.

Horse Lore _____

The phrase "tall in the saddle" comes from Western riding. The upper body should remain erect and in the center of the saddle, shoulders square, chin up, thighs and knees in contact with the horse. The body is allowed to lean forward at the waist (actually, it's more like hollowing your back) at the jog, slightly more forward at the lope, and a bit more at the hand gallop. The legs and feet should never change position.

Racing Against the Clock: Gymkhana

Gymkhana is an Indian term meaning games with horses, an ancient tradition that was brought to Europe in the nineteenth century by British army officers and then spread to America, particularly the Western states. These games are very popular and now venues for them can be found all over the country, but they have their roots in the West. In Gymkhana events, speed and precision are everything—the fastest one to do it right wins.

Tall in the saddle: the classic "stock," or Western, seat.

Barrel Racing

Barrel racing is the most popular Gymkhana event and one of the fastest-growing sports in the country (there's even prize money). The sport requires a fast, supple horse who can move swiftly and make tight turns around three barrels set in a triangular pattern, going either clockwise or counterclockwise (the fastest horse around all the barrels wins—touching a barrel is okay, but knocking over a barrel gets a penalty of five seconds). This used to be a girls-only sport, but now there are divisions for both sexes and all ages from children to seniors.

Pole Bending

Pole bending is another popular Gymkhana event where the horse must weave around poles (think slalom skiing).

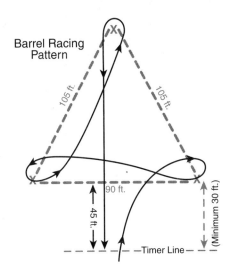

A barrel racing pattern can be run either to the right or left (see our Quarter Horse color photograph for a team in action).

Cowabunga: Stock Classes

Stock work requires stock (cows to you city slickers). These events mimic what a cow pony does in real life when working cattle.

Roping

Roping is a sport in which you need a horse with speed and agility and a good sliding stop. A roping horse and rider follow a calf at a distance where the rider can rope it. When cued the horse slides to a stop, faces the calf and backs to keep the rope taut enough so the calf won't slip out, but not tight enough to hurt it. The rider jumps off and ties the calf. The fastest calf roper wins.

Team Roping

Team roping is when two horses and their riders chase a steer. One rider, called the header, ropes the steer's horns and the heeler ropes one or both of the steer's back feet almost simultaneously. Both

horses then stop, face one another, and back just enough to stretch their ropes to keep the steer immobile. This takes precision timing and a well-trained mount.

Team Penning

Team penning is a cutting contest where a team of three riders work together to cut three head of cattle from the herd and then drive them into a pen within a set amount of time. This is fun to watch because the cattle never seem to get the idea that they're supposed to stay penned.

Cutting

Cutting is a sport where the horse does all the work while the rider tries to stay out of his way. A good cutting horse must have cow-sense, great stamina, intelligence, agility, speed, and enjoy (like herding dogs) moving cattle around. The point of the contest is to cut a cow from a herd and prevent her from returning by staying between the cow and the herd.

Oh, What a Beautiful Morning: Western Pleasure

The term says it all. Western pleasure class shows off the comfortable gaits and training of a Western horse at the walk, jog (slow trot), and lope (canter). The Western pleasure walk should be rhythmic and ground covering. The Jog should be slow and cadenced. The lope, also known as the "rocking horse" gait, is a lightly collected, slow, smooth, three-beat gait.

In this class the emphasis is on pleasure, and the horse should appear to be a pleasure to ride. Transitions should be invisible to the spectator, and the horse is ridden on a loose rein with a curb bit, snaffle, or hackamore with bosal (depending on his age). In advanced stock seat equitation classes, the ability to stop square and balanced and the ability to back up may be called for, in addition to the execution of a reining pattern and being judged at the walk, jog, and lope on the rail.

Dressage American Style: Reining

Reining is an American-made sport dominated by American-made Quarter Horses. Another fast-growing sport, it was officially recognized by the U.S. Equestrian Team in 1998, and is on its way toward becoming an Olympic event.

Reining is easily the most spectacular of the Western disciplines. It took the turns and fancy footwork of the working cow horse— spins, sliding stops, lead changes, rollbacks, changes of speed and direction—and turned them into an art form. Reining horses are ridden on a loose rein, mostly from the seat and back of the rider, which makes good reining partnerships really a matter of trust.

In a typical reining pattern, the horse gallops, goes into a sliding stop, spins, and comes out of the spin in a gallop on the opposite lead. The spin is a move that really gets the crowd going. In one spin, the horse turns 360 degrees (that's four *Western pivots* in smooth succession) on his hindquarters, and most reining patterns require four 360 degree turns in rapid succession.

 From the Horse's Mouth _____

To understand how a reining horse spins, you must know the **Western pivot.** The pivot is a 90-degree (quarter-turn) turn to either the right or the left. The horse rocks back on his haunches, and his front feet leave the ground completely until the pivot is complete.

Logs and Streams and Things That Go Bump in the Night: Trail Classes

Nature happens, and trail classes delight in making it happen on cue. Show ring trail classes feature a series of artificial obstacles, meant to represent real-life elements, such as water, barrels, mailboxes, and poles. These are negotiated in order, at various specified gaits, with a time limit.

Backward and in Heels: Sidesaddle

Someone once paid Ginger Rogers the ultimate compliment, saying that she could do everything Fred Astaire could, only "backward and in heels." The same might be said of sidesaddle, once the only way women could ride, and now enjoying a resurgence.

Invented in medieval times so privileged women could watch their knights in battle (riding astride was considered vulgar), developments in the saddle, in which the leg is secured between two pommels, meant that women could jump and gallop with the best of them. Once transported to America, sidesaddles migrated to the West, also, and are now to be found for all the major disciplines—saddleseat, hunt seat, and Western. A challenging technique in which a long whip takes the place of the suspended leg, the costumes and comportment required transport you right back to the nineteenth century.

Dorothy Mayo in great sidesaddle form on El Greco.

Speak English: The English Tradition

If the ghosts of the Spanish Conquistadors hover over Western riders, the ghosts of country squires and cavalry officers hover over English ones, because we owe this tradition to the hunt field and the military. Emphasizing daring on the one hand and decorum on the other, so-called English riding has given rise to a wide range of activities that appeal to both the bold and the meek, from dressage to show jumping to saddleseat.

The basic technique, as for Western riding, calls for a centered rider sitting relaxed and tall, with legs lightly in contact with the horse's sides. (English saddles are sparer and lighter than Western ones, and keep the rider's body closer to the horse.) The reins are held in two hands, forming a straight line from the horse's mouth to your flexed elbow (this is probably the thing you will hear most often as a beginner rider—"keep that elbow flexed!").

A Contradiction in Terms: Hunt Seat

Take a look at any old hunting print and you'll see people going over fences as if they're on their way down a dip on the roller coaster at Disney World. Even today, riding in actual hunts requires more guts than finesse. "Hunt seat" is an invention of the show ring—an idealized performance by horse and rider of the perfect form on the flat and over fences. Defined by the trainer George Morris in the 1960s, it is the dominant equitation style, taught to scores of eager teens, and also defines a big part of the show circuit.

Up and Over: Show Jumping

People were probably testing their horses over obstacles long before the camera immortalized them. But show jumping became a common feature of shows and fairs in the nineteenth century, and got a real push, so to speak, from military competitions established early in the twentieth century. With the development of the forward seat by Italian Cavalry officer Frederico Caprilli, the sport became safer and more generally popular, and is now one of the staples of the show ring—and the riding school.

At the higher levels riders have to be part mathematician and part daredevil, as both precision and guts are required to get your mount over a course of fences that might be as high as five or six feet.

Horses, too, need to be bold and athletic—the field is dominated by Thoroughbreds, sport horses, and Warmbloods. Happily, if *your* blood is beginning to go to your head, it is possible to have a lot of fun, once you've safely mastered the basics, over more modest courses.

Plain English: the basic English seat.

Tall in the saddle, the classical way: the basic dressage seat.

Horse Lore

Puissance, French for "force" and "power," is the name given to the most spectacular of the jumping competitions, where a single artificial brick wall is raised by increments, sometimes reaching up to seven feet before a pair fails to clear it.

Horse Ballet: Dressage

Strictly speaking, *dressage* is not a direct descendant of the English (tradition), as it comes from the classical riding (tradition) established in the sixteenth and seventeenth centuries that spread throughout Europe. But it is more closely associated with English riders.

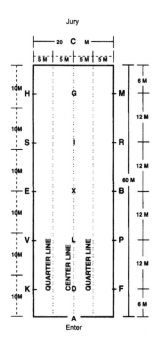

Alphabet soup. The standard dressage arena is 20m × 60m, and rimmed with letters at which the various test movements are performed.

Dressage tests the harmonious bonding of horse and rider through the performance of a range of schooling exercises that increase in complexity as the pair progress through various levels. Tests are performed in two different sizes of rectangular arena, and the various movements are performed at different letters rimming and bisecting the space.

From the Horse's Mouth

Dressage is the French word for training, and classical dressage is designed to train and test the horse, through a series of school movements, in suppleness, straightness, impulsion, and collection, in harmony with the rider.

A comparison with competitive ice dancing may be appropriate, especially with the recent introduction of "freestyle," or musical *kur* tests, in which the rider performs a choreographed series of school movements to music.

Saddleseat English Pleasure

This exciting discipline is not as widespread as hunt seat or some Western forms, but has a loyal following in and out of the saddle: these animated horses can really get a crowd going. Saddleseat classes (pleasure and equitation) are offered for American Saddlebreds (of course), Arabians and Half-Arabians, Morgans, National Show Horses, and Shetland and Welsh ponies. What the mounts have in common is their high step and elevated head carriage. To help create this effect, the saddle—which is very flat—is placed well behind the horse's withers so as not to hinder the front leg action, and the rider has a long stirrup. The horse is ridden with a double-bit bridle, usually with a colored browband and noseband, with the reins in an elevated position.

Saddleseat is judged on the performance, manners, suitability, conformation, responsiveness, and animation displayed in the three basic gaits—walk, trot, and canter.

Steel Magnolias: Gaited Horses

The working life of the Southern plantation owners and the need for a comfortable horse with a ground-covering stride helped establish the various gaited horse breeds like the Saddlebred (who could easily walk between the rows of planted crops without trampling them), the Missouri Foxtrotter, and the Tennessee Walking Horse. The natural high-stepping action of these horses also gave rise to a dapper riding style that is no longer the exclusive domain of Saddlebreds. Arabians, Morgans, National Show Horses, and American Shetlands are high-stepping their way around a show ring near you.

Extreme Sports

For every discipline we've discussed, there is a version that asks you to go the extra mile, and two of most demanding are growing in popularity: three-day eventing and endurance.

Hat Trick: Three-Day Eventing and Horse Trials

For today's multitaskers, three-day eventing (also called just "eventing") is the premiere sport, and is enjoying its largest-ever participation level. Another legacy of military competitions, eventing tests the horse and rider in three phases—dressage (is he controllable?), cross-country jumping (is he hot to trot, or, rather, *gallop?*), and show jumping (after all that running, is he still supple and sound?). The upper-level competitions also include a steeplechase and competitive trail phase, and fences that look as if *they'd* make good rides at Disney World. But the nice thing about eventing (or horse trials, as the less-strenuous competitions are called) is that organizers have embraced the adult amateur and made a real attempt to provide fun competitions at the lower levels.

A related sport also growing in popularity is the hunter pace, in which teams of horses compete against an ideal hunter's time over an outdoor course of about a mile and a half. These lighthearted competitions often feature amusing theme fences (one had an overturned canoe reading *HMS Titanic*) and picnic lunches.

Horse Lore

In the summer 2000 Olympics, Three-Day Event Team member David O'Connor won the United States's first-ever individual gold medal in this event, which has been an Olympic sport since 1912. Exhausted on the final day of show jumping, he almost went off course, but was corrected by the cries of thousands of spectators.

Trail Riding up a Notch—Endurance and Competitive Trail Riding

Endurance riding tests the—well, endurance—of horse and rider, over courses all over the world that range from 50 to 100 miles per day or a set number of miles per day over 4 to 6 days. Terrain is sometimes rugged, and these timed courses require peak fitness from both horse and rider. To win in endurance, your horse must cover the trail in the shortest amount of time and have passed the multiple vet checks along the way.

Endurance horses must be part long-distance runner, and part racecar. They must be able to take all kinds of new experiences in stride, be responsive to their riders, stand quietly without being tied, and be calm enough to endure the pit crew who rush in to wipe him off and check his heart/pulse/lungs—all while he's eating!

Arabians, the world's original endurance horse, hold the most records in worldwide endurance riding and the best complete 100-mile races in less than 10 hours, but any horse and rider team with sufficient grit and conditioning can compete.

Competitive Trail Riding differs from endurance. Horses generally travel 25 to 50 miles in an event. The object here is not to come in first, but to finish in the allotted amount of time with your horse passing mandatory vet checks along the way. The winner has the horse in the best physical condition after the race and is also judged on the quality of their ride.

Both endurance riding and competitive trail require that horse and rider be in the best possible physical condition.

Go, Team!

If you like to play in company, you might want to look into two riding disciplines that have that team spirit: polo and drill teams. In international competition, of course, each country has a team, but the riders actually ride as individuals.

Not Ralph Lauren: Polo

Polo has been the game of choice for snobs since ancient Persia, where it was played outside the mosques, and many cultures have a version of it. The most familiar was brought back from India by British officers, and involves four players per side scoring by hitting a ball through a goal with a long bamboo mallet. How do they do this? By riding really, really fast, on specially bred polo ponies (many are bred in Argentina, polo's leading nation). Originally called "hockey on horseback," the game is just as ferocious, but has a loyal (and, it must be said, well-heeled) following in many resort communities. Many players are semi-pros.

Fat of purse and not faint of heart? Give it a try.

About Face: Drill Teams

Two's company, and so is twelve. Drill teams, the stuff of marching bands and parades, are rising in popularity, and involve riders from many different styles. Some "teams" are composed of just two riders performing classical dressage movements, while others go the whole flag-waving hog. Teams are great for youngsters, a good way to get young horses disciplined, and fun if you like performing for a crowd. Most are grass-roots groups, so you may have to rely on word of mouth, or check local magazines and papers, to find one.

Out of the Saddle

Not all horse sports require you to get on a horse, and you can be both thrilled and charmed by the alternatives.

Surrey with a Fringe on Top: Driving

A fast-growing sport with fascinating accessories, driving can be roughly divided between social (pleasure driving of carriages and related vehicles) and macho (so-called combined driving is three-day eventing on wheels, involving a dressage phase, a marathon, and an obstacle course). Pleasure drivers compete in a wide range of vehicles harking back (and sometimes actually coming from) the eighteenth and nineteenth centuries, from elegant phaetons to humble governess carts, and dress accordingly. Combined driving uses sturdy vehicles and teams of one to four horses, and is judged on time and accuracy rather than turnout. There is also competitive trail driving, which follows the same rules as for trail riding. And for real speed demons, even professional harness racing is trying to interest amateurs.

(© Lori Steffensen)

Combined driving: a natty turnout for a tricky course. Katana Rubinstein with Morgan Rohan Shadowfax.

Swimsuit Competition: Halter and Showmanship Classes

No horse is just a pretty face, but sometimes the pretty face is just what the judges want to see. Halter classes (sometimes called "in hand") are common at breed shows to assess the conformation and movement of a horse of any age against its breed's standards. Showmanship classes, common for juniors, test the handler's ability to show off the animal.

Lilliputian Larks: Minis

Will they still love you when you're 64? Here's one part of the horse world that can comfortably take you right into your golden years, but has a loyal following of all ages. In our space-deprived era, Minis are thriving (you don't even need a horse trailer—minivans work just fine), and not only as grazing lawn ornaments. They are shown in a wide range of competitive settings, including in-hand halter, jumping, and driving, but the one competition they win hands down is for cuteness.

(© Karen Winston)

Thistle Meadows Dark & Debonaire, 32-inch Mini stallion, jumping a picnic bench. Owned by Solar Wind Miniature Horses, Perkasie, Pennsylvania.

Couldn't I Just Ride?

Don't let all this talk of competitions intimidate you if all you want to do is take your horse out and enjoy nature. You still need to learn to ride (duh) and this will involve making some decisions about which style and which traditions (clothes!) appeal to you, but your newly found skill doesn't have to take you any farther than the nearest trail. Many local riding clubs, in cooperation with landowners and the National Parks system, are working to keep trails open for riders, so that on some weekends you can see America the way your grandparents might have seen it.

And for you free spirits, there is always bareback riding (to be done only if you know your animal well, know how to ride, and are properly helmeted!).

A Word About Togs

We talked about basic riding gear in Chapter 15, but as you begin to explore the various disciplines you'll discover that each comes with its own range of dress codes and gear, from the sleek black jacket of the hunt rider to the brilliant palette of the Western pleasure competition and saddleseat, to the defensive upholstery of the polo player. So be prepared to do a little shopping.

The Least You Need to Know

- There two basic riding traditions, Western and English, from which many competitive disciplines have come.

- There's a horse sport for every type of horse and rider, and the talents and temperaments of each.

- And it's not only riding—driving, halter classes, and work with Minis can satisfy your horse craving without you ever leaving the ground.

- The various styles of riding share a "basic seat," but differ in look, approach, training, and goals.

- It's okay to want to just ride.

Chapter 17

A Leg at Each Corner: Choosing a School

In This Chapter

- How to rate a riding school
- How to pick an instructor
- How much to pay, and how often
- What lessons can and can't do

It happens all the time: You turn down a date with a person in order to keep one with a horse. "I don't want to cancel my riding lesson," you tell your friend who asks you to the movies. Same old story, every Wednesday (or Thursday, or Friday). Be ready for the come-back. "What's the matter?" someone always has to ask. "Don't you know how to do it yet?"

Nobody really knows how to ride. Sincere students are the ones who admit it. Everybody else teaches. You need to figure out who has something to say that you need to hear.

It sounds paradoxical, but in order to really have fun on a horse, you have to take lessons. It's the only way you can get on top of the discipline of riding and make it work for you.

Riding teachers used to make house calls. That's becoming increasingly rare. If you don't own a horse, and even if you do, you're going to have to choose where to learn how to ride. Here's how.

Sty or Stylish?

After you've asked in tack shops and at shows, and picked the brains of everybody you can think of, plan to visit a few places and figure out if they're worth your time and money. First impressions are important. Some riding schools look like goat farms run amok, and some look like Sonoma County spas. But just because a place has a cappuccino machine doesn't mean the teaching's any good, and some of the most rustic establishments are kept that way on purpose to discourage students who are afraid of getting dirty.

Finding the right place to begin your journey on horseback shouldn't take forever. If you want to shorten the process, look for the bare essentials. Where's the …

- Phone?
- Water?
- Toilet?
- Owner?

If they're not within easy reach, leave.

Secondarily, you should be able to locate the following:

- Grain room
- Hay loft (you want to know the horses are eating and the hay bill is paid)
- Vet's telephone number

- 🏚 Price list for lessons

- 🏚 Practice ring

- 🏚 Manure pile or dumpster

As suburbia engulfs a lot of old riding schools, you need signs that they've adapted. If the place is close to a noisy road, it needs a good sturdy fence to keep wayward horses and riders where they belong.

Follow Your Nose

There's a certain homey odor to a well-used barn. It'll tend to smell of hay, dirt, old wood, warm fur, and just a bit of manure. You shouldn't be able to detect the strong smell of ammonia that comes from urine. If you walk in and your eyes start to water, you have a problem.

Healthy horses have a distinctive, musky smell. Their skin shouldn't reek of excrement or the funky tang of long-accumulated sweat. They should be relatively clean. They should be dry (unless they're standing in a nonfreezing downpour). They shouldn't be obsessively looking for something to eat. You should be able to easily see where the water supply is, and where dinner is served. Their manes shouldn't be long and tangled. They shouldn't be bony, though once in a while a superannuated one flatly refuses to gain weight no matter how much it is fed.

Nose in the Air

Lots of fancy riding establishments deliberately appeal to the snob factor in their clients. They'll make you look good while you're learning, but they probably won't push you too hard or teach you too much.

Nose to the Grindstone

So you're standing in the driveway, looking at the horses milling about in the corrals, admiring the architecture (French Provincial? Early Hardscrabble?) and wondering whether to give the place a tumble.

Whoa! _____

You don't want to see the boss yelling at staff, or treating them like lackeys. People who work at stables don't make much, and they're the ones who handle all the animals. If they don't look reasonably happy, beware.

Take a gander at the horses, the other students, and the teachers before you decide.

You can tell about how stable a stable is by how they treat their help. If you don't see anybody working, the place is getting by on a shoestring. That's acceptable as long as it's clean and everybody seems content.

The Old Gray Mare

A good educational institution has tenured professors. They're the grouchy ones with hair growing out of their ears. Ask to be introduced to their riding school equivalents, the *schoolmasters*. What are their names? Expect to meet Star, Brandy, Midnight, and Bob. How old are they? Average age will be well over 15 (25 is old for a horse). They won't be a thrill to ride, but they know every facet of the business, including how to both annoy and take care of you. It will probably be hard to get them going, and at the end of an hour (these wise old guys also know how to tell time), they'll take you to the center of the ring, crane their heads around, and look at you as if to say, "Time's up. Get off my back."

From the Horse's Mouth _____

Cherish the **schoolmasters,** highly experienced and educated horses used for lessons. Treat these horses like the royalty they are. The very best thing you can do for them is to groom them thoroughly, ride them as well as you can, groom them again after your ride, and, perhaps least important, give them treats.

If the barn doesn't have school horses, you're supposed to ride privately owned horses. This isn't a good deal. If they've got a discernible turnover in school horses, this is an even worse deal.

Equipment Check

Ask the barn manager to give you a tour. Can you see the tack room? Rows of saddles and bridles should be hanging on (labeled) racks. They shouldn't be covered with dust, or lying on the floor. Ask to see the school stuff (some horses and tack will be privately owned, and therefore off-limits to you). Is it cracked and shaggy? This isn't great. It's rare that tack breaks when you're using it, no matter how bad it looks, but when it happens it's awful beyond belief.

Ten O'Clock Scholars

Barns are usually full of kids. They're the ones who keep the sport going. Do they know what's going on and participate in it, or are their parents using the barn as a substitute daycare center? Experienced kids 12 and older should be able to help you find a saddle, a bridle, or a horse.

Watch the Kids Ride

Are they on horses (or, ideally, ponies) that suit them in terms of temperament? Do they demonstrate basic control and maintain safe conduct on horseback? Is there a staff member to help them if they don't? If they're not wearing helmets, you're either having a bad dream or the stable management is totally out to lunch. Complain. Then leave.

Drop In on an Adult Group Lesson

Observe the group dynamic. People should be relaxed and attentive, and they should look like they're having a good time. If they're scared, or bored, ask them why.

Whip Cracker or Horse Whisperer? Vetting Instructors

Riding is a yelling sport. Think about it. If you're going around in a circle with four other people going clip-clop-clip-clop and getting all out of breath, you're not going to hear somebody who's trying to communicate in a normal tone of voice. But there's yelling, and there's *yelling*.

Short of actually getting to know them—which is nearly impossible—here are a few things you can discover about an instructor:

- Is the instructor certified? There are a couple institutions that give certification courses in the United States. If the teacher is accredited by the BHS (British Horse Society), you're golden. But American certification isn't all that widespread. Don't turn down somebody just because they don't have a pedigree.

- Do they know CPR? Most don't, but it's a definite plus.

- Do they bother with basic horse-handling skills? They should.

- Will they be available to coach you at competitions? Will they be a pain and insist on going even when you want them to stay home?

- Can they easily identify what you're doing wrong? And can they explain in understandable terms how to fix it?

- Do they welcome reasonable questions, or seem irritated by them?

- Are they sarcastic? Snappy? Bored?

- Do they demonstrate understanding of a working adult's time and money constraints? Do they give homework or exercises to help you improve?

- Do they place the welfare of students and horses above winning?

And, of course, the Big Two: Do the lessons start on time? Does the teacher show up?

Horse Sense

Discussing theory is important, but teachers who spend the first 10 minutes and the last 15 of an hour-long lesson talking to you are sandbagging. Lots of them do it. Don't let them. You're paying to learn to *ride*.

Mr. Fix-It: Clinics

A product of this promotion-savvy age, a riding clinic is an intensive series of classes and/or lectures by a respected professional. You might spend a weekend riding and observing, using either your own horse or one you've leased. You're going to be spending a lot more for each session with a clinician than with your regular teacher; if you're interested in a training philosophy but don't have the money or the horse, ask about auditing. There's sometimes a fee for this, but it's much cheaper than riding.

You'll be put in a group with others (supposedly) at your skill level. Here are a few suggestions to help them, and yourself:

Horse Whispers

"A perfect book on riding could only be written by a horse."

—Vladimir S. Littauer

- 🐎 Prepare just as you would for a college seminar: Read the book first, then watch the video.

- 🐎 The other students paid the same big fees as you did. Respect their time and their needs. If you use the clinic as a substitute for weekly instruction, they're going to know it—and they might not forgive you.

- 🐎 Write down what you've learned, and use it in your practice later.

Show Them the Money: What It Costs

At the moment of this writing, the going rate for an individual hour-long lesson is between $35 and $50. Your first lessons will be individual

ones; you'll save money once you get into a group, where you'll probably be paying $25 to $35. Groups are more fun, and bring distinct advantages. You can relax and try to feel out your horse while the instructor is focusing on someone else. You can learn from watching other people ride. Few people—and no horses—can study jumping for a whole hour. The horses often perform better when their friends are in the room, too. If you need to focus on a particular problem, training issue, or competition requirement, you can always schedule individual lessons as needed.

How Often?

Plan on a lesson a week, for starters. Once you move up to two, you need an alternate approach. Tough as it is for people just getting into horses, the lessons you take might be the only opportunity to practice. If you keep at it for long enough, many sympathetic riding professionals may be impressed enough by your initiative to cut a deal with you so you can practice without going broke. This is a delicate matter; it's getting a service for free that others pay for. But it's something to keep in mind as you prepare to climb the learning ladder.

Clinics are another kettle of fish. You can pay anywhere from $65 (for a single session in a group, for instance) to $2,000 for a whole weekend.

Great Expectations

Riding is such an organic process that it's hard to say how fast you should be learning it. You owe it to yourself, however, to get a grip on whether your lessons are getting you anywhere.

Right away, you should be getting indoctrinated to how a horse should be led to the mounting block, how to get on, how to sit, and how to hold your hands. During your first few lessons, the teacher may want to keep you on the lunge line so you don't have to worry about steering or brakes. Be encouraged. He or she cares that you start out right. Learn to love the small steps, and bask in the glow of each achievement, whether successfully mounting for the first time or *posting the trot.*

From the Horse's Mouth

Learning to **post the trot** is an initiation rite. It's one of the hardest things you have to learn. Be patient with yourself. You'll feel like a broken marionette at first, but before you know it you'll be bobbing up and down like a smooth piston.

Second Gear: Posting the Trot

Just as soon as you're feeling secure and in control at the walk, it will be time to start all over again, but this time you'll be going (literally) a bit faster—at the trot. The trot is a bouncy gait and the way to ride it comfortably (for you and the horse) is by learning to post. Posting (also called rising) is not difficult—once you understand the dynamic. When a horse trots (remember, two legs on the same side move at once) there will be a natural "rise" to the gait. Posting is merely taking advantage of this so that you can rise along with the horse's rhythm instead of bouncing against it. Sit up straight, relax your ankle and hip joints, keep your shoulders back, heels down, hands steady, and squeeze your legs to cue him into a trot. Let the natural rise of his body lift you up off your seat and then back down (gently) on the next stride.

Of course, like everything else in this sport, there's a lot more to it than that, but this is the basic principle. Although posting is more common in English riding, Western riders (outside the show ring) also post the trot; it makes a long ride more comfortable for rider and horse.

What Lessons Will and Won't Do for You

Lessons will not …

- Conquer deep-seated fear.
- Tame your intolerance or too-quick temper.

- Change a devil-may-care attitude about horses into automatic skill and concern.

But they will …

- Identify attitude problems you didn't know you had.
- Push you bit-by-bit beyond your comfort zone.
- Help you appreciate small, subtle signs of progress.
- Show you how to be in the moment with a horse.

The Least You Need to Know

- Your safety and the health of the horses are more important than anything.
- The better you ride, the safer you'll be; take the time to pick the right school and teacher for you.
- Be tolerant of teachers and reverent of horses.
- Be patient with yourself—riding is a complicated and rewarding process.
- Everyone needs lessons, because none of us will ever ride perfectly. The point is to keep getting better.

Chapter 18

From Stick Horses to the Real Thing: Getting Started with Horses

In This Chapter

- ▣ The best age to start riding
- ▣ Kids and ponies
- ▣ Pony on board? What you're committing to
- ▣ Adult riders

What is it that draws people into the world of horses? Usually it's a chance encounter—a pony ride in a park, a summer at camp, a visit with friends who coax you into the saddle. The fuse is lit, and boom! Little kids clamor for ponies, teenage girls swoon over horses, adults start relationships with four-footed friends that take on all the seriousness and reverence of marriage.

They all have one thing in common: They ride because they want to. This is one sport where forcing yourself or someone else to participate doesn't work.

Riding Off into the Sunset

If we only could, sometimes, but that's what riding is—escape. When you're on the back of a horse you are not on this earth. You have escaped the routine of your daily life, and all that matters is staying on and having a good time. Keep in touch with that idea, and the fun factor will stay alive.

It doesn't matter how old you are when you get the urge to tackle the mysteries of the saddle. There's a size, temperament, and breed of horse or pony for everyone—no matter what their age, physical build, or body fitness.

Learning techniques differ for every stage of life, as do physical limitations. Take these seriously, but remember, there are riding experiences that work for just about everyone. To ride on your own, you should have the balance to keep yourself upright when the surface underneath you is tippy—think paddling a canoe—and you should be potentially able to exert, at the very least, five pounds of pressure on the reins for a start. Very little kids can't do this, which is why they ride on the leadline until they're bigger.

Whoa!

We know you're eager to get your toddler in the saddle, but riding instructors ask that you wait until she knows her right from her left. Trained horses and ponies can tell the difference, and horse and rider should be going the same way.

Arthritis and other physical (and neuromuscular) challenges make balance and control difficult for many people, old and young. But they don't have to forego the joy of being on horseback. Horse therapy programs get a lot of people into this sport.

The Perfect First Horse

When choosing a first horse or pony for an inexperienced rider (of any age), consider these points:

- Look for a quiet animal who is respectful of his handler.

- Watch for pinned ears or other unacceptable behavior, such as kicking or biting.

- Choose the animal who is tolerant of the fumbling beginner. Will it stand quietly while the novice figures out what strap goes into what buckle?

- Don't be afraid to consider an older animal. Older mares, past their foaling years, don't exhibit the quirks of younger mares in heat. Most horses in their 20s are still willing to work, and ponies even more so.

Mommy, I Want a Pony!

Hearing this may make you want to crawl into a hole (and take your checkbook with you). But consider the benefits of having a kid who wants to ride. Riding is a commitment of mental energy, physical activity, and practice. And kids who ride have a source of comfort that the rest of us envy.

First and foremost, a horse or pony is a sensitive friend. Developing intuition about the world around them is a tough process for the very young, because they're not allowed to act on their gut feelings in most situations (and they shouldn't be). But learning to ride is a time of supervised experimentation. How is the horse feeling? The child has to concentrate on figuring it out. What should I do to get Star's attention? A riding teacher provides the exercises that help the child influence the animal. How much force should I use to assert myself? This is a delicate topic for most of us. Children who ride deal with it every time they mount up.

Horses Teach Responsibility ...

Those lucky kids who commune with ponies every day! They learn responsibility: Riding an ungroomed, unfed animal is a major sin. They'll need to learn task organization: Feeding (and mucking), grooming, tacking up, warming up, and practicing are complicated. They learn confidence: What could be more thrilling than to be partnered by someone much bigger than you?

... and Confidence

Riding always incorporates a certain amount of insecurity. Children learn to test the boundaries of their comfort zones, to push themselves bit by bit into the unknown. And if they're responsibly taught, they do it with compassion.

... and Social Skills

There are two great ways for kids and ponies to connect with and learn about each other: 4-H and Pony Club, both of which have chapters all over the country.

4-H has its roots in the rural farming tradition, but this is changing in the horse end of the organization. 4-H now sends equestrian teams to big regional exhibitions, and is renowned for its outreach programs. Check around, there will probably be a 4-H program in your community.

Pony Club, which began in Britain as a rather strict society for tiny members of the gentry, has loosened up a bit, and is a great way to introduce kids to the basics. It's devoted almost exclusively to the English tradition, but emphasizes total horsemanship (you learn about the horse, inside and out), not just riding and showing. It conducts rating tests to help monitor progress: A is the pinnacle of equestrian achievement, and D is just entry-level walking and trotting. A lot of Olympic show jumpers began in Pony Club, which has local and national team competitions. (And for your inner child, there are now adult Pony Club teams.)

Horse Whispers

Eight is the ideal age to begin riding lessons. Before that, give 'em pony rides. The attention span just isn't there.

—Lisa Thorsey, riding instructor

Whee!

Riding involves risk. Everybody falls. But kids hang by their knees, they bike downhill without touching the brakes. It's a rare pony that will crash into a stationary object. They're way too smart for that. Riding provides a sense of achievement that few other activities can match. And young people who aren't athletic in any conventional sense often discover true grace on horseback.

> **Whoa!** _____
>
> Don't think a child can handle a young horse (they can't) or that they'll grow up together. That's fine for puppies and kittens (maybe), but "green" horses are dangerous for inexperienced riders, and even experienced ones. Put the kid on a pony! A kid is a lot closer to the ground when they fall. Not *if* they fall, *when* they fall.

My Little Pony

Here are some reasons why a pony is the perfect mount for a child:

- Ponies are custom-made for kids, and boy, do kids appreciate it.
- Choose the right-size pony and the child will be able to catch, groom, pick out feet, tack up, and mount without help.
- Kids aren't intimidated by something they can see eye-to-eye with. Ponies are the traditional child's mount.

To Buy or Not to Buy?

A child can get a lot of riding done without a pony of their own. But if conditions are right, you have the space and the inclination, go for it—but only if Junior has proven by constant begging, finishing household chores on time, and practicing diligently, that a pony would get the right care and attention.

Horse Sense _____

Kids grow. Ponies don't. But animals don't outgrow their usefulness, or their right to a comfortable, productive life. If you must pass your pony on to another household, choose it yourself, and make sure Mr. Pony gets proper care, shelter, and exercise.

Kids Will Be Kids

If you decide to buy, better get handy with that pitchfork and wheelbarrow: Mr. Pony is a family pet, not just a project. You'll inevitably be running interference when the younger generation gets sick, has too much schoolwork, or simply spaces out. Animals shouldn't suffer because young people have short attention spans or mind-boggling agendas.

Ah, Youth ...

When adolescence comes knocking, most kids' minds are anywhere but on their responsibilities, or they suddenly have too many. But years and years of evidence has shown that the young pony rider who's graduated to horses often remains loyal to his or her steed throughout the turbulence of growing up. A horse is a confidante and a sincere flatterer, especially for teens who are groping for identity. A horse knows who you truly are.

Horsing Around

Teenagers can be incredible riders. They're light and flexible, and they're not afraid to experiment with different techniques. They also haven't completely learned to be embarrassed by romantic urges that can't be satisfied. They really throw themselves into the ring. And here's a special dynamic not to be dismissed: Two teenagers who are friends and both ride have access to their own world of fun and adventure. Horses strengthen their camaraderie and give a touch of magic to the everyday world. She's getting exercise, too. (Yup, most teenage riders are girls. At this stage, the discipline is in sync with many of their social and emotional needs.)

Gimme Shelter

But the parents still have an important job to do: They have to provide constancy in the lives of both the rider and the horse. An animal with a horse's needs can't be simply shuffled off to another home once it's outlived its usefulness. You have to watch it like a hawk, every step of the way. Kid going to college? Why not keep the horse and learn to ride it yourself? With all those years of training in old Brandy, he's probably a gem. Whatever you do, don't just make that horse disappear. That's getting the kid off the hook, and sentencing the horse to a very uncertain future.

Tall in the Saddle, Long in the Tooth

Of course, you might not be within earshot when somebody's little Johnny or Susie screams for a pony. Your kids might be out of the house, and, finding nobody else at home, the riding bug bites you instead.

You might as well give in. Get out the Advil and sign up for a stretch class, though. Your body is going to be taxed in interesting ways—and you'll be the better for it.

The Voice of Experience

Learning to ride is a very different deal when you're grown up. For one thing, acquiring motor skills is difficult for most mature people. But the balance and flexibility you need to ride are very useful in trying to preserve an able, useful body. The great thing about being an adult rider is precisely that sense of escape that enchants the kids. You can forget the mutual funds and the peeling paint, and see nature a little more closely than before. A quiet trail ride on a fall afternoon can make you feel glad you're alive.

Been There, Done That

But don't think you won't have to deal with frustration. You can't expect to achieve the same degree of success with horses as you've had with your job or your children. You have to work things out on the horse's time clock, not your own. This, believe it or not, is a blessing. It teaches you to slow down. And who doesn't need to do that?

Mature adults are taught to disregard the emotional rumblings we have that tell us we're lonely or that we feel out of sorts with the world around us. We're supposed to always be able to cope. With horses, you don't have to pretend. You can seek out the friendship you needed when you were little. And you can find it.

Back to the Future

You may have picked up this book because you rode as a kid and are thinking you might go back to it. Good for you, but be prepared for a whole new world, and an older you. Don't expect to immediately recover the blithe confidence and flexible joints of your youth. Expect more trepidation, and expect to be told that some of the things you remember are all wrong! But be patient—you and your inner Pony Clubber will soon be as one.

The Least You Need to Know

- Learning to ride and take care of a pony or horse is a good way for a child to take responsibility, learn respect, and gain confidence.

- Kids and ponies have a special bond: Start a kid out with a pony they can learn to groom and saddle all by themselves safely.

- 4-H and Pony Club provide great opportunities for children to join the horse community.

- A pony becomes a responsibility for the whole household—be sure you're ready.

Part  5

Horse Heaven

You've decided to become a horse owner, and suddenly you have dozens of questions. Where will you keep him? Do you have the time and energy to have a homestead horse? Or is a boarding situation right for you?

Then there's actually buying the beast. Welcome to the world of dealers, deceptions, and best intentions. We'll steer you through the hazards, and remind you to be realistic, patient, and get that vet check! Once you've taken all the necessary steps, you'll need to know if the price is right.

We'll also give you a quick glimpse of the joys and perils of horse shows, and how to tell if they're right for you, and some information on caring for older horses.

LH Endless Luv, Half-Arabian Pinto Mare (owned by PJ Dempsey, Saylorsburg, Pennsylvania).

(© *Equine Photography by Suzanne, Inc.*)

Chapter 19

A Horse of Your Own

In This Chapter

- Why are you buying a horse?
- The backyard horse
- Boarding options—what to look for, what you'll pay

You think marriage is a big commitment? It's nothing compared to horse owning. In addition to love, honor, cherish, and obey (well, they're *supposed* to obey you, but that's another matter), there's feed, groom, shoe, muck out, insure, trailer, or board, travel, and pay, pay, pay. Not that we want to discourage you—like marriage, the rewards are well worth the risk—but it's important to know what you're getting into *before* you wake up the proud owner of 1,000 pounds of love.

And Why Are You Doing This?

Right answers:

- I want to create a real partnership with one animal.
- I need access to a horse 24/7 because my lesson time isn't taking me as far as I hoped. Having easy access and getting used to riding only one horse will help me to focus and advance.

- I am interested in competing.

- I've done a lot of background research and looked around, and I'm pretty sure that an Arabian/Thoroughbred/Morgan/ Appaloosa is right for me.

Wrong answers:

- My friend has one.

- He's pretty.

- She's a champion, so I can get to the top really fast if I buy her.

- It's so romantic to own a horse!

- I like the clothes/tailgate parties/people you meet.

- I can afford it, so why not?

All right, we've got your list, and we're checking it twice. Assuming you pass, the first thing you need to think about is where your horse is going to lay his head (or whatever). The two principle options are at home, if you have sufficient land, or a property with a barn; or at a boarding facility of some kind. Each comes with different issues with regard to your time, responsibilities, and costs.

Home Is Where the Horse Is

If you are fortunate enough to be a landowner, there are certainly advantages to keeping your horse at home. He will be under your eye, always accessible, you will have full input into his care and feeding, and you might save on board, though the expenses related to getting your property horse-ready may level these savings. Here are some issues to bear in mind:

- **Facilities.** Do you have a barn already, and is it in good condition? If not, you many have to face building or renovation costs. Stalls need to be at least 12 foot by 12 foot, and 14 foot by 14 foot for larger horses. You will also need to consider such issues as access, ventilation, and materials (wood, concrete, steel, etc.). You will also need somewhere for your feed, supplies (and there'll be a lot), tools, and tack.

Pasture. If you've been reading closely, you'll know how vital this is for a healthy, happy horse. Very limited pasture will affect the amount of time he can be turned out, and what he will be able to eat when he's there. Even if you have land (you need at least one acre per horse), you will now need to have the soil tested to see if it will produce sufficient good-quality forage, and you'll need to check it over for poisonous plants (see Chapter 6). If you have running water, it, too, will need to be tested, and if you don't, you'll need to provide tubs. And you will need to check your fence line to see that it is horse safe.

Manure happens. If you've reached this stage, you are probably already familiar with the one common feature of all equine landscapes: the unsightly manure pile. And never mind unsightly—in many regions, they are illegal. You will need to look into disposal—do you have land you can fertilize, and the right equipment for spreading? Manure should be composted first to help it break down and reduce flies, so you'll need to build a compost shed (Cooperative Extension offices can usually help with this). If you don't want to deal with it, is there someone you can pay to take it away, or enough gardening neighbors to give it to?

Flies happen. We've been over this. One of the constant aggravations to the horse and horse owner will become your responsibility to monitor and alleviate.

Zoning. Don't care for those bikers down the road? Can't believe they put a mall up near the woodland? Want to introduce a horse to the neighborhood? All these issues involve zoning—legal ordinances, specific to each region, county, neighborhood, and road, about the appropriate use of land and property. Your neighbors may be no more thrilled to see you and your manure pile than you are to see them—and if there's a zoning restriction, they'll move fast.

- **Insurance.** Becomes much more complicated and expensive, especially if anyone will be riding on your property.

- **Time.** This is crucial, because if you're keeping your horse at home he becomes a 24-hour-a-day job—every day, holidays included.

- **Companion animals.** As we've said, single horses are likely to be anxious and lonely, so your initial investment may need to include a companion animal for your companion animal.

- **Time off.** Forget going away unless you can arrange for a reliable barn sitter.

> **Horse Sense**
> Don't know where to begin? Relax, this is an industry, remember? Horse magazines (see Appendix B) are full of ads for builders, consultants, and prefab barns, stalls, and fences. Or ask someone who has done it.

The Daily Grind

Most of us know how to budget our money, even if we don't always *do* it (did you really need that Hermes scarf, now that you're getting the real thing? And forget that executive toy—Napoleon's executive toy was a horse). But we are much less efficient about budgeting time, which we always think will infinitely expand. A typical horse day starts early, but will vary depending on circumstances. At the very least, though, it will involve:

- Bringing horses in from pasture and feeding and watering

- Cleaning stall if horse is stabled indoors or kept inside for any part of the day or removing manure piles from the pasture

- Checking him over for injuries that might have occurred in the night—scrapes, cuts, bruises, bug bites

- Grooming

- Riding and/or schooling

- 🐴 Cooling off and grooming

- 🐴 Night feeding and watering, taking them back out to the pasture or bedding them down in their stalls.

The Upside

Yes, there is an upside. Any time of the day or night you will be able to kiss or pet a velvety nose if you feel the urge. That, in and of itself, may justify the time and effort. And your horse is likely to greet you in the morning with something more enthusiastic than "Where's the paper?" or "I've used up all the milk."

And You Thought It Was Just for Your Car: Insurance

Insurance is an important factor, especially in America, land of the litigators. If you keep a horse on your property, you will need to beef up your liability insurance, and you may also wish to insure the horse itself, both at home and when traveling to shows. A number of companies now specialize in equine insurance, but rates can still be substantial for total coverage. Check with your carrier before building the barn.

Whoa!

If you keep a horse, or horses, on your property, you should have notices warning that children cannot touch them, play with them, or enter a pasture without an adult present. Put your "hands off" policy in writing, and pass it out to your neighbors. Why? In law, horses are deemed an "attractive nuisance." This is defined as an artificial condition (like a swimming pool) that might attract children and cause harm, and is the responsibility of the owner.

Horse Hotel: Boarding

You've taken a long, cold look at your handkerchief-size garden, remembered that your neighbors complain if your trellis rose crosses into their side of the fence, noticed that your Palm Pilot features

16 meetings and 4 out-of-town business trips. So instead of building that barn, find your horse a boarding situation. But wait, you're not off the hook yet. This decision (the wisest course for many busy professionals and weekend riders) comes with another list of questions and considerations.

Where Is It?

If the barn isn't within convenient driving distance, trust us, you won't be going there often. Try to find something that's no more than half an hour away. When you consider that the average time spent away from home will be at least three hours when you factor in grooming time and chatting with your barn friends, the last thing you want is to add in a long commute—and your family won't be thrilled, either.

Board Is Not Board Is Not Board

There's money in horses, big and small, and many people are eager to make a living from your leisure. These days, board can mean anything from a place for your horse to hang his halter to the horse equivalent of an exclusive boarding school. These are the establishments that will add schooling to feeding—to the Ritz—luxurious accommodations, and all the extras. The three basic types of board are as follows:

 Horse Sense
What's your dollar buying? Most board includes basic feed (grain and hay). Dietary supplements, medications, veterinary bills, and shoeing are the responsibility of the owner, and most barns will arrange for you to be billed separately for them.

- **Pasture board.** The least expensive, this involves your horse being outdoors all year 'round, usually with a shed of some kind for shelter in really rough weather. Hardy ponies and other hard-wearing types often do well in these conditions, but they don't suit many thin-skinned, nervously intelligent, or, let's face it, expensive horses.

- **Basic board.** The horse has an assigned stall and usually some turnout, meaning that the horse gets to spend at least part of the day, and sometimes night, outdoors, in a pasture.

- **Training board.** Becoming commonplace in areas of the country with well-to-do clients who are focused on competition, this sort of board is offered by training barns and includes daily schooling as well as basic care.

Is This Your Type of Place?

In addition to the simple question of what level of care your horse is receiving, there are a host of questions about what kind of environment he'll be in. In some cases, you'll wind up boarding where you're training, or looking for a place that allows you to school your horse as well as feed him. If you have bought your horse at or brought your horse to your training barn, some of these questions will already be resolved. Otherwise, here's what to consider:

- Where can you ride? Is there an indoor, as well as an outdoor, arena or pasture you can ride in? (Why does this matter? Because that sylvan landscape, that fall foliage, is going to turn into a snow-covered dome, or at least bitter, nasty sludge sometime during the year, and you don't want to be going through your paces in all that.) Is there limited access? And what's the footing like?

- Are these your type of people? No, we don't mean did they go to the right schools. We mean things that really matter: Are they your type of riders? There is no greater loneliness than being the only dressage person in a barn full of hunter/jumper types, or the only one who thinks trail riding is for looking at leaves and covered bridges, while your barn mates are obsessed with interval training and keep looking at their big sports watches.

- Are there training/competitive opportunities? If you are interested in showing, your barn may be horse central. Do they offer rides to shows (if you aren't going to buy a trailer) and help you prepare for them? Are there clinics and guest instructors?

- Will your horse's stall be roomy, and allow him to see other horses? Is there good ventilation? Is there turnout available (a crucial issue), and if so, for how long and with whom? If weather conditions and your horse's health and temperament permit, your best bet is someplace where turnout is the norm, with the stall in reserve for feeding, really bad weather, and show days.

- Does the barn seem clean and tidy? While busy stables are never going to look like five-star hotels, stalls should be clean (or being cleaned), there should be no dangerous tools in the aisles, mounds of dust, open feed bins, or protruding hooks. And a cloud of flies around the manure pile may mean it isn't cleared much.

- Is the barn on a regular schedule in regard to feeding and turnout? As you've learned, horses are creatures of habit and an irregular schedule can cause physical and emotional problems (see Chapter 10).

- What additional services does the barn offer? These might include (in addition to training) blanketing, additional turnout, regular worming, and *hot walkers* (usually only at up-market barns, these are people who will cool down your horse while you're cleaning your tack, etc., so you can leave more quickly). What arrangements are made for shoeing and veterinary care?

- Ambience. It's that indefinable something, like body chemistry. Does the staff seem warm, or snippy? Do the clients seem happy, or gossipy and disgruntled?

The Ritz, or Motel 6: Boarding Costs

Costs vary considerably from area to area, with the East Coast winning the prize for most exorbitant. An average for basic board (per month) is between $200 and $450, but in Sarah's area of upstate New York $500 is standard, with training boarders paying between $650 and $750. (We did hear of one barn that was charging a breathtaking $1,200 each month—we only hope these horses had a mini bar and chocolates on their pillows each night!)

Horse Sense _____

In the absence of the *Michelin Guide to Horse Hotels*, here are some places to look for boarding situations:

🐴 **Classified ads, especially in horse magazines and local papers.** Don't just check under "horses"—listings for livestock, farms, rural properties might also include boarding prospects.

🐴 **Word of mouth.** Ask around at your lesson barn— which may also be one of your options—at the tack shop, and check with local riding groups.

🐴 **Roadsides.** Keep an eye open as you drive. Would-be boarders often post notices.

Can You Get It Wholesale?

If you're still dead set on a horse, but are hoping there's some way to keep down boarding costs, here are some low-budget options:

🐴 **Share boarding.** You and another rider share your horse or hers. For this delicate arrangement to work well, you need someone with similar riding goals, at a similar level to you, and with a different schedule. You will split the board costs, and will need to work out in an agreement letter what other costs and responsibilities you share.

🐴 **Working it off.** Some barns will consider letting you work off part of your board if you will agree to care for your own horse and help out with others.

🐴 **Barter.** Again, this really depends on your individual circum-stances, and is likely to be possible only if you have a personal relationship with the barn. But if you have a marketable practi-cal skill, from fence building to tax preparation, it's worth a try.

🐴 **Cow country.** In rural areas in the West and even in the East, some ranchers and farmers have extra barn and/or pasture areas available for rent (and sometimes even free). You must still care for your own horse and supply the food (and maybe the shelter or fencing).

A Hobby Is a Type of Horse, but a Horse Is Not a Hobby

Before we lead you through the exciting, but (horse) hair-raising, business of actually obtaining a horse (in Chapter 20), we just wanted to make this one last point. Horse ownership takes time, money, and dedication, and it doesn't matter if you board your horse out or he bunks in your backyard. Horses are lots of work, every day. If you board, you'll have to make time to get to the stable. Lots of us do this, but be aware that having a horse, like parenting a child, will change your life. It also helps to have understanding friends (a person who doesn't mind if you come to lunch in your breeches, and faintly fragrant) and family (particularly your mate) who like horses and know how much it means to you to have one in your life, and don't mind doing a little more around the house to make it possible.

The Least You Need to Know

- Horse ownership is like marriage—a huge commitment with both perils and rewards.

- If you plan to keep your horse at home, you've taken on a 24-hour-a-day responsibility, rain or shine. Are you ready?

- Boarding is the best option for many busy riders with careers, but be sure you know what to look for, and choose carefully for both your horse and yourself.

- In the long run, the cost of the horse is the least expensive part of horse ownership.

Chapter

High Horse Hopes: Shopping and Buying

In This Chapter

- 🎞 Planning your purchase: know what you want
- 🎞 Where to look
- 🎞 What to ask
- 🎞 Making the offer
- 🎞 Other options

You're really going to do it—buy a horse. Now comes the hard part—finding what you want. The more care, patience, and self-control you exercise now, the more likely it is that you'll make a happy horse marriage (and they don't come with in-laws!).

You Can't Always Get What You Want ...

You know the rest. The first thing you need to do is think seriously about what you're buying this horse for—and there is no other thing we can think of that needs to combine utility and companionship the

way a horse does. You don't want to take long strolls with your SUV, and your Pekinese doesn't have to work for a living.

By *seriously* we mean make a list:

- **What are you hoping to do with the horse?** There are good horses to be had in all categories, but your search will be different if you are looking for a horse to compete seriously with, regardless of discipline, or if you are just looking for a good trail buddy (really good horses can be both).

- **What level rider are you?** Be honest and realistic. If you are a newcomer, or a tentative intermediate rider, you should be looking for a safe, well-schooled horse who can show you the ropes.

- **How much time do you plan to devote to riding?** Again, the type of horse you will be happy with will depend partly on how much time you have to devote to riding. Don't buy a high-maintenance performance horse if all you have is an hour or two a week, unless you're prepared to pay for someone to work him. Even then, absentee horse ownership shouldn't be your choice.

Horse Whispers

Many people have sighed for the "good old days" and regretted the passing of the horse, but today, when only those who like horses own them, it is a far better time for horses.

—C. W. Anderson

- **Are you attracted to any breed/type?** If you've begun to read about horses (here, for instance) or been to shows, or met some prospects at your lesson barn, you may have already developed an affinity for a particular breed, especially if it's one that's linked to your discipline of choice.

- **What type of personality are you looking for?** Come on, you know you have one. Do you like your dogs/cats/men/women/horses placid or feisty, cuddly or aloof? It won't matter (or not much) how terrific a performer your horse is if you don't feel comfortable around him.

How much can you spend? One school of horse buying says, "decide how much you want to spend, then double it," because you may well be unrealistic in your estimates. That experienced show horse in the prime of life is going to cost more than your computer, trust us. Do some research (we'll talk pricing in a later section), then set realistic limits.

(© Lori Steffensen)

Appaloosa Sugar's Domino, owned by Tina Veder, shows why sometimes wishes are horses.

That's You—What About Him?

Once you've taken stock of your own aims and limitations, the whole world of horses (within reason) awaits you. Here are some key things to consider.

Breed and Type

Do your homework, find out about the different breeds, and see if one might be right for you and your goals. Starting competitive trail riding? Maybe there's an Arabian in your future. Western pleasure or Gymkhana? Think Quarter Horse. Drawn to horse trials? Peruse those sport horse listings (carefully!). Drawn to dressage?

Warmbloods are us. On the other hand, there are many fine animals out there of mixed parentage, and sometimes type matters more than pure breeding—your trail horse needs to be sturdy, your sport horse quick, and your dressage mount physically capable of performing the advanced moves necessary to this discipline.

Sex and Size

As we said in Chapter 9, there are some definite sex-related character-istics, and you need to decide whether they are significant factors in your decision. And size is likely to matter a lot more than gender. You need to be safe, comfortable, and effective on your horse—and his own comfort is important, too. There are no hard-and-fast rules—small women often pilot large horses, and men have won medals on dainty mares. But if you are merely a passenger, or the animal is sink-ing under your weight, it's going to do neither of you much good.

All Horses Are "Pre-Owned": Experience

The toughest call of all, because there are so many gradations and degrees. At one extreme, there is "green," which can mean anything from has barely been ridden to hasn't had a lot of formal experience; at the other is "made," which can mean anything from knows the basics to has recently retired from the international circuit. As we've said, the right degree of schooling will depend a lot on where you are with your riding, and what you have to offer the horse in terms of training. A green horse is likely to cost less initially, but you will prob-ably need to have professional help in bringing him along; a "made" horse will have a certain amount under his belt, but don't think of him as a shortcut to greatness.

Not Older, Better

Chances are, an older horse will come with more experience, but some come with more wear, requiring special feed, shoeing, and general tender loving care to keep them at their best. While some conditions, such as a little stiffness, are common and can be kept at bay, older horses may well have more serious conditions—such as hoof and leg injuries—that aren't as easy to spot, and should be vetted carefully.

He's the One: Chemistry

Buying a horse is like buying a house. You have a list of prerequisites, and any number of houses may fulfill them, but only one feels like home. If he doesn't make your heart beat faster, he may be still be a nice horse, but he's not *your* horse.

Roundup: Where to Look

There are nearly seven million horses in this country, but when you're trying to buy one, sometimes you find yourself wondering where they all are. Happily, a combination of tried and true, and high-tech, sources will help you find your true friend:

- **Classifieds.** As with stables, the majority of horses for sale are still listed in papers and magazines.

- **Click on horse.** The digital equivalent of classified ads, with the added advantage that you can consider prospects from around the country, view pictures and performance histories, and correspond with the owners, without ever leaving your desk (although you have to do that at some point).

- **Word of mouth.** Ask your instructor. Spread the word at your riding school, tack shop, and horse show. As soon as you announce you're in the market, everyone will know of at least one horse you must see. The trick is learning how to pan for gold.

- **Horse shows.** Many owners use competitions to display their prospects—check bulletin boards at shows and on stable doors for "For Sale" signs. And you'll have a chance to see the prospects performing.

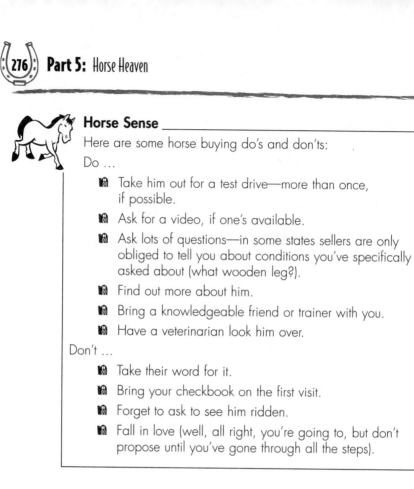

Horse Sense

Here are some horse buying do's and don'ts:

Do ...

- 🐴 Take him out for a test drive—more than once, if possible.
- 🐴 Ask for a video, if one's available.
- 🐴 Ask lots of questions—in some states sellers are only obliged to tell you about conditions you've specifically asked about (what wooden leg?).
- 🐴 Find out more about him.
- 🐴 Bring a knowledgeable friend or trainer with you.
- 🐴 Have a veterinarian look him over.

Don't ...

- 🐴 Take their word for it.
- 🐴 Bring your checkbook on the first visit.
- 🐴 Forget to ask to see him ridden.
- 🐴 Fall in love (well, all right, you're going to, but don't propose until you've gone through all the steps).

Eyeballing: What to Look For

We recommend that you bring a knowledgeable friend or your instructor with you to look at prospects—it takes a lot of years in the horse business to spot the subtle clues that might mean trouble, and unlike new clothes, you can't just exchange a horse for one that fits better.

Here are a few tips:

- 🐴 If possible, ask to see the horse untacked, so you can get a sense of how he is to catch and handle

- 🐴 Ask to see him ridden before you ride him, so you can see how he moves and responds to a rider

- 🐴 Don't just ride him, handle him. Does he seem nervous on the floor or in the stall? Is he touch-shy? Can you pick up his feet? Does he look you in the eye?

- What's his overall appearance? Any noticeable conformation defects, scars, corrective shoes? Does he look healthy?

- Is he a people person?

Background Check: What to Ask

Try to find out everything you can about your prospect: what type of work he's done, age, breeding, any vices, why he's being sold (take the answer to this with a grain of salt). If you're planning to show, be sure he loads and trailers so you don't waste frustrating hours trying to get a balky animal into your rig or end up with one who will kick at the walls trying to break out, once inside.

Horse Sense

Be sure to compare the environment and training regime of any horse you are considering with the one that you'll be placing him in. A high-powered performance horse used to focused work on a daily basis can turn into a nervous wreck if you suddenly reduce him to a diet of occasional lessons and hacks. This is not only discouraging, but can be dangerous, as horses like this don't have outlets for their nervous energy.

Consider the Source

Other than the local supermarket, horses are to be found from an amazing number of sources, and context can affect your prospect's potential health, the availability—and accuracy—of the information you get, and how much you need to be on your toes.

Horse Dealers: The Second Oldest Profession

It's not by accident that horse dealers have been compared to used-car salesman. It's not that they're all crooks, but there's a strategic level of fuzziness about the information they give out, and they essentially look upon horses as a commodity—"Have I got a deal for

you!" Often, they've bought at auction, or from another dealer out of state, and may not know much more about the animal than you do. If there's a paper trail, it may be thin, or fictitious, but if he's claiming that the animal is registered, your persistence should be rewarded. Always, they will be trying to put the best four feet forward, and you should be alert for vagueness, implausibility, and, in worst-case scenarios, active manipulation. (Drugging horses to make them appear calm is very common—another reason why a vet check is crucial as well as a second surprise visit, if you're serious.)

Homemade Horses: Breeders

Unlike dealers, if you buy from a breeder there is likely to be a strong investment in the condition and reputation of their animals, since these reflect the condition and reputation of their barn. Buying from a breeder isn't foolproof, but you'll have the added advantage of checking out other horses they've bred (either from buyers or in the show ring) or, perhaps, even the relatives of the horse you are considering. It is also possible that you can get a better price from a breeder who is willing to forego extra dollars if their animal is going to a good home.

Check around. Like we said, there are good horses everywhere and from a variety of sources—the trick is how to know when you've found the perfect one for you.

"Off to College" and Other Stories: Individuals

In many areas the most likely source for your eventual horse is his previous owner, and while there are many straightforward reasons for a sale—she's college-bound, moving up in competition, has outgrown her horse, has moved on to boys, etc.—without close questioning on your part the seller may forget to mention that the horse cribs like a beaver, will not go across water, shies if the wind shifts, cannot keep weight on, or any one of a dozen other flaws.

"He's Been in the Ribbons at Dublin" and Other Stories: Trainers

Increasingly, in competitive areas of the country, individual horse professionals, often based at training barns, are also in the selling business on the side. Unlike dealers, they don't preside over a lot full of anonymous horseflesh, but instead are purveying to the high end of the market, and almost always seem to have something fresh off the boat (or plane) with many unverifiable overseas credentials. Here, too, be sure to verify any story if you can, and think seriously about whether the $35,000 price tag (we kid you not) is worth being able to say that your handsome gray just flew in on the Concorde.

 Horse Sense

Depending on your needs, do not underestimate the potential of a senior. A well-trained veteran of the show ring may come at a bargain price if his previous owner is moving on to a younger horse with more of a future.

You've Found Him and You Can't Live Without Him

This is the hardest stage to reach, and the one that is most crucial to your future safety and happiness. Here's what to do before planning a welcome home party.

Call the Vet

The single most important stage of horse purchasing is being sure you are acquiring a sound animal who can do the work required of him. Never buy a horse without a thorough check by a veterinarian—called vetting. If you don't know one personally, get a recommendation, and be sure, of course, that your choice is someone other than the owner's own vet.

The first thing the vet will ask is what you plan to do with the horse. No animal is perfect, and she will be making an assessment

based on your needs. Next, she'll ask how far you want to go—if you are buying a performance horse, x-rays, though an additional expense, are recommended in addition to the basic physical. If it's an older horse, you may even want to consider ultrasound. Otherwise, your vet will ask to see the horse walked and trotted out, will examine him physically for conformation defects, condition of the legs and lungs, scarring, flexion, vision, and other basic functions, and will give you a report detailing the up- and downsides of this particular animal (there will always be both). After that, it's up to you.

How Much Is That Pony in the Window? Making an Offer

Again, horses are like houses. There's an asking price, usually based on local market value, and sometimes there's a little wiggle room. Know what you want to spend before setting out, so that you're not wasting your own or the seller's time.

Price ranges vary dramatically around the country and by breed. It's possible to buy a perfectly decent horse for several thousand dollars or even less; and sometimes a buyer beware special. A seasoned performance horse that can cost $15,000 in an affluent area may be had for $6,000 in another area. (This is another good reason for checking the Internet for prospects—even with shipping, and traveling to ride, you might get a much better deal out of state.) Sellers who are willing to "deal" can usually be expected to come down a few thousand on a high-end horse, and a few hundred on a lower-priced one; but if you're in a competitive area, they may not budge.

Penning Them In: Legal Issues

What you don't know *will* hurt you. Once you're committed, be sure to execute a formal buyer's agreement, stating the purchase price (you will need this for any insurance or appraisal situations) and including a clause stating that the animal is returnable, and your money refundable, if any undiagnosed condition surfaces within two weeks of purchase.

Whoa! _____

Be wary of the ad for an inexpensive horse that "does it all." Stop and think about it. If he is so great, why is he a bargain? Like anything in life, there's usually a reason it's cheap. But, as with any bargain, if you know what you're looking for and have the ability to recognize a horse diamond in the rough, or one that has just had some hard luck or a cosmetic flaw that the present owner just can't live with—you just may get the buy of your life.

Getting Him Home

Some sellers will be willing to deliver your horse, but this is usually your responsibility. Be sure that your barn is ready to receive him; that you've checked on his diet and have a couple of meals already packaged (even if you are changing his feed, you'll want to do this gradually); that you've got shipping boots (horses can easily bang themselves up in trailers, and should travel in tall padded boots that wrap around the legs from the knees to the edge of the hoof); and that you've allowed enough time to get him loaded and comfortably settled.

Calling Him by Name

Chances are your horse will come with a name he recognizes and responds to, unless you buy a foal. Can you change it if you don't like it? Some say it's bad luck, and some breed registries won't allow a registered-name change (especially if the horse has offspring or has earned points in showing). If you're applying to a registry, some allow you to check your choice on their websites. You could always just change his barn name, but why bother if your horse knows and responds to his name?

When choosing a name, our advice is to come up with one that is easy to pronounce and won't be mangled over the P.A. system when you're announced as a winner at a show or rodeo. Pick something positive, prefix it with your stable name, or add a spicy tag to a boring name (Sarah's horse arrived as "Jonathan" which made him sound like a blind date; now he's Jonathan Swift).

Hello, Horse–Good-Bye, Bank Account

No matter what you pay, the horse is still the cheapest part of horse ownership. Everything costs—choose one or more from this list: board, or bedding and feed; vet checks; inoculations/worming; shoes, blankets, coolers, sheets; buckets; tack; insurance; trailers or transport; trainers; clinics; horse shows; riding clothes; stuff!

Take a look at this sample horse budget:

Board: $400

Farrier: $50 to $100 every six weeks if you shoe all around

Wormer: $10 a month

Vet: $30 a month for routine visits

Extras: $45 a month—supplements, extra turnout, dry cleaning

Training: $150 (lessons once a week and the odd clinic)

Transport: $50 a month (or invest in a trailer for a mere $3,000 to $7,500)

Shows: $1,500 including entry fees and travel expenses during the season

And this is assuming your horse stays healthy, and *before* all those catalogs start rolling into your mailbox.

Gotta Get a Horse!

If you can't afford to buy one right now, there are other options:

- **Leasing.** As with cars, and probably for the same reason—the economic crunch—leasing is becoming a popular option. Owners with no time to ride or also faced with economic problems may lease the animal for a limited period (a year, or the summer, for example). Financial arrangements vary, and should be put in writing—you might be responsible for part of the board, or other fees, or pay a set amount to the owner. Spell out your agreement in writing.

- **The gift horse.** Here's one case where you do need to look the horse in the mouth, and every other place. Miracles do happen, and people have gotten remarkable animals from owners more concerned about an animal's well-being than money, but more often than not, "free" means unsaleable. There are a variety of reasons—age, medical issues, behavioral problems, or rescue (see the following section). We'd love every story like this to have a happy ending, but be sure you read between the lines before you say "Yes."

Politics Aside

It's not our intention to rub any horse hair the wrong way, and it's hard to make jokes when there are abused, unwanted, and homeless equine victims of the down-turned economy (it costs money to own a horse). For all sorts of reasons, there are foals and horses out there who need homes. Check out these possibilities:

- **Mustangs.** The Bureau of Land Management has been adopting out horses and burros for many years now. Check out their website (see Appendix B) for the details and adoption sites. There are rules you must follow to own one of these special horses, so be sure you're willing to abide by them.

- **Premarin foals.** Premarin foals are the result of the hormone replacement drug Premarin, made from PREgnant MAre uRINe. Any hormone beginning with "pre" is made from pregnant mare urine. This seemingly unwanted side effect of pregnancy has doomed more foals than we care to think about to a slaughterhouse future, but they are adoptable if you know where to find them. Many of these foals are registered and there are a number of draft crosses (the bigger the mare the more urine she makes). We've listed the website in Appendix B; check it out.

- **Off the track.** If you adopt a horse off the track, have reasonable expectations. The horse may have some physical problems due to injuries and may need medical attention. The horses with the most potential are already earmarked for trainers. If your horse doesn't come from a trainer, you will need to invest in one. Remember, these are horses who pretty much go at one

speed and need to be retrained. Check out their websites (see Appendix B). We know a number of people who went this route and were very happy with their horses. Adoption fees range from $1,000 to $3,000.

- **Auctions.** At one end of the spectrum there is the Keeneland Thoroughbred auction, followed by auctions from various breed associations down to the auctions patronized by the "killers." True, you may find a bargain there, a good horse who has fallen on unfortunate circumstances. Beware, though, of unscrupulous sellers and forged registration papers. Know what you're looking for and take an experienced horseperson with you. Know what you want to spend and stick to it. Just be realistic as to what you can find at this type of auction.

- **Rescue.** We've mentioned a few prominent rescue organizations in Appendix B, but you can also find these organizations on the web or through local horse people. Sometimes they will have a table at a county fair, horse show, or horse expo.

- **Don't forget our other equine friends.** Burros and Donkeys need homes, too. The Bureau of Land Management (BLM) rounds up Burros along with the Mustangs, and many horse rescue organizations also rescue these guys. If you are interested in adopting a longear, query The American Donkey and Mule Society (see Appendix B).

The Least You Need to Know

- Know what you want and how much you're prepared to spend.

- Don't rush your fences, or your horses. Take your time, get to know your prospect well, and—the hardest thing—be ready to move on.

- Horses aren't see-through: The vet check is crucial.

- Forget that face lift/sports car/world tour: Your money's already spent. (But spent well.)

Chapter  21

Going Gray: Seniors

In This Chapter

- Keeping your old guy young at heart and hoof
- From feed to feet: senior products
- Retirement options
- The hardest choice: euthanasia

When people talk about "the graying of America," they usually mean the advance into late middle age of the baby boomer generation. But a parallel trend exists in the horse world. Better care and nutrition have improved and extended the working life and general lot of older horses. The senior scene is particularly germane to beginning riders and/or first-time owners, because older horses are often more affordable and give great value for money in terms of experience. So if you wind up owning or sharing a horse with a few miles on him, here's how to keep him tuned up, and what to do when his best days are behind him.

Whoa!

If you notice any change in weight in an older horse, call the vet. There are any number of health problems that could be responsible. Getting the right diagnosis quickly will help you treat the problem before it causes larger health issues.

The Fountain of Youth: The Aging Process

Ponce de Leon, the explorer who searched for the fountain of youth, hasn't had any better luck with horses than with people. We are all growing old together, and for many of the same reasons. As we age, cells cease to replenish, bones grow brittle, blood sugar levels become problematic, circulation is compromised, muscles, tendons, and sinews stiffen, and the body does not as easily convert nutrients into energy. That's the bad news, but it doesn't mean you and your horse should catch the next bus to Florida.

When is old for a horse? Every horse is different, but around the late teens is when you might begin to see some signs of aging, although some horses don't show any sign until their early 20s. Once your horse reaches his mid- to late teens, keep a vigilant watch, so you can spot symptoms that indicate he might be slowing down or in need of extra care. Here's a useful checklist:

- **Dental problems.** Teeth begin to angle sharply downward, and are more prone to splintering, making eating difficult. Be sure that you have your older horse's teeth checked regularly, as dental problems contribute to ...

- **Eating problems.** Older horses sometimes begin to "quid," dropping food out of their mouths, and have trouble eating their hay. Because food is not being properly processed or digested, this in turn leads to ...

- **Weight loss.** Which may also be a sign of other forms of deterioration or sickness.

- **Thyroid problems.** Older horses commonly develop benign tumors of the thyroid gland. Nothing is done about these tumors unless they cause problems.

- **Cataracts.** Even though these can impair vision, most horses learn to function well in spite of having them.

- **Cushing's Disease (pituitary tumor).** This is the most common endocrine disorder of senior horses and is the result of increased cell growth of the pituitary gland. The classic signs are: Excessive hair growth which tends to be long and curly and does not shed in the spring, laminitis, no energy, thick neck, pot belly, decreased muscle mass. Keep in mind that not all horses exhibit these signs, but if you notice that your horse is not acting like his normal self, call the vet. The disease can be diagnosed with a blood test and is treatable with medication.

- **Aches and pains.** Watch for signs of arthritis and other forms lameness and general stiffness.

- **Coat.** Older horses don't shed out as easily and they are more prone to skin infections and irritations.

- **Feet.** Hooves become more brittle with age.

- **Crankiness.** This you'll recognize with no trouble.

"Oy!" you're thinking, but be honest: Isn't *your* medicine cabinet filled with vitamin supplements? Aren't *you* buying more low-fat products? Isn't that tennis injury from twenty years ago beginning to twinge again? All you need is love, and a little help from your (horse's) friends.

Horse Lore

Horses are like people—some get old early, some never do. A prime example is Elmer Bandit, a gray, home-bred, Half-Arabian out of a Hancock Quarter Horse with a dash of Percheron. In 1986, at the age of 15, he was the North American Trail Ride Conference's inaugural Hall of Fame inductee. Today he still goes more than 1,000 miles each year in competitive trail rides. Forget being put out to pasture for this horse.

"It's Good for You": Senior Feed

As we keep saying, it's a great time to be a horse. As *we* get older, people keep telling us what we can't eat, and steak and chocolate give way to low-fat foods and Metamucil. Meanwhile, back at the barn, horses are the beneficiaries of decades of nutritional research and there is a plethora of yummy feed products on the market specifically designed for seniors. (Just look at any issue of those horse magazines you're going to be reading soon.) These are fortified with the vitamins and minerals that older horses need higher concentrations of. Different hay mixes, containing more digestible grasses like timothy and brome grass, may also be called for.

 Horse Sense

If you're keeping your horse at home, you may benefit from some suppliers' sophisticated marketing strategies. Major drug and feed companies such as Pfizer and Purina have created "wellness" programs—often with discounts and free advice—if you commit to their products exclusively. This is clearly enlightened self-interest on their part, but probably worth checking out.

Been There, Done That: Riding Him

Your senior probably has a long (maybe even distinguished) career behind him, so you can focus on quality, not quantity, in your training and showing program. Don't school compulsively, or enter every show on the calendar. Here's what's important:

- **Warmups.** A good warmup is important for all horses, but especially for seniors, whose creaking joints and stiff muscles simply will not respond as quickly at 16 as they did at 6. Be careful, too, about riding on hard surfaces—with decreased elasticity, these can provoke not only discomfort, but actual lameness.

- **Easy does it.** Concentrate on long walks and trotting over soft ground. If you're keeping him fit for competition, short

(three- to five-minute) canters are fine as long as he has plenty of down time in between. And pay attention to his response: If he sounds winded, or seems tired, slow down!

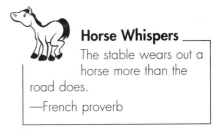

■ **Weekend warrior?** Not a good idea. Try to ride, or have your horse ridden, most days. It's much harder for an older horse to be idle for five days out of seven and then suddenly be asked to rev everything up.

■ **Going for the gold.** If you and he have had a thriving competitive partnership, it may be hard to cut back, but you'll lose him a lot faster if you don't pick and choose. And when you're making your picks, think about things like time of year (monsoons? heat waves?), distance, accommodations, wait time.

Horse Whispers

The stable wears out a horse more than the road does.

—French proverb

Senior power: Winchester, a 19-year-old Thoroughbred, showing good form over a hunter pace fence.

 Horse Sense _____

> If you don't exercise a senior equine regularly, you're asking for trouble. Regular, low-impact exercise will lubricate stiff joints, tone muscles, stimulate appetite, and keep him in a good mood. Instead of long, hard workouts a couple times a week, do easy, shorter workouts more often during the week. Be consistent in your schedule and don't give him days off at a time—he will stiffen up. Even if you only have 15 minutes to ride, do it. Nice long walks on the trail (with the occasional trot and canter) are good for the soul (yours and his).

We Have the Tools, We Have the Technology: Senior Strategies

It's the little things. Everything that applies to keeping a horse fit and happy is slightly altered by the aging process:

- **Shoes.** Adjustments in shoes, hoof angles, or padding can relieve stress on aging legs and back muscles.

- **Supplements.** In addition to special feeds, a variety of supplements are available to counteract the changes that come about in old age. These include glucosamine/chondroitin (every mammal of our acquaintance—dogs, cats, people, and horses—is on this stuff) and others like MSM, and the usual range of vitamins and minerals.

- **Spa treatment.** Now may be the time to try (with guidance!) some of those alternative therapies, such as massage (good for aching muscles), chiropractic (a horse with a long working life may well be literally "out of joint"), naturopathic medicine, or acupuncture.

- **Friends.** No, not Jennifer Aniston. Older horses need compatible stable and pasture mates to minimize rites of challenge and possible injury.

🐴 **A soft bed, or the equivalent.** Peat moss is a good choice because it's less dusty, and more cushion-y. Outside (regular turnout is even more important for seniors to prevent stiffening) there should be some sort of shelter.

From the Horse's Mouth

A horse is considered a senior when he reaches the age of 15. What this means is that he's started on the road to old age. This does not mean that you should immediately change his work routine—he'll let you know when he's starting to feel the effects of the number of years he's walked the earth.

Moving On

Things change. A change of job or locale, a change of fortune such as divorce, illness, or injury, waning interest, or new interests, might affect your ability or willingness to keep a horse, and while a younger horse can usually be sold, this is not always a viable option with an older animal. More difficult even than sudden lifestyle changes is coming to terms with the fact that you will not be able to move forward with your senior—he is no longer up to the level of work you need to do, or you have outgrown his particular set of skills. Nevertheless, he remains, at the very least, your responsibility, and more likely a friend and companion for whom you want the best. Following are some options (see Appendix B for contact information).

Time for Golf: Retirement

While not as prevalent as retirement communities for humans, there are a growing number of retirement facilities for horses opening around the country if you do not have the land to simply put your old friend out to pasture. You will have to continue to pay board (most places try to keep this as low as possible) and should be sure to check out the establishment before committing to be sure it is right for your animal. Like all boarding arrangements, there are different types of retirement situations. Depending upon what part of the country you

live in, there may or may not be stalls provided, but only run-in sheds, which are fine in warm climates.

Good-Bye, Mr. Chips: Schoolwork

Many riding schools and training barns are happy to have schoolmaster horses donated to them, and this is an especially good choice if your older horse is still fit and active and would clearly be bored and wasted standing around doing nothing all day. Sarah's old Thoroughbred, Winchester, no longer able to jump, found a splendid home with a nearby lesson barn where he makes beginners his own age feel elegant and safe, and enjoys autumn trail rides. Again, be sure you know the physical circumstances and reputation of the barn you are donating to—you don't want your horse to wind up as the equivalent of a galley slave. You should also work up an agreement letter that stipulates a trial period, and gives you some control over your horse's fate once he is no longer able to work.

Lending a Hoof: Hippotherapy

As we saw in Chapter 2, riding programs for people with emotional problems and physical disabilities are growing around the country. Most are nonprofit operations, and are always in need of safe, well-schooled horses (and equipment) for their work. Because of their special needs, they have strict criteria—horses usually need to be on the small side to facilitate mounting; should be strong, fluid movers, because the motion of the horse's body is what benefits the disabled rider; and should be relatively spook-proof, because beach balls and wheelchairs will become part of his world.

Horse Whispers

Old minds are like old horses; you must exercise them if you wish to keep them in working order.

—John Adams

Free to a Good Home ...

If your horse is still able to work, he may be a dream come true for someone who cannot afford to buy a new horse. This sort of situation

is usually uncovered by word of mouth and notices in local papers and tack shops. Again, be very careful to review the situation before making a commitment—if the person can't afford to buy, can he/she afford to keep? Or someone may just be looking for a companion animal for another horse—as long as it doesn't turn out to be the equine equivalent of the Odd Couple, this is often a restful option for your social senior.

A Friend in Need ...

Horses' basic needs don't change with age, and one of these is companionship. You may be able to find your friend a home with another horse who needs company. This might be an older horse also heading for retirement, or a younger horse looking for a steadying influence. Again, research the possibilities carefully, keeping your horse's needs and temperament in mind (if he's an alpha type he might terrorize some more timid soul, and if he's a milquetoast you don't want him to be henpecked). Be sure to visit the barn, and work out any legal details about expenses and liabilities.

Until Death Do Us Part ...

We hope euthanasia (or "putting down," as it's more commonly called) is an option only when your old friend is experiencing measurably decreased quality of life; it should not be a convenient way out of an inconvenient situation. If you must make the ultimate choice, your vet can advise you (lethal injection is the commonest form of euthanasia), and recognizing the growing bond between riders and their older animals, there is a substantial body of literature and therapeutic programs to help you cope.

Here's when it's probably time:

- He's experienced a mortal injury. It happens, and your responsibility is to release him from pain and suffering as soon as possible.

- He's got a serious break. This is of course a decision between you and your vet, and there have been some miraculous recoveries, but sadly, many horses never really heal, and—a tough reality—the costs of trying can be stupendous.

- He has a chronic condition that is ceasing to respond to treatment, and he is obviously in constant pain and discomfort.

- Dramatic deterioration—a horse who can no longer eat, or stand safely, or be turned out with others, has ceased to have the sort of life you would want for him.

In the long run, pay your friend and companion the greatest compliment you can: Imagine yourself in his place, and allow him the same dignified release from suffering that you would wish for.

From the Horse's Mouth _____

Even though you've always let your vet decide on which medications or treatments to use to keep your horse healthy during his lifetime, the decision to put your horse down is yours and yours alone. For any owner, this is the toughest decision you'll ever have to make and there is no way around it. All you can do is what you think is best for your loyal friend and longtime companion.

The Least You Need to Know

- Advances in nutrition and health care mean many horses are still thriving in their teens and 20s.

- Changes in diet and exercise, and maintenance attentive to his special needs, will help keep your senior going strong.

- When it's time to part with your senior, there are many options, from full retirement to a new life as a school or therapy horse.

- Recognize when euthanasia, the hardest decision you'll ever have to make, is the right choice.

Chapter 22

"Look What We Can Do": Showing

In This Chapter

- When it's time to consider showing
- How to prepare yourself and your horse
- What to do on the day
- Lists are your friend—and we've provided one
- After the show

Purists will tell you that competition is just schooling in dress clothes, but we know better. Showing is, at least in part, showing off—your horse, your riding, that canter transition you finally nailed, and yes, those snazzy duds you just ordered. Is it for you? What's in it for you (and your horse)? Really, only time will tell, but here's a preview.

Why and When

The purists are partly right. Formal competition is a great way to test your developing skills, not only against other riders (if you really need

that thrill, stick to marathons) but against the standards of the discipline itself. A show gives a finite goal to the infinite tasks of refining your riding, and your relationship to your horse. And if you got into riding partly for the social side, it's a great way of bonding with your fellow riders (there's nothing like meeting at 6 A.M. over the manure pile for breaking the ice).

When will be a matter for you and your instructor to decide. Happily, this doesn't usually have to be in some unforeseeable future when you are perfect—many shows have friendly low-level competitions such as pleasure and equitation classes, or are what are known as "schooling shows" with modest classes and courses designed to give you and your horse experience.

Horse Lore

There are more than 14,000 sanctioned, and thousands of unsanctioned, horse shows held each year.

Choosing a Trainer

If showing is one of the reasons you got into riding, and if you own a horse, now may be the time to look for a trainer, as opposed to simply a riding instructor. Of course, this can sometimes be the same person, especially if you board where you are taking lessons, but school instructors are often fully engaged with a long list of clients, or are only qualified to help you with the basics. A trainer will focus specifically on you and your horse, help you design a program and set achievable goals, and coach you at shows if you feel you need it.

Horse Sense

You've made the decision to show. PJ figures that her first two ribbons cost her about $300 apiece when she totaled up show expenses, new show clothes, and motel room (she even borrowed the Western show bridle and saddle pad). Be prepared to spend—but if you ask her, it was worth it.

Costs

We gave you a little glimpse in Chapter 20, but frankly, that was the low end. If all you're interested in is appearing in your local show once or twice a summer, showing will not have a significant impact on your wallet. But if you are looking at serious competition, you're also looking at serious money.

Aside from your trainer, who might be getting $40 to 50 an hour (if you only use an instructor, that will be significantly less and probably negotiable), there are entry and stabling fees (ranging from $20 to $200), travel and transportation, food and lodging, special equipment, show clothes (for Western classes you need to invest in a good pair of chaps and a good hat, so the initial layout might be high, but once bought you'll be fine until you want to change colors). And for competition on the "A" circuit (USA Equestrian–accredited shows are ranked according to level of competition and entries), where frequency builds points and can affect placement, you could be looking at many thousands of dollars a year if you're planning on progressing to regional or national competitions. (Don't blanche—at the cheap and cheerful end, for most of us it's in the hundreds of dollars.)

 Horse Sense _____

When your class ends, before you walk off to accept your ribbon, take the time to thank your horse with a nice rub on the neck and a few kind words for a job well done. He deserves it. If you don't win, do not punish him. Ever! Go kick a trash can if you must, but don't take out your frustration on your horse.

Going for the Blue: Preparation

You're already goal-oriented, or you wouldn't be riding. Showing just requires you to sharpen your focus. You and your instructor will probably discuss a program of lessons and exercises leading up to the show. These will focus on weak spots (you're having trouble

keeping your rein contact steady, or your horse keeps taking the wrong lead, or you don't mind jumping hedges, but brick walls have you spooked) and refine strong ones. If your competition involves pattern work, as dressage and reining do, most instructors advise against drilling these to death—your horse will get bored, and begin to anticipate. Instead, you'll work separately on the elements that make up the pattern, so you can turn in a finished, but vital, performance.

And be sure to remember to build in some long walks and days off. Otherwise you and your horse will arrive at the show panting with anxiety or bored to death from doing the same routine without a break. Not only does this take away all the fun (showing is fun), but can actually lead to accidents: if you are tense and distracted, so are your muscles, your coordination, and your judgment, and you'll communicate this dither to your horse.

Going for the Blue: Admin

The first leg is easy: Formal shows have entry forms you are required to fill out between four and six weeks in advance; local shows usually post notices and have a pay-at-the-door policy. For shows with multiple classes, fees are per class; for single events (like horse trials) there is one fee. Be sure to get these forms out on time if there is a deadline—many shows are overbooked quickly. You and your trainer will have determined what level/class/division you and your horse belong in.

Whoa!
Remember, you're doing this to have fun. If competing isn't fun, don't do it. Riding is a wonderful sport that can rejuvenate you. Ride where you want, when you want. Do what's best for you and your horse.

This is also the time you'll be planning on overnight accommodations for you and your horse if needed (in general, if you have to drive more than two hours each way, you'll want to stay over); stabling at shows is usually also at a premium, which is another reason to stay on top of your paperwork. While you are striving to be your elegant best at the show itself, there is little glamour behind the scenes, and you'll get to know more about Motel 6 than you ever wanted to.

"Where Did I Put ...?": Right Before the Show

Seasoned campaigners plan for shows with the aplomb of jet-setters, but your first couple of times out you'll feel as if you've signed on for a cross between a wedding and an invasion. The list is your friend, so much so that some organizations actually include show checklists to give some parental guidance to their frazzled riders.

In addition to all that packing, here are some other things you'll want to keep in mind:

- Many classes require detailing—braided manes and tails, or set tails for saddle horse. Have you left enough time for this, or hired someone to do it?

- All official shows (and some organized trail rides) require a negative test for Equine Influenza, known as a Coggins test. You'll have this blood test done yearly at the time your horse gets his vaccinations, but now is the time to remember where you put that slip the vet gave you (PJ keeps copies everywhere—at the barn, in the car, etc.—in plastic self-sealing sandwich bags so they don't get dirty). (Some states also require rabies certificates.)

- If you're traveling with other riders from your barn, you can all help each other (riders are a very generous lot, as a rule), but if you are solo, try to persuade a friend to help out. It's not only a little dispiriting to compete alone, it can be chaotic, as you try to groom your horse/find your number/visit the ladies' room, all at the same time!

Event Checklist

This list, although comprehensive, is not inclusive. Use the blank spaces offered to add items not mentioned here.
Good luck, drive safe and happy travels!

❑ **SHIPPING**
❑ Shipping Halter
❑ Cotton, Leather Lead
❑ Chain
❑ Head Bumper
❑ Shipping Boots
❑ Bell Boots
❑ Bandages and Cottons
❑ Pins, Tape
❑ Tail Bandages
❑ Travel Sheet, Rug
❑ Surcingle and Pommel Pad
❑ Watering Bucket
❑ Water Jugs, with fresh water
❑ Full Hay Net
❑ Coggins Test, Health Certificate
❑ _____
❑ _____

❑ **FEED**
❑ Hay and Hay Net
❑ Grain, stored in trash can or pre-mixed in plastic bags
❑ Measuring Can
❑ Vitamin Supplements
❑ Electrolytes, Salt
❑ Carrots, Apples
❑ Grain Bucket
❑ Water Buckets (2)
❑ _____

STABLE
❑ **MANAGEMENT**
❑ Stall Guard
❑ Toolbox, with:
❑ Screw eyes
❑ Double-end snaps
❑ Hammer and nails
❑ Screwdrivers
❑ Pliers, wire cutters
❑ Tape measure
❑ Duct tape
❑ Scissors, knife
❑ Manure Basket
❑ Apple Picker
❑ Pitchfork
❑ Shovel
❑ Broom
❑ Rake
❑ Hose
❑ Hot Water Heater
❑ Fan
❑ Extension Cord
❑ Scrub Brush
❑ Hay String, Rope
❑ Chairs
❑ Writing Paper and Pen
❑ Shavings, Straw
❑ _____

❑ **GROOMING**
❑ Washing Buckets
❑ Shampoo, Color Enhancer
❑ Sponges

❑ Sweat Scraper
❑ Towels
❑ Show Sheen
❑ Brushes
❑ Curry Combs
❑ Mane Pulling Combs
❑ Tail Brush
❑ Clippers
❑ Blade Wash, Lubricant
❑ Stable Rag
❑ Baby Oil
❑ Fly Spray
❑ Hoof Pick
❑ Hoof Oil or Polish
❑ Thrush Treatment
❑ Turpentine
❑ Vetrolin
❑ Checkerboard
❑ _____
❑ _____

❑ **BRAIDING**
❑ Stool
❑ Spray Bottle, Sponge
❑ Mane Comb
❑ Hair Clips
❑ Yarn
❑ Needle and Thread
❑ Pull-through
❑ Scissors
❑ Rubber Bands
❑ Braid Tape
❑ _____
❑ _____

❑ **TACK**
    Saddles, dressage and jumping
❑ Saddle pads, pommel pads
❑ Girths, extras
❑ Breastplates
❑ Overgirth
❑ Extra Stirrup Leathers and Irons
❑ Bridles
❑ Martingales
❑ Extra Bits
❑ Extra Reins
❑ Halters
❑ Lead Rope
❑ Galloping Boots
❑ Polo Bandages
❑ Bell Boots
❑ Weight Pad and Lead
❑ Lunge Line
❑ Side Reins
❑ _____
❑ _____

❑ **BANDAGING**
❑ Standing Cottons
❑ Bandages
❑ Tape, Pins
❑ Sheet Cotton
❑ Liniment

❑ Alcohol
❑ Poultice
❑ Paper Bags, Paper
❑ Towels
❑ Plastic Wrap
❑ _____
❑ _____

❑ **MEDICAL KIT**
❑ Antibacterial Cream
❑ Betadine Solution, Scrub
❑ Gauze and Gauze Pads
❑ Sheet Cotton
❑ Spider Bandage
❑ Hock Bandage
❑ Icthamol
❑ Witch Hazel
❑ DMSO
❑ Hydrogen Peroxide
❑ Bandage Scissors
❑ Tape
❑ Vetrap, Elastoplast
❑ Twitch
❑ Epsom Salts
❑ Thermometer
❑ Vaseline*
❑ Band Aids*
❑ Paper Towels
❑ _____

❑ **HORSE CLOTHES**
❑ Stable Sheet
❑ Rug
❑ Anti-Sweat Sheet
❑ Wool Cooler
❑ Dress Sheet
❑ Surcingle and Pommel
❑ Pad
❑ Fly Sheet
❑ Fly Mask
❑ Rain Sheet
❑ Tail Bandages
❑ Quarter Sheet
❑ _____

STUD KIT/
❑ **HOOF CARE**
❑ Studs
❑ "T" tap
❑ Wrench
❑ Stud hole plugs
❑ Lubricant, WD-40
❑ Spare Horseshoes
❑ Easy Boot
❑ Clincher, for nails
❑ _____

❑ **RIDER'S ITEMS**
❑ Breeches
❑ Belt
❑ Boots
❑ Boot Pulls
❑ Boot Jack
❑ Spurs and Spur Straps
❑ Shirts

❑ Stock Tie and Pins
❑ Jacket
❑ Helmet
❑ Helmet Covers
❑ Gloves
❑ Equipment Bags
❑ Mirror
❑ Dressage Whip
❑ Jumping Bats
❑ Rain Gear
❑ Sweater, Jacket
❑ Sunscreen
❑ Band Aids
❑ Running Shoes
❑ Barn Boots
❑ Work Clothes
❑ Dress Clothes
❑ Toilet Kit
❑ Alarm Clock
❑ Sewing Kit
❑ Omnibus
❑ Rule Book
❑ Medical Armband
❑ Body Protecting Vest
❑ Insect Spray

❑ **TRAVEL**
❑ Map and Directions
❑ Truck and Trailer Registration
❑ Truck and Trailer Jacks
❑ Spare Tires
❑ Flares
❑ Flashlight and Batteries
❑ Tool Box
❑ Kleenex
❑ Cooler and Ice
❑ Food and Drinks
❑ Cash
❑ Credit Cards
❑ Mobile Phone
❑ _____
❑ _____

❑ **UPON ARRIVAL**
❑ Prepare Stall
❑ Locate Water Outlet
❑ Stable Horse
❑ Prepare Stall Card, with:
    Horse's name, Rider's name, Hotel name & Emergency phone numbers.
❑ Pick up Competitor's Packet
❑ Locate Warm-up and Competition Areas
❑ _____
❑ _____
❑ _____
❑ _____
❑ _____
❑ _____
❑ _____
❑ _____
❑ _____
❑ _____
❑ _____

It's all in the details. The United States Eventing Association (USEA) actually provides a competition "checklist" in its quarterly event handbook.

Down to the Wire: At the Show

The first rule of showing is: Allow more time than you think you need. Nothing will doom a showing experience more than arriving late and trying to push yourself and your horse through myriad tasks and your warmup. Arrive at least two hours before your class/event phase (if you are stabling, you might even want to bring your horse over the day before, if this is feasible). Here's what to make time for:

- **Reporting to the show secretary.** This person will check you in and give you your all-important competitor's number and information packet. Class or start times will either be assigned in advance or listed in the program, but this is the time to double-check them—cancellations can sometimes speed up the proceedings, while crises like accidents can slow them down.

- **Walking your horse around the grounds to get him accustomed to the sights and sounds.** Showing can be traumatic for horses (new herd, new smells, new saber-tooth tigers in the form of bicycles and scooters, *noise*); letting him adjust will help his performance in the ring. Some trainers even recommend lunging a horse to settle him down.

- **Walking yourself around.** If you are doing a course of some kind (trail, jumps, patterns, cross country) it will usually be posted and available for walking sometime before the class begins. And you'll need to know where things like the food and the toilets are.

- **Setting up.** For events within driving distance, you'll be showing from the back of a trailer, and want time to get your horse acclimatized and safely secured (outside with a release knot or inside if he is nervous—this very much depends on the temperament of the horse), and your gear out and ready. You'll want to groom your horse before setting out—an open field is no place for heavy-duty cleaning, but you'll be putting the finishing touches on just before you go into the ring.

From the Horse's Mouth _____

1st Place	Blue Ribbon
2nd Place	Red Ribbon
3rd Place	Yellow Ribbon
4th Place	White Ribbon
5th Place	Pink Ribbon
6th Place	Green Ribbon
7th Place	Purple Ribbon
8th Place	Brown Ribbon

The practice of awarding only two ribbons (Grand Champion and Reserve Champion) is based on the same practice as beauty pageants (Winner and Runner Up)—one functions as a spare in case the other is deemed unsound.

It's Your Turn

Miles of platitudes have been written about developing the winning edge, and the power of positive thinking—and the five-minute show jumper, no doubt—and we won't add to them here. It's idiotic to tell you not to be nervous about something that's bound to get your adrenaline flowing, or not to care about winning when you're in a *competition*, for heaven's sake. You'll have to find out for yourself how it feels, but if you're lucky, it will feel exactly like a wedding—the trappings are fun, but it's the partnership at the heart of things that matters.

 Whoa! _____

Butterflies? Stage fright is natural, and often goes away the minute you get into the ring or on the course and have your riding to focus on, but real numbing fear is a sign that you aren't ready to show. Don't force yourself, or let anyone else force you—you'll be miserable, and it's dangerous. There are plenty of shows, and your time will come.

After the Show

Your horse comes first; be sure he's cooled down, fed, and watered before you settle back for that celebratory meal or obsessive post-mortem (whatever your show mode turns out to be). There's often some delay in posting results at shows, and if you're showing with a group you may be waiting on different people's schedules. First thing, be sure to return your number to the secretary. Many shows are run on tight budgets and replacing supplies is costly.

Horse Sense
Every time you handle a horse you train it, whether you mean to or not.

Horse Sense

You know you're a Horse Person if:

- 🐴 Your horse gets new shoes more often than you.
- 🐴 Your spouse does something nice and you pat him/her on the neck and say "good boy/girl."
- 🐴 You show up at business meetings only to have some-one reach over and pick out the piece of hay stuck in your hair.
- 🐴 You get funny looks from nonhorsey people when they get in your car and notice the whips and spurs in the back seat.
- 🐴 You say "Whoa" to everyone, your dog, cat, spouse, and kids.
- 🐴 You've cornered the market on carrots and no one in your family eats them.

Show Duds

Take care of your show duds.

After a show be sure to clean all of your tack well, clean and press your show clothes, and organize them in their own garment bag so you are able to find them and keep them fresh for the next

show. If you show Western, you've got lots to keep track of: earrings, necklaces, shirt studs, cufflinks, hairpins and bands, and makeup. A small tackle box works well for this. Store your show gloves in your hatbox. Store expensive chaps inside out and in a chaps bag.

It's a Stage, Little Grasshopper

Save the real analysis of what went right or wrong for the next day (when you will be giving your horse time off, we might add), or your next lesson. Then, choose one thing to work on—don't try to get it all right in re-runs.

This is the end of our book but just the beginning of your life with horses. Happy trails!

The Least You Need to Know

- Shows are a fun way to see how far you and your horse have come, but be sure you're ready.

- Serious showing can be expensive, but you can enjoy yourself at lower level shows without taking out a second mortgage.

- Details, details, details: Preparing ahead of time prevents chaos on the day.

- Allow (much) more time than you need.

- It's only a show.

Appendix

Glossary

above the bit   Horse is carrying his head too high trying to evade contact with the bit. *See also* behind the bit and on the bit.

action   How high a horse lifts his feet and legs when it walks, trots, and canters.

aids   The arm, leg, shifts of body weight, and words used to cue a horse.

amble   A smooth gait in which horse walks with his front legs and trots with his hind legs.

barrel   A horse's belly.

barrel racing   A Gymkhana event in which a horse and rider race a cloverleaf pattern around barrels.

bay   A brown horse with a black mane and tail.

bosal   A stiffened noseband used with a hackamore bridle.

bradoon   A lightweight snaffle bit that's part of a double or full bridle.

breastplate   A wide leather or cloth band attached to both sides of the saddle, running across the horse's chest, that keeps the saddle from slipping backward.

brown   A horse color. Just what it sounds like. If the mane and tail are black, it's a bay.

canter   One the three basic gaits; its three-beat, waltzing rhythm inspired "The William Tell Overture" (and the theme from *Bonanza*).

cantle   The back of a saddle.

caulk   A metal projection on the bottom of a horseshoe to aid in traction.

cavesson   The noseband of the bridle on its own headpiece. Also a halter-like appliance used in lungeing horses.

cinch   One of the two terms that describe the piece of tack that holds the saddle on the horse. *See* girth.

coldblood   A mixed-breed or purebred draft horse. *See* hotblood.

colic   A painful, potentially fatal digestive ailment caused by intestinal blockage, trapped gas, or other irritants.

colt   A male horse younger than four years. Three-year-olds are still considered colts.

combined driving   Like eventing but with carriages. *See also* eventing.

competitive trail riding   A form of competition in which horses and riders cover a longish distance (25 to 50 miles) within an allotted time, and are then checked for fitness and stamina (conditioning).

contact   The connection made between the bit and the rider's hands with the reins.

corrective shoeing   A farrier's arsenal of tricks for helping horses with physical defects or lamenesses retain their soundness.

cremello/perlino   A creamy off-white colored horse with blue eyes that is often mistaken for white. Rare.

cross-ties   A pair of ropes or straps attached to either side of a horse's halter (connecting him to poles or walls) to hold him still while grooming or tacking up.

croup   The top of the rump.

curb bit   A type of bit with a long shank that puts pressure on the horse's lower jaw.

curb chain   A strap or chain that attaches to both sides of the curb bit and rests under the horse's chin.

curb rein   The lower rein on a Pelham bridle.

D-ring snaffle   A popular, mild bit jointed in the middle or straight with D-shaped rings instead of the more usual round ones.

discipline   (1) (verb) Not reprimanding. Firm but nonabusive correction of a horse's misdeeds. This may involve positive or negative reinforcement. (2) Discipline (noun) is also the term used to describe riding styles, e.g., dressage, Western pleasure, etc.

dorsal stripe   A line of dark hair from the base of the mane to the top of the tail common to some breeds and colors of horses and ponies, such as duns. *See* primitive marks.

double or **full bridle**   A bridle with two bits—curb and bradoon—popular in the old days but now used only in high-level dressage and English saddle-seat riding. *See also* Weymouth.

draft horse   A thickset type of horse, originating in Europe, used for pulling and as contributing stock to the breeding of warmbloods. *See also* warmblood.

dressage   A popular, competitive form of riding, derived from the training of war horses, in which the horse's gaits and movements are extremely regulated. The "ballet" of the equine world.

electrolytes   Gatorade for horses, to keep their body chemistry balanced in times of excessive sweating. Dandelions contain natural electrolytes.

endurance riding   A long-distance (50 to 100 miles) run on horseback. Endurance horses are checked frequently on course for medical indications of exhaustion, and not allowed to continue if they are stressed.

Eohippus   The ancient knee-high ancestor to modern horses. (Synonym: Hyracotherium.)

equitation   Horse show classes (English and Western) judging the form, appearance, and performance of a rider.

Equus caballus   The scientific name for modern horses.

eventing   The three-phase competition (dressage, cross-country, and stadium jumping) used in Olympic competition. Often done at more elementary levels and lower fence heights, when it is known as horse trials.

extension   When a horse reaches way out with his forelegs during a gait, and stretches his back.

feathers   Silky hairs descending from the fetlock joint—common in draft horses.

fetlock   A horse's ankle joint.

filly   A female horse younger than four years. Three-year-olds are considered fillies.

floating   Filing, as in teeth. Horses' teeth are floated with a rasp.

foal   A horse in its first calendar year of life.

Forest Horse   A term for one of the modern horse's close ancestors (along with Tarpan and Przewalski's horse).

foundation   Original stock to which a breed can be traced.

founder or **laminitis**   Painful disease of the hoof that results in lameness. A badly foundered foot can curl up like an elf shoe.

frog   Triangular, fleshy shock-absorbing pad on the bottom of a horse's hoof.

gaited   Adjective signifying that a horse is one of the plantation breeds (Missouri Foxtrotter, Tennessee Walker, Saddlebred, and even some mules) having high "action" and ground-covering steps.

gallop   A fast canter. The fastest gallop is a four-beat gait (and also a hair-raising experience).

gelding   A castrated male horse.

girth   One of two terms used to describe the strap that runs under the horse's belly to hold the saddle on. Girth is an English term; cinch is Western. *See* cinch.

gray   The term used to describe horses that range in color from dark gray to white, but have black skin. The key is the skin color. Black skin = gray. Pink skin = albino (white).

green   An unschooled or inexperienced horse.

hack   A term used for a trail or pleasure ride. Also means a horse used for riding (or, to make things more complicated, a horse and carriage for hire—hence, hack license).

hackamore   A bitless bridle. *See* bosal.

half-ass   A colloquial term for Onager, or hemionid—a subspecies of Equus sharing both horse and ass characteristics.

halter   A simple leather or nylon device horses wear on their heads to facilitate being groomed, led, or tied.

hand   The principle unit of measure for horses. A hand is four inches.

hay belly   A big, round barrel horses get from eating inferior hay.

headstall   The bridle minus reins.

heavy horse   A draft horse.

herdbound   A horse who won't leave his friends.

hippotherapy   A form of physical therapy using a horse's natural movements to treat people with disabilities.

horn   (1) Hard fingernail-like material in a horse's hoof. (2) The projection on the front of a Western saddle.

horse   An *Equus caballus* more than 14.2 hands high.

hotblood   An Arabian, Barb, or Thoroughbred horse.

hunt seat   A seat with a slight forward lean, used in foxhunting and jumping.

Hyracotherium   The more scientifically accepted term for Eohippus.

imprinting   Acclimatizing a newborn foal to human contact.

jog   A Western gait—a slow trot.

laminae   Layers of tissue inside a horse's hoof.

laminitis   *See* founder.

lead   (1) (noun) The "rope" that is fastened to a halter to lead a horse (think leash). (2) (verb) To guide a horse by walking next to it holding its rope or reins.

livestock   Animals kept for use on a farm or bred and sold for profit. This is also the federal government's current classification of horses, even those used solely for pleasure riding or kept in the back yard.

lunge   The act of exercising a horse by standing on the ground and controlling the horse by means of a very long rope (long line) as the horse moves in a circle around you. Also spelled *longe*.

lope   The Western term for (slow) canter.

longear   An affectionate term used to describe all mules, donkeys, and their kin.

martingale   A leather device made of interlinking straps meant to keep the horse's head low. There are several types, including Standing, Running, and Irish.

Merychippus   An ancient (but after Hyracotherium) ancestor of modern horse.

Mesohippus   An ancient (but after Hyracotherium) ancestor of modern horse.

Mini or **miniature horse**   A specific breed of small-scale horse, with its own registry.

moon blindness   Painful eye inflammation that can blind horses.

mule   A hybrid animal with a jack (male donkey) for a sire and a mare for a dam. Mules can't reproduce. The opposite arrangement—a jennet, or female donkey for a dam and a stallion for a sire—is called a hinney. Hinnies are rare.

navicular disease   A bone degenerative condition in the foot causing lameness.

near side   The left side of a horse as viewed from behind. *See also* off side.

off side   The right side of a horse as viewed from behind. *See* near side.

on the bit   When the horse's hocks are engaged, the head is on the vertical (more or less), and the rider is in light contact with the horse's mouth. The desired frame, as opposed to above the bit (horse's head is raised and poll is stiff) or behind the bit (horse tucks mouth in toward chest).

palfrey   A medieval lady's gentle horse.

pastern   The bone between fetlock (ankle joint) and hoof that influences springiness of gait.

Pliohippus   An ancient (but after Hyracotherium) ancestor of modern horse.

pommel   The bump at the front of an English saddle.

pony   An *Equus caballus* shorter than 14.3 hands high.

posting   A rising and sitting motion in the saddle synchronized to the motion of the trot (also called rising).

prepotency   A genetic term meaning the ability to breed true to type for generations. Certain stallions are said to be prepotent; some breeds, such as Arabians, are prepotent because they can pass along their traits to other breeds.

primitive marks   Dark marks or stripes on a domestic equine's coat indicating genetic throwback to ancient origins. Most common—the dorsal stripe (with intersecting crossbar across the shoulders), also known as the St. Andrew's Cross. Zebra stripes on the legs of domestic horses, ponies, and longears are also seen. *See* dorsal stripe.

Przewalski's horse   Also known as Asian world Horse, these are the closest breed to prehistoric Pliohippus.

rack   A Saddlebred's high-stepping, dramatic show gait.

reining   A Western discipline, based on the movements used to herd cattle, featuring the turns and fancy footwork of the working cow horse. An exciting show ring spectacle.

roan   A horse color consisting of different colored hairs mixed together. Gray, black, and white hairs make a blue roan; red and white make a strawberry roan.

round pen   A small exercise pen used in training horses.

schoolmaster   A highly experienced and educated horse used for lessons. It frequently knows more than the student (or the instructor).

scratches   A painful skin disorder located on the back of the pastern that can make horses lame.

saddleseat   The seat used in riding gaited horses. The rider sits farther back than a hunt seat rider does, to facilitate the upward movements of a gaited horse.

seat   The part of a rider's posture that influences a horse's steering and balance. It resides in—you guessed it—the hips and rear. Seat also means ability to stay in the saddle.

shank   The straight part of a bit to which the reins are attached; longer on many Western bits than on English bits.

snaffle   The mildest bit, with a plain or jointed bar, comes in many different styles

spook   When a scared horse leaps sideways or up.

stallion   An uncastrated male horse.

stock seat   The long-legged seat used in Western riding.

stud   A metal projection on the bottom of a horseshoe to aid in traction; a working stallion.

stud farm   A place where horses are bred. 'Stud' is not a synonym for stallion, except colloquially.

tack   Any piece of equipment that is used to maintain, train, ride, or drive a horse—saddles, bridles, reins, blankets, bits, halters, and harnesses are all tack.

Tarpan   One of the modern horse's close ancestors (along with Forest Horse and Przewalski's horse).

team penning   Three horses and riders working together cut three head of cattle from a herd and drive them into a pen.

team roping   Two horses and their riders chase and catch a calf.

thrush   Same as in people—a fungal infection. Horses get thrush in their feet.

trot   The horse's two-beat, up-and-down gait.

turnback   The post-riding grooming session (which may also include watering and a bath).

turnout   (1) (noun) A horse's time spent out of doors, also called pasture time. (2) (verb) The act of physically walking the horse to his pasture or corral.

tusk   An extra tooth male horses get. Also called a *tush*.

twitch   A device used for making nappy horses stand still for the vet.

vaulting   A sport wherein one person (or a whole team) executes acrobatic movements on the back of a moving horse.

vices   Damaging habits horses often pick up through stress and/or boredom. Common vices are cribbing (chewing wood), weaving (leaning weight back and forth while obsessively swinging head), and wind-sucking (gulping air, which can lead to colic).

warmblood   Formerly a term applied to half-hotblood, half-coldblood horses, warmbloods are now breeds in their own right. They originated in Germany, the Netherlands, and Scandinavia.

Western Pleasure   A variety of horse show class that demonstrates the comfortable gaits and training of a Western horse.

weymouth bridle   A type of full or double bridle.

wind   A horse's capacity for breathing efficiently under stress. Can be improved through exercise.

withers   The bump between the horse's shoulder blades at the base of the neck. A horse's height is measured from the ground to the top of his withers.

wolf teeth   Horses' wisdom teeth, located in front of the molars.

Appendix  B

Resources

Magazines/Periodicals

Magazines and periodicals are the best way to keep current on what's happening in the horse world, including the latest fashions for horses and people, book reviews, new products, amusing stories, and practical information about horse care and riding.

General Interest

The Chronicle of the Horse
www.chronofhorse.com

Discover Horses at Kentucky Horse Park
301-977-3900

Equus
www.magazines.com

Horse Illustrated
www.horseillustratedmagazine.com

John Lyons Perfect Horse
perfecthorse@myexcel.com

Ride with Bob Avila
www.horse.com

Young Rider
www.fancypubs.com

English

Practical Horseman
PracHorse@aol.com

Western

Horse and Rider
www.hrsenrider@cowles.com

Western Horseman
www.westernhorseman.com

Longears

Brayer Magazine
www.lovelongears.com

Miniature Donkey Talk
www.miniaturedonkey.net

Mules and More, Inc.
mules@socket.net

Special Interest

America's Barrel Racer
www.americasbarrelracer.com

Arabian Horse World
www.ahwmagazine.com

The Blood-Horse
www.bloodhorse.com

Draft Horse Journal
www.drafthorsejournal.com

Dressage Today
www.primediamags.com

The Gaited Horse
www.thegaitedhorse.com

The Holistic Horse
www.holistichorse.com

Hunter and Sport Horse
www.hunterandsporthorsemag.com

Miniature Horse World
www.amha.com

Natural Horse Magazine
www.naturalhorse.com

Ropers Sports News
www.roperssportnews.com

Trail Rider Magazine
www.trailridermagazine.com

Books

You can never have enough horse books. Every one will give you a new perspective, provide just a bit more information.

A Horse Around the House, Second Edition, by Patricia Jacobson and Marcia Hayes. 1999. Crown Publishers. 500 pages.

This one's been around for a long time for a good reason: It's simply the best, friendliest, and most comprehensive all-around horse care book available.

Book of Horses: A Complete Medical Reference Guide for Horses and Foals, by Members of the Faculty and Staff, University of California, Davis, School of Veterinary Medicine, edited by Mordecai Siegel. 1996. HarperCollins. 526 Pages.

Covers a lot of the same ground as Veterinary Notes for Horseowners, but, in addition, dispenses warm, friendly advice on all aspects of medical care.

Centered Riding, by Sally Swift. 1985. St. Martin's Press. 198 pages.

This pioneering work teaches the rider to use creative imaging to achieve harmony with the horse for a natural way of riding.

Definitive Donkey, by Betsy and Paul Hutchins, Revised and edited by Leah Patton. 1999. 320 pages.

The most comprehensive and best-selling book available on the subject.

Horse Watching, by Desmond Morris. 1988. Crown Publishers. 160 pages.

The tag line on the front cover says it all: "Why does a horse whinny and everything else you ever wanted to know." A delightful book that helps you understand why horses do the things they do.

The Encyclopedia of the Horse, by Elwyn Hartley Edwards. 2001. Dorling Kindersley. 440 pages.

A true encyclopedia, in full color, of the complete evolution of the horse from domestication, to breeds (even obscure ones), to the different styles of riding.

Natural Horse-Man-Ship: Pat Parelli's Six Keys to a Natural Horse-Human Relationship, by Pat Parelli. 2002. Lyons Press. 232 pages.

This is a book to teach people the language of horses for more effective communication.

The Natural Rider, by Mary Wanless. 1987. Simon & Schuster. 320 pages.

A revolutionary method of teaching riding by using the right side of the brain to unite the mind and body to teach truly natural riding.

The Nature of Horses: Exploring Equine Evolution, Intelligence and Behavior, by Stephen Budiansky. 1997. Free Press. 240 pages.

Uses the findings of modern scientific research to explain what makes a horse tick.

The Principles of Riding: The Official Handbook of the German National Equestrian Federation, Revised Second Edition. 1997. Half Halt Press. 174 pages.

An excellent book of basics for horse and rider.

Western Horsemanship, by Richard Shrake. 1987. Western Horseman. 144 pages.

The complete guide to riding Western horses.

The Whole Horse Catalog, Revised Edition, by Steven D. Price, et al. 1993. Fireside Books. 288 pages.

A general guide to owning, maintaining, buying, and enjoying horses, with expert advice on stabling, equestrian activities, health, tack, and horseshoeing.

Veterinary Notes for Horseowners: An Illustrated Manual of Horse Medicine and Surgery, Eighteenth Edition, by M. Daniel Hayes, et al. 2002. Simon & Schuster. 880 pages.

This massive volume was first published in 1877. It's the *Merck Manual for horses*.

Breed Associations

Alphabetical by breed:

Appaloosa Horse Club, Inc.
2720 West Pullman Road
Moscow, ID 83843-0903
208-882-5578
Fax: 208-882-8150
www.appaloosa.com

Arabian Horse Registry of America, Inc.
PO Box 173886
Denver, CO 80217-386
303-450-4748
Fax: 303-450-2841
www.theregistry.org

International Arabian Horse Association
(also Registers Half-Arabian and Anglo-Arabian)
10805 E. Bethany Drive
Aurora, CO 80014-2605
303-696-4500
Fax: 303-696-4599
www.iaha.com

Belgian Warmblood Breeding Association/North American District
136 Red Fox Trail
Chapin, SC 29036
803-345-5588
Fax: 803-345-0806
www.belgianwrmblood.com

American Buckskin Registry Association, Inc.
1141 Hartnell Avenue
Redding, CA 96002
916-223-1420
www.americanbuckskin.com

Clydesdale Breeders of the USA
17346 Kelley Road
Pecatonica, IL 61063
815-247-8780
Fax: 815-247-8337
www.clydesusa.com

American Connemara Pony Society
2360 Hunting Ridge Road
Winchester, VA 22603
Phone and fax: 540-722-2277
www.acps.org

American Donkey and Mule Society, Inc.
PO Box 1210
Lewisville, TX 75067
972-219-0781
Fax: 972-420-9980
www.lovelongears.com

The Friesian Horse Association of North America
PO Box 11217
Lexington, KY 40574
www.fhana.com

American Haflinger Registry
2746 State Route 44
Rootstown, OH 44272
330-325-8116
Fax: 330-325-8178
www.haflingerhorse.com

American Hanoverian Society, Inc.
4067 Iron Works Parkway, Suite 1
Lexington, KY 40511-8483
859-255-4141
Fax: 859-255-8467
www.hanoverian.org

International Sporthorse Registry and Oldenburg Registry North America
939 Merchandise Mart
Chicago, IL 6064
312-527-6544
Fax: 312-527-6573
www.isroldenburg.org

Lipizzan Association of North America
PO Box 1133
Anderson, IN 46015-1133
765-644-3094
Fax: 765-641-1205
www.lipizzan.org

American Miniature Horse Association, Inc.
5601 South IJ 35W
Alvarado, TX 76009
817-783-5600
Fax: 817-783-6403
www.amha.com

American Morgan Horse Association, Inc.
PO Box 960
Shelburne, VT 05482-0906
802-985-4944
Fax: 802-985-8897
www.morganhorse.com

American Mustang and Burro Association
(Registers wild equine and their offspring adopted through the Bureau of Land Management [BLM] or any of the recognized placement programs)
PO Box 788
Lincoln, CA 95648
530-633-9371
Hotline: 1-800-US4-Wild or
916-632-1855
www.bardalisa.com

American Paint Horse Association
(Only horses of Paint, Thoroughbred, or Quarter Horse Breeding)
PO Box 961023
Fort Worth, TX 76161-0023
817-834-2742
Fax: 817-834-3152
www.apha.com

Palomino Horse Breeders of America
15253 E. Skelly Drive
Tulsa, OK 74116-2637
918-438-1234
Fax: 918-438-1232
www.palominohba.com

Paso Fino Horse Association, Inc.
101 North Collins Street
Plant City, FL 33566-3311
813-719-7777
Fax: 813-719-7872
www.pfha.org

Percheron Horse Association of America
PO Box 141
Fredericktown, OH 43019-0141
740-694-3602
Fax: 740-694-3604

Pintabian Horse Registry, Inc.
(Horses must possess more than 99 percent Arabian blood)
PO Box 360
Karlstad, MN 56732-0360
218-436-7768

Pinto Horse Association of America, Inc.
(All spotted horses except those with Appaloosa, Mule, or Draft breeding)
1900 Samuels Avenue
Fort Worth, TX 76102-1141
817-336-7842
Fax: 817-336-7416
www.pinto.org

Pony of the Americas Club, Inc.
5240 Elmwood Avenue
Indianapolis, IN 46203-5990
317-788-0107
Fax: 317-788-8974
www.poac.org

American Quarter Horse Association
PO Box 200
Amarillo, TX 79168-0001
806-376-4811
Fax: 806-349-6401
www.aqha.com

American Saddlebred Horse Association
4093 Iron Works Parkway
Lexington, KY 40511-8434
859-259-2742
Fax: 859-259-1628
www.saddlebred.com

American Shetland Pony Club
(Also registers all ponies
48 inches and under)
81-B E. Queenwood
Morton, IL 61550
309-263-4044
Fax: 309-263-5113
www.shetlandminiature.com

American Shire Horse Association
PO Box 739
New Castle, CO 81647-0739
970-876-5980
Fax: 970-876-1977
www.shirehorse.org

National Show Horse Registry
10368 Bluegrass Parkway
Louisville, KY 40299
502-266-5100
Fax: 502-266-5086
www.nshregistry.org

American Show Pony Registry
(*see* American Shetland Pony Club)

Federation of North American Sport Horse Registries
(Represents interests of all European-origin breed registries and promotes breeding of sport horses in North America)
4067 Iron Works Parkway, Suite 1
Lexington, KY 40511
859-255-4141
Fax: 859-255-8467
www.sporthorsefederation.org

Tennessee Walking Horse Breeders' and Exhibitors' Association
PO Box 286

Lewisburg, TN 37091-0286
931-359-1574
Fax: 931-359-2539

The Jockey Club
(Thoroughbreds)
821 Corporate Drive
Lexington, KY 40503-2794
859-224-2700
Fax: 859-224-2710
www.jockeyclub.com

American Trakehner Association, Inc.
1514 West Church Street
Newark, OH 43055
740-344-1111
Fax: 740-344-3225
www.americantrakehner.com

United States Trotting Association
(Standardbreds)
750 Michigan Avenue
Columbus, OH 43215-1191
614-224-2291, ext. 3209
Fax: 614-224-4575
www.ustrotting.com

American Warmblood Registry, Inc.
PO Box 211735
Royal Palm Beach, FL 33421-1735
209-245-3565
Fax: 775-667-0516
www.americanwarmblood.com

Swedish Warmblood Association
(Fully associated with the Swedish Warmblood Association in Sweden)
PO Box 788
Socorro, MN 87801
505-835-1318
Fax: 505-835-1321
www.wbstallions.com/wb/swana

Welsh Pony and Cob Society of America, Inc.
PO Box 2977
Winchester, VA 22604-2977
540-667-6195
www.welshpony.org

Catalogs

You can never have too many clothes or too much tack. With that in mind, check out some of the following catalogs. Most of these catalogs sell an assortment of clothing (for humans and horses), tack, practical gizmos you can use at home and in the barn, shoes, boots, books, car mats, and even house wares. If you're like us, you'll find something in every catalog that you absolutely "need" and can't live without whether you own your own horse or not.

Call to request a catalog or check out the websites.

Back in the Saddle
1-800-865-2478
www.backinthesaddle.com

Chariton Vet Supply
1-800-648-7837
www.charitonvet.com

Chicks Discount Saddlery
1-800-444-2441
www.chicksaddlery.com

Country Supply
1-800-637-6721
www.countrysupply.com

Equine USA
1-800-648-1121
www.stagecoachwest.com

Hitchingpost Supply
360-805-1673
www.hitchingpostsupply.com

Hobby Horse (Show) Clothing Company
1-800-569-5885
www.hobbyhorseinc.com

Libertyville Saddle Shop, Inc.
847-362-0570
www.saddleshop.com

Millers Equestrian Mall
1-877-HORSE00
www.equestrianmall.com

Miller Harness
1-800-553-7655
www.millerharness.com

Nasco Horse Essentials
1-800-558-9595
www.eNASCO.com

National Ropers Supply
1-800-GO-ROPIN
www.nationalroperssupply.com

Rider's Warehouse Superstore
770-569-9609
www.riderswarehouse.com

Rod's Western Palace
1-800-325-8508
www.rods.com

SS Schneiders
1-800-365-1311
www.sstack.com

Sergeant's Western World
1-800-383-3669
www.sergeantswestern.com

Sheplers: The World's Largest Western Stores and Catalog
1-800-835-4004
www.sheplers.com

Smith Brothers
1-800-433-5558
www.smithbrothers.com

State Line Tack
(specify English or Western)
1-800-228-9208
www.statelinetack.com

Valley Vet Supply
1-800-356-1005
www.valleyvet.com

For miniature horses:

Mini Express Miniature Horse Tack
717-362-MINI (6464)
www.miniexpress.com

Supreme Equine Design
1-800-447-6053

Sew Your Own
English and Western clothes, carry bags, dog blankets, horse blankets. For a catalog of patterns:
SuitAbility
1-800-207-0256
www.SuitAbility.com

Organizations

The American Horse Council
1700 K Street NW
Suite 300
Washington, DC 20006
202-296-4031
Fax: 202-296-1970
www.horsecouncil.org

Gladstone Equestrian Association
PO Box 119, Hamilton Farm
Gladstone, NJ 07934-0119
908-234-151
Fax: 908-234-0863
www.gladstonedriving.com

National 4-H Council
7100 Connecticut Avenue
Chevy Chase, MD 20815
www.fourcouncil.edu

National Barrel Horse Association
725 Broad Street
Augusta, GA 30901-1050
706-722-7223
Fax: 706-722-9575
www.ngha.com

National Cutting Horse Association
4704 Highway 377S
Fort Worth, TX 76116-8805
817-244-6188
Fax: 817-244-2015

National Reining Horse Association
3000 NW Tenth Street
Oklahoma City, OK 73107-5302
405-946-7400 (No Fax given)
www.nrha.com

United States Dressage Federation
220 Lexington Green Circle, Suite 516
Lexington, KY 40503
859-971-2277
Fax: 859-971-7722
www.usdf.com

United States Pony Clubs, Inc.
4041 Iron Works Parkway
Lexington, KY 40511-8462
859-240-PONY (7660)
Fax: 859-233-4652
www.ponyclub.org

USA Equestrian, Inc.
4047 Iron Works Parkway
Lexington, KY 40511-8483
859-258-2472
Fax: 859-231-6662
www.equestrian.org

Hippotherapy and Therapeutic Riding

North American Riding for the Handicapped Association (NARHA)
(Queries regarding Hippotherapy, Equine Facilitated Psychotherapy and Equine Experiential Learning can also be directed here)
PO Box 33150
Denver, CO 80233
1-800-369-RIDE or 303-452-1212
Fax 303-252-4610
www.narha.org

Horses in the Hood Los Angeles
(A nonprofit, public benefit corporation that provides horse day camps for at-risk youth and other residents selected by the Watts organizations)
310-559-9841
www.horsesinthehood.org or
www.hhla.org

Holistic Medicine

The following associations have referrals to veterinarians who practice various types of alternative medicine for pets ranging from holistic veterinary care, herbal medicines, homeopathy, nutrition therapy, to chiropractic.

American Holistic Veterinary Association (AHVMA)
2218 Old Emmorton Road
Bel Air, MD 21015
410-569-0795
Fax: 410-569-2346
www.ahvma.org

American Veterinary Chiropractic Association (AVCA)
442154 East 140 Road
Bluejacket, OK 74333
Phone and fax: 918-784-2231
www.animalchiropractic.org

The Association for Complimentary and Alternative Veterinary Medicine (AltVetMed)
www.altvetmed.com

Equine Welfare, Rescue, and Adoption

Many of these organizations are supported by donations, so if you can't adopt a horse, maybe you can contribute to its support until it finds a loving home.

Adopt-a-Horse Ltd., Inc.
7609 W. Josephine Road
Lake Placid, FL 33852
863-381-4483
Fax: 863-382-4483
zeke@strato.net

Saves racehorses and other breeds from slaughter.

American Horse Protection Association, Inc.
1000 29th Street, N.W., #T-100
Washington, DC 20009
202-965-0500
Fax: 202-965-9621

A nonprofit organization dedicated exclusively to the welfare of all equines, both wild and domestic.

B.R.R.R.O.
Burro Rescue-Rehab-Relocation Onus
PO Box 222
Cheney, WA 99004
509-235-2255
brrro@cet.com

Hooved Animal Humane Society
10804 McConnell Road
PO Box 400
Woodstock, IL 60098-0400
815-337-5563
Fax: 815-337-5569
www.hahs.org

Dedicated to the protection of hooved animals through intervention and education; 98 percent of work is done with horses.

Horse Lovers United, Inc.
PO Box 2744
Salisbury, MD 21802-2744
410-749-3955
Fax: 410-742-6928
www.horseloversunited.com

Finds new homes for Standardbreds and other breeds. Horses are retrained for new careers and placed in new homes with adoption agreements.

Government Sources

Bureau of Land Management
Wild Horse and Burro Program
U.S. Department of the Interior
18th and C Streets, N.W.
Washington, DC 20240
202-452-5073
www.blm.gov/whb

General Interest/Expos/ Museums

Equine Affaire
136 E. High Street
London, OH 43130
Phone and fax: 740-845-0085
www.equineaffaire.com

Equitana USA
1199 S. Belt Line Road, #100
Cappell, TX 75019
1-888-HORSES-1 or 972-906-6780
www.equitanausa.com

The Kentucky Horse Park
4409 Iron Works Parkway
Lexington, KY 40511
1-800-698-8813
www.imh.org/khp/

Twelve hundred acres dedicated to man's relationship with the horse. Two museums, theaters, and 50 breeds of horses (some famous) on display to look at and pet. An amazing place. You must check this out if you're a horse lover.

Rider Safety

The American Medical Equestrian Association
5318 Old Bullard Road
Tyler, TX 75703
903-509-2374
Fax: 903-509-2474
horsesafty@aol.com

Index

Q-R

T